ROCHDALE AFC

A Who's Who
1973 to 1999

Steven Phillipps

A *SoccerData* Publication

Published in Great Britain by Tony Brown,
4 Adrian Close, Toton, Nottingham NG9 6FL.
Telephone 0115 973 6086.
E-mail soccer@innotts.co.uk
www.soccerdata.com

First published 2015

© Steven Phillipps 2015

All rights reserved. No part of this publication may be reproduced, stored in a retrieval system, or transmitted in any form, or by any means, electronic, mechanical, photocopying, recording or otherwise without the prior permission in writing of the Copyright holders, nor be otherwise circulated in any form or binding or cover other than in which it is published and without a similar condition including this condition being imposed on the subsequent publisher.

Cover design by Bob Budd.

Printed and bound by 4Edge, Hockley, Essex
www.4edge.co.uk

ISBN: 978-1-905891-95-5

PREFACE

Rochdale recently completed 108 seasons as a professional club and as noted in the first two parts of this work (covering 1907 – 1939 and 1939 – 1973) over 1800 players have appeared in the first team in competitive games. This third volume covers the period 1973 to 1999, a period of fairly unrelieved gloom for Dale supporters. Starting with a catastrophic relegation back to Division 4, all the club had to show for the next 25 years was one cup run and one ultimately unavailing promotion chase. Indeed, it took 16 years before they managed a top half finish. Although the players from this era are largely well known, some had long non-league careers, some details of which are uncertain. As with the previous volumes, I have therefore included details which, while likely true, are not completely certain (and are clearly marked as such). Also continuing the style of the earlier volumes, the players appear in the text in the order in which they made first team appearances for Rochdale, so that there is also an underlying narrative history of the club over the years in question. A total of 372 players are included in the present volume (taking the overall tally to 1559), and as in the previous books, these range from full internationals and league championship winners to local juniors with just the odd senior appearance to their credit. All players chosen among the (ever increasing number of) substitutes are included, even if they never left the bench.

Steven Phillipps
July 2015

ACKNOWLEDGEMENTS

The details contained within these pages have been acquired over a period of many years with the help of many Rochdale followers and statisticians of other clubs. Special thanks go to Mark Wilbraham for the use of his archive of official Rochdale AFC photographs and Tony Brown for readily agreeing to publish these volumes.

1983: The Greenhoff brothers arrive at Rochdale

ROCHDALE AFC HISTORY 1973 TO 1999

Relegation

After topping the table early in 1972-73, Dale had eventually finished 13th in Division 3, though only five points behind the side in seventh place. This was their second best finish since the formation of national third and fourth divisions. Nevertheless, the Board had decided not to renew manager Dick Conner's contract at the end of the season and after a brief period in which secretary Gus McLean was acting manager, the new man appointed to the job was Oldham youth team coach Walter Joyce.

Unfortunately, the outcome almost rivalled the disastrous days of the early thirties, indeed Dale managed to win even fewer games than in the infamous 1931-32 season. The new manager almost immediately dismantled Conner's team, moving on most of the experienced players and replacing them largely with untried youngsters, indeed 23 different players were used in just the first 14 games. The first victory came at the end of September, but the second – and only other – did not arrive until January, when Shrewsbury were beaten in front of just 957 fans. Dale had fallen to the bottom of the table in November and remained there for the rest of the season. The final 22 games brought no further successes and just nine points. With a total of 21, Dale thus added to their record low points tally for Division 3 North by claiming the same record for Division 3. The match against Cambridge, on a Tuesday afternoon (due to a power workers' strike) attracted a 'crowd' of officially 588, though many observers thought the real figure was even lower. Unsurprisingly, the average league attendance slumped from 3186 to 1890. To add to the misery, Dale went out of the FA Cup to Southern League Grantham.

Division 4

Despite their relegation, Walter Joyce retained a substantial number of the squad, while adding some experience including Neil Young, a league championship and FA Cup winner with Manchester City. A victory over Barnsley ended a run of 25 games without success, but Dale never looked like making a challenge towards the top of the table and, indeed, after a run of only three wins in 19 games only a last day victory over Swansea kept them out of the bottom four. Meanwhile, young striker Alan Taylor had been sold to West Ham for £40,000 and after two goals on his debut in the FA Cup quarter-final, amazingly he repeated this in the semi-final and the final itself. Dale certainly needed the money from the transfer, average home attendances falling to around 1500.

The 1975-76 season started in more promising style, with seven victories and only four defeats in the first 14 games. Dale also managed a decent cup run, taking first division Norwich to three games in the third round. However, after a nine match unbeaten run in mid-season, they won only one of the last 14 and ended in 15th place, having scored a meagre 40 goals and figured in nine goalless draws.

Most of the young hopefuls were released at the end of the season, and the manager, too, left 'by mutual consent'. Coming in was 1950s Dale player Brian Green, a successful coach and manager around the world. However, arrivals on the playing front were scarce and Dale started the season with just 14 pros and injuries cut this to 11 even before the season kicked-off. Against the odds, Green's side were third in early October and suffered only two defeats in the first 16 games. Further injuries and departures depleted the side further, though, and Dale gradually slid down to finish 18th. They picked up only 11 points in the second half of the season and unsurprisingly, after signs of improvement, crowds dropped back below 1000 for some games.

Summer signings numbered just four as Green's attempts at further shoestring recruitment foundered, and Dale were forced to start the 1977-78 campaign with 13 players including two goalkeepers. Indeed, with two players suspended, Dale could only muster nine professionals and two apprentices for the first league game: Ted Oliver, at 16 years 5 months, became easily Dale's youngest ever FL player. When Dale played Leeds in the League Cup, the visitors had more internationals than Dale had professionals. Green soon resigned to take up a coaching position at Leeds and a more recent ex-player, Mike Ferguson, took up the reins. Dale were already bottom, and didn't look like moving from there, and they were guaranteed to finish in the bottom four as early as March. They collected a mere 24 points, just two of them away from home, and lost 30 of 46 games. Most of the late season home games were reported to have attendances just over 1000, but it later transpired that chairman Fred Ratcliffe had demanded - with a re-election vote on the horizon – that no sub-thousand crowds be admitted to. In fact, the real attendances had dipped as low as 734 (the average was only 1275).

Mr Ratcliffe's advocacy, and Dale's relative success until the last couple of years, kept them in the League at the AGM, though Southport, next-to-bottom for the last three seasons, lost their place. Matters on the pitch weren't any better, though, and it took Dale 14 games to notch their first victory (though they weren't bottom – Halifax had a run of 22 games from which they picked up five points). Five consecutive defeats without a goal scored, including a humiliating defeat by Cheshire League Droylsden in the cup, saw Mike Ferguson lose his job, and he was replaced by former coach Peter Madden as caretaker boss. Quickly recruiting some experienced heads, Madden oversaw a remarkable 4-0 away win at Scunthorpe, Dale's best away victory for over 20 years, before giving way to former Burnley player Doug Collins who became player-manager. Atrocious weather meant that Dale didn't play at home between December 9th and March 10th. However, the backlog of games played a part in what became known as 'the Great Escape'. Dale – still on just 13 points at the beginning of March - remarkably won nine of their last 10 home games and seven of the last eight games of the season to climb out of the re-election places at the last gasp.

Confidence was high at the start of 1979-80 and the manager persuaded the Board to sanction the signing of England youth team captain Alan Weir for a record £12,000. The optimism quickly faded, though, with just one victory in 17 games. In November, new chairman Andrew Hindle sacked Doug Collins and replaced him with former boss Bob Stokoe who since leaving Spotland the first time had found fame at Sunderland. A couple of league wins and progress to the third round of the FA Cup revived hope (the game at Bury was watched by a crowd of 10,739, six times the league average), but following a 5-1 defeat by Tranmere, Stokoe attempted to fine his players for "lack of effort". This escalated into a dispute between the Football League (who supported the legality of Stokoe's move) and the PFA before Stokoe withdrew the fines a month later. In the meantime his side had beaten Doncaster but then launched on possibly the worst run of non-goalscoring ever seen – just one goal in 15 games, with nine blanks in succession. Unsurprisingly they finished last with only 27 points and a lowest ever 33 goals. At the FL AGM, Dale came up against a concerted campaign by top non-leaguers Altrincham to gain a league place and when the votes were counted they read Rochdale 26, Altrincham 25, with two not cast as the clubs' representatives missed the meeting. It was rumoured that both had promised their votes to Altrincham, but one way or another, Dale had survived by the skin of their teeth.

Bob Stokoe

Off the field the club was running up huge losses and at the end of the season it was revealed that the ground had been sold to an anonymous buyer, which later transpired to be a business owned by the then chairman, who had since resigned. Stokoe, too, resigned, saying the job was too big for him, and Peter Madden once more stepped into the breach.

The Eighties

Madden started by giving the existing players a fresh start and then recruiting a number of Yorkshire based players, as he had when caretaker a couple of years earlier. Remarkably, 'Madden's mercenaries' as they were dubbed by the press, lost only once in the first six games and, though not able to mount a serious challenge towards the top, remained competitive throughout the season, almost doubling the previous season's goals tally in finishing 15th. (They were only six points behind the side in 7th). Attendances were up 25%, too, to 2460. Moreover, after the ins and outs of the past few campaigns, Madden used only 17 players and four of those played no more than five games. Nigel O'Loughlin became the first player for a decade to complete 200 FL games for the club.

Though Madden continued his policy of consistent team selection, 1981-82 (the first season of three points for a win) saw a return to a struggle nearer the bottom of the table after only one victory in the first ten games, the main problem being a lack of goals. In the end, despite decent runs of form from time to time, Dale finished 21st, one point short of safety from re-election. Fortunately, all the bottom four were comfortably re-elected this time. Nevertheless, the club continued to lose money, the home game against Crewe which attracted only 1060 fans actually making a loss at the gate, after expenses were taken into account.

The first team squad for the new season was thus limited to just 13, with numbers made up by a succession of trialists and loans. Unsurprisingly performances suffered as a result, with just two league successes by the end of October. Indeed, Dale never seemed able to string two decent performances together and in March the Board decided on a change at the top and brought in former Manchester United star Jimmy Greenhoff as player-manager. Jimmy brought in brother Brian as coach and his first two games were both won, but form then reverted to what it had been before, and it took a point from the last game for Dale to reach the sanctuary of 20th place. The most remarkable result was a 6-4 defeat at Aldershot. Attendances at a couple of games dropped below 1000 again.

Off the field, financial affairs had taken an odd turn when the former chairman's company which owned Spotland went into liquidation and the new chairman, David Kilpatrick was able to negotiate a re-purchase of the ground for a knock-down valuation – and even managed to borrow the money to buy it from the local council. Since the ground sale back in 1980, debts of £250,000 had been cleared thanks to the efforts of Messrs Kilpatrick and Graham Morris, the financial director.

The summer saw the arrival of former Manchester City and England star Mike Doyle and a new record signing in Bury striker Steve Johnson for £13,500. The season was almost a replay of the Doug Collins era, though, as Greenhoff hardly ever played and eventually resigned after exactly one year in charge with Dale back in the bottom four again after one winless run stretched to 12 matches. Senior pro Les Chapman was made caretaker manager but improvement was only marginal and Dale failed by two points to get out of the re-election zone. Again, though, the vote went the way of the existing league clubs.

1984: Vic Halom meets the players

The next man in the Spotland hot seat was the Barrow manager Vic Halom, an FA Cup winner in his days at Sunderland. Despite another new record signing, Les Lawrence from Aldershot for £15,000, Halom's tenure could not have got off to a much worse start as all the first five games were defeats. With his side bottom of the table in November, Halom gradually turned things round with some further signings, not least striker Steve Taylor from Stockport. Indeed, despite using 37 different players, Dale had reached a relatively prosperous 17th by the end of the season, picking up 24 points from the last 14 games. The victory at Hereford was their first south of Birmingham for nine years. Attendances remained low, however, averaging just 1450.

Dale briefly headed Division 4 in the early weeks of 1985-86 after their best ever start of four wins and a draw. At Christmas, they were still in contention and Steve Taylor had already scored 21 goals, netting in seven successive games, the best run since Jimmy Wynn in the thirties. Dale had also reached the third round of the FA Cup where they went down only 2-0 to Manchester United in front of a 40,000 crowd. A controversial defeat at Stockport and the end of a 19 game unbeaten run at home precipitated a slump in the second half of the season, only a draw in the last match keeping them out of the bottom four, though 55 was their best points return since the introduction of three points for a win. Steve Taylor won the fourth division 'golden boot' with 31 goals, 25 in the league matching Reg Jenkins' post-war best return from 1964-65. Off the field David Kilpatrick was replaced as chairman by comedian Tommy Cannon.

Early in the following campaign Steve Taylor, who had personally scored half of Dale's goals over the last two years, was sold to Burnley for £20,000 and victories were hard to come by. By the time Dale were 3-0 down at home to Torquay, one of only two sides below them in the table, the crowd were calling for the manager's head. Even though his side came back to draw 3-3, Vic Halom was removed the following week and shortly replaced by ex-Leeds boss Eddie Gray. With the side who finished bottom now facing automatic relegation, there was no immediate improvement and by late February Dale still had just three victories to their credit. Fortunately at this point, with a number of new signings including former Rangers and Scotland star Derek Parlane, Dale went eight games without defeat. Even so, subsequent defeats saw Dale at the foot of the table again in mid-April and, according to at least one newspaper 'needing a miracle' to stay up. They still had six games left to play in the last 15 days of the season, though, and managed another escape act by winning four of them, the most dramatic a 5-3 defeat of Halifax with the season's heroes, the on-loan Lyndon Simmonds and skipper John Bramhall, both netting. (Remarkably, centre half Bramhall scored nine league goals). Despite, or perhaps because of, the tense finish, attendances averaged over 2000 for only the second time since relegation.

In many ways 1987-88 was even more of a struggle, though the collapse of Newport County, who finished 19 points behind anyone else, meant there was no real danger of relegation. Despite the arrival of new record £20,000 signing Mark Gavin, only two of the first 18 games were won and successive away games in October were lost 6-1 and then infamously 8-0 at Orient. Off the field an EGM was called by shareholders to insert a clause in the club's Articles of Association to the effect that the board could not sell the ground or use it as security for a loan without the consent of a full shareholders meeting. Chairman Tommy Cannon and other members of the board took this as a vote of no confidence and resigned. Former financial director Graham Morris told the meeting that in his view the club was insolvent and he and various other earlier directors were voted back onto the board to try and save the club. Cost cutting led to the sale or release of relatively high earners and the side for the rest of the season included numerous local lads, the 13 man squad for some games containing nine teenagers. Form, in fact, dramatically improved, Dale taking 34 points from a run of 23 games, though they still only finished 21st again.

Danny Bergara

Eddie Gray left for Hull in the summer and the other big news was that Rochdale Hornets would in future share Spotland with the Dale, following the sale of the Athletic Grounds. The intriguing choice as the next manager was Uruguayan Danny Bergara, the Sheffield United coach. His team proved somewhat erratic, not winning any of the first five games of the season but then winning all the next five. South American style certainly brought goals to Dale's early season games with a rare 4-4 draw (at Hereford), a 4-3 cup defeat and three 3-3 draws, but the good form soon petered out. It was mid-March before Dale managed their second victory in 18 games, but after securing some breathing space with three wins in a row, Bergara quit and moved to Stockport. Dave Sutton, recently retired as a player because of injury took over a caretaker until the appointment of another ex-player Terry Dolan as the new boss. Dale played out the season well clear of relegation, ending in 18th place, the eighth time in succession they had finished between 17th and 22nd

The Nineties

With pretty much a clean slate – only four of the previous season's players reappeared - and with David Kilpatrick, back as chairman, able to report a sizeable profit, Dolan's new team were finally able to break the club's 15 year run of bottom half finishes in 1989-90. They hovered around mid-table for most of the season, being consistently inconsistent with victories generally followed by defeats, and were eventually placed 12th with 20 of each and just six draws. Nevertheless, this was the first time that Dale had had even a passing interest in the play-offs, introduced three years earlier, ending just five points behind the side in seventh spot. Attendances recovered somewhat, as a result, edging back above 2000, where they stayed for the next seven years. The main feature of the season, though, was a remarkable cup run which took them to a fifth round tie at Crystal Palace where they went down 1-0 to the eventual finalists, the first time Rochdale had ever made it to the last 16. The result which Dale fans still recall gleefully from this era, though, was the 1-0 win at Burnley with nine men.

The following season began with two 4-0 victories and just one defeat in the first 12 league games saw Dale as high as 2nd in the table. This wasn't maintained, though, and the end of the campaign again saw Dale finish 12th, though they achieved it rather differently, with no fewer than 17 draws. By this time Terry Dolan had left for the manager's job at Hull and Dave Sutton was back in charge, this time on a more permanent basis. His first game in charge had seen goalkeeper Keith Welch sent off, his subsequent suspension breaking a run of 188 consecutive FL games since his debut.

In the summer of 1991 Welch was sold to Bristol City for easily a new club record fee of £200,000 and the incoming record was broken, too, when Andy Flounders arrived from Scunthorpe for £80,000. Dale again got off to a great start with five wins and three draws and this time they did keep it going. Indeed, when the table was recalculated in late March, following the mid-season demise of Aldershot, Dale were in 5th place and had suffered only five defeats. Only three points behind the third placed side with six games to go, but hampered by injuries, they disastrously lost five of them and the defeat by champions Burnley, in a game postponed until after the season should have finished, left them three points short of even the play-offs. Average attendances reached 2784, the best since 1972-73.

Dale found themselves in Division 3 in 1992-93, as the formation of the Premier League saw the other divisions renumbered. In points terms the season saw a slight downturn, runs of good form being interspersed with strings of defeats as they finished in 11th. In fact, with the side in 7th place having an unusually low number of points, Dale retained an interest in the play-off places until the last couple of games. There were some memorable moments, too, such as Flounders' 50 yard lob over the stranded Lincoln 'keeper. A new Main Stand was opened on Boxing Day, the first stage of an ambitious plan to redevelop the stadium

Dave Sutton

Dale briefly led the table at the start of the following campaign, winning six of the first eight league games, earning Dave Sutton a manager of the month award. Although not able to keep up this pace, they did again remain in contention throughout the season and for the second time in three years still had a chance of a play-off spot at half time on the final day, before finishing 9th. They also netted six for the first time since 1968-69 when they beat Northampton 6-2. A less pleasant episode was the 'battle of Turf Moor' when Dale's FA Cup tie with Burnley ended with one Dale player in hospital, three players sent off and three penalties awarded.

Unfortunately, after beating a young Manchester United side – Beckham and all – in the pre-season Lancashire Cup and winning three of the first four league games, the next term was a disappointment. Centre half Alan Reeves, player of the year for the last three seasons, was sold to Premier League Wimbledon for a new record £300,000, but it was a lack of goals as much as the defence – though a spectacularly unsuccessful loan spell for 'keeper Matt Dickens didn't help - which cost Dale points and Dave Sutton his job. After trying to recruit from outside, the board eventually confirmed Sutton's assistant Mick Docherty as the new man in charge. A decent run of form in the new year, with only one defeat in 13 games, still didn't change Dale's position just below half way in the table, but they did reach the Northern Final of the Auto Windscreens Shield. In the first leg, skipper Andy Thackeray chose to play into the teeth of a gale at Carlisle and Dale conceded three first half goals, only for the wind to disappear after the break to deny Dale an equal advantage, the Cumbrians eventually winning 5-3 on aggregate. A notable occurrence was the selection of a Dale player for a senior international match for the first time since World War I, when Neil Matthews was selected for Northern Ireland 'B'. At the end of the season long serving midfielder Shaun Reid was sold (for the second time) after accumulating 240 FL appearances over his two spells with the club, his total of 314 games the most since Reg Jenkins and Graham Smith over twenty years earlier.

The 1995-96 season followed a somewhat familiar pattern with a good start – 18 points from the first 10 league games and 48 goals in the first 23 games in all, the best in the country - followed by a steady decline, to again finish 15th. They did reach the third round of the FA Cup but were trounced 7-0 at Liverpool, Ian Rush netting the goal he needed to be the FA Cup's all-time leading scorer. A more positive result was a 4-0 victory at Barnet, the club's first ever success in London at the 41st attempt spread over 75 years! Steve Whitehall netted 20 league goals and 24 in total, the next best to Steve Taylor in the last 30 years.

Two weeks after the season ended, Mick Docherty was sacked and Graham Barrow was appointed in his stead. Two of the leading players, Paul Butler and Jason Peake, also moved on, their transfers eventually netting some half a million pounds to boost finances hit by continued low gates. None of the new boss's first six games was won, but after perversely gaining a first victory when reduced to nine men against Doncaster, an eight game unbeaten run stabilised things and Dale's position oscillated around the middle of the table thereafter. The reserves, on the other hand, won 13 games in a row and ran away with the Pontins (Central) League Division 3 title. At the end of the season, Dave Thompson, who had made his debut back in 1981-82, was released after 266 FL games in his two stints at Spotland (leaving him fourth in the all-time rankings), while Steve Whitehall was sold to Mansfield after notching 95 goals in all games, the third highest ever after Reg Jenkins and Bert Whitehurst. At the other end of the age range, Centre of Excellence product Stephen Bywater was selected for the England under-16s. He made his senior debut the following year in an AW Shield game when still only 16 and was then transferred to West Ham for £300,000 plus add-ons.

Dale gained five home wins out of six at the start of 1997-98 and ended the season with another seven home wins out of eight (by an aggregate of 20-3), giving them the second most home successes in the division (though average attendances didn't reflect this, at only 1847). However, a dreadful away record - 17 defeats in 23 games - left them down in 18th though with the same points tally as the previous term and a positive goal difference. One of the away defeats (unsurprisingly) was at Orient when Keith Hill was sent off for supposed handball after 19 seconds and Dale finished with nine men, losing 2-0 to two penalties. Further ground development saw the opening of the new WMG stand at the completely rebuilt Pearl Street End. Unfortunately crowds in the new stands were no higher, while fans had also polarised into pro- and anti-Barrow factions who actually came to blows on occasions.

In 1998 Dale managed to reach the final of the pre-season Lancashire Cup for the first time since it took on this format, but lost to Wigan. With the manager concentrating on the defensive side of his team, the goals dried up, just 42 in 46 games, the lowest in the division, and Dale slipped another place to 19th. Finally with one match of the season to go, Barrow was sacked, leaving youth coach David Hamilton in charge for the final game.

It was now 25 years since relegation to the bottom division and for much of that time survival until the following season had had to be considered a success. Dale had managed two 12th placed finishes under Terry Dolan, one serious promotion push and a couple of other challenges for the play-off places under Dave Sutton, but had finished in the bottom half in the other 20 seasons. As 1999-2000 approached, the club were therefore in the familiar position of seeking yet another new manager to try and lead them out of the lower reaches of the table.

1975-76: Back, left to right. Joyce (manager), Townsend, Cooper, Mountford, Whelan, Oliver, Poole, Summerscales, Hanvey, Mulvaney, Horne, Campbell (coach). Front: Hallows, Ainsworth, Fielding, Tobin, Murty, Lacey, Hulmes, Sweeney

1980-81: Back; Probert, Snookes, Senior, Hilditch, Burke. Centre; Hoy, O'Loughlin, Seal, Wann, Cliff, Weir, Taylor, Madden (manager). Front, seated; Oliver, Esser, Wellings, Jones, Martinez. On ground; Lambert, Stanley

1984-85: Back; Thompson, Edwards, McMahon, Lawrence, Conroy, Hanvey, Cooke, McCluskie. Front; Heaton, Keegan, Diamond, Griffiths, Chapman, Reid

1988-89. Back; Walling, Armitage, Mellish, Smith, Smart, Welch, O'Shaughnessy, Copeland, Mycock, Beaumont, Jones (trainer). Centre; Harris, Simmonds, Lomax, Bergara (Manager), Sutton, Reid, Frain. Front; Lucketti, Worsley, Hancox, Buckley, Appleby, Hughes, Hedderman, Allen.

NOTES TO WHO'S WHO

In the following section, players are listed in the order of their Rochdale competitive debuts. An alphabetical table of the players, with the seasons played and appearances and goals in the various competitions is appended. Games counted for these purposes are the Football League (and play-offs), the FA Cup, the Football League Cup (under various sponsors' names), the Associate Members Cup from 1983-84 (aka the Freight Rover Trophy, Sherpa Van Trophy, Leyland DAF Cup, AutoGlass Trophy, Auto Windscreens Shield, LDV Vans Trophy, Johnstone's Paint Trophy) and the last few years of the Lancashire Senior Cup as a first team competition (1973-74 and then 1982 to 1996 and 1998 as a pre-season tournament). 'Other' games include the pre-season Charity Rose Bowl games against Oldham Athletic (played irregularly between 1981 and 2007) and the Isle of Man summer tournament in 2002. Substitute appearances are denoted by + signs. If a player was named as substitute, but without making an appearance, this is denoted +0.

In the individual players' career details, FL appearances for any club are given in square brackets. In addition, Scottish League appearances are denoted by ScL. After the formation of the Alliance League, later renamed the Football Conference, at the top of the non-league game in 1979, appearances at this level are denoted 'Conf'. Details for the 'new' Football League Divisions 1, 2 and 3 after the renumbering in 1992-93 are labelled Division 1+ etc. Appearances in the North American Soccer League (1967 to 1984) are given as NASL. A £ sign indicates that a fee was paid for the player's transfer, but the amount is not known. Under 'Honours', players (or managers) who were with a club at some point during a season in which a championship or promotion was obtained, but were no longer with the club at the end of that season, have the relevant honour in brackets, as do players who were unused substitutes in cup finals etc. Probable but unconfirmed details are contained in curly brackets. An asterisk denotes that a player was still at the final club listed as of the end of the 2014-15 season. In the few cases where relevant, FL appearances are also up to the end of 2014-15. In the dates of birth, if no precise date is known, JFM signifies the first quarter of the year (January, February, March) and so forth.

Keith Hanvey 1973-77, 1984-85

Born: Manchester 18.1.52
6'1" 13st
Defender
FL Apps/Gls 136/10 Total Apps/Gls 161/11
Career: Ashton College, Manchester C. 9.70, pro 8.71, Swansea C. 10.7.72 [11/-], Dale 19.7.73 [121/9], Grimsby T. 7.2.77 £12,000 [54/2], Huddersfield T. 7.78 £14,000 [205/14], Dale 7.84 [15/-], retired injured 12.84.
Huddersfield T. commercial manager 1988, Bradford C. commercial manager 1990, Leeds U. commercial manager 1993 to 2002
Honours: Division 4 champions 1980, Division 3 promotion 1983

Walter Joyce's first signing for Dale, Keith proved one of the most successful. His sole appearance for Manchester City was against Airdrie in the Texaco Cup just after turning pro, and he made his league debut for Swansea a year later. Despite Dale's relegation and some injury problems, at Spotland he remained a regular at left back and then centre back for four seasons, also being the side's top scorer for a time when he netted four times in the first seven games of 1976-77. Sold later in the season, he subsequently had a long spell with Huddersfield helping them rise from the fourth to the second divisions. He had a final season with Dale, curtailed by an ongoing pelvic injury and Ron Atkinson sent a Manchester United XI to play Huddersfield at Spotland for his benefit game (making him the last Dale player to have a testimonial). Keith later returned to Huddersfield as their commercial manager and took similar roles at Bradford City and Leeds before starting his own sports hospitality company.

Stephen Frank (Steve) Arnold 1973-74

Born: Willesden 5.1.51
6'0" 12st7
Midfield/central defender
FL Apps/Gls 37+3/1
Total Apps/Gls 40+3/1
Career: Crewe A. app 28.9.66, pro 14.1.69 [13+2/-], Liverpool 9.9.70 £12,000 [1/-], Southport loan 27.1.72 [16/3], Torquay U. loan 1.9.72 [2+1/1], Dale 12.6.73 [37+3/1], Weymouth 7.74, Dorchester T. loan, retired cs.76. Connah's Quay Nomads 8.78. West Kirkby 1982 to 1985-86

A promising midfielder as a youngster at Crewe, Steve was signed by Liverpool, but played only one game for them, when Bill Shankly rested his entire first team ahead of the Fairs Cup semi-final against Leeds in 1971. Signed for Dale by Gus McLean while they were between managers, he scored probably their goal of the season in the rare victory over Southend with a storming run from half way, but was unaccountably used as a central defender for most of a disastrous season in which Dale conceded 111 goals in all games. Despite a decent run in the Southern League with Weymouth, he left the game when only 25 but later played some minor football.

Alan David Taylor 1973-75

Born: Hinckley 13.11.53
5'7" 11st
Forward
FL Apps/Gls 55/8
Total Apps/Gls 62/10
Career: Preston NE app 10.69, Lancaster C., Morecambe, Dale 11.5.73 £2500 [55/8], West Ham U. 25.11.74 £40,000 [88+10/25], Norwich C. 8.79 £90,000 [20+4/5], Vancouver Whitecaps summer 1980 £90,000 [58/23 NASL] to 1983, Cambridge U. loan 10.80 [8/2], Cambridge U. loan 10.81 [9+1/2], Hull C. 12.83 [13+1/3], Burnley 6.84 [60+4/23], Bury 6.86 [55+7/10], Norwich C. 9.88 [1+3/1], Bury Town 1989-90, Thetford T. player-manager, Dereham
Honours: FA Cup winners 1975, Anglo-Italian Cup final 1975, European Cup Winners Cup final 1976

Dick Conner's final signing, Alan made his debut as a 19 year old in the first game of 1973-74. Playing wide on the right or as a striker he managed only one league goal in Dale's catastrophic relegation campaign but was one of the few players to enhance their reputations and after seven goals early the following term was transferred to West Ham for £40,000. Having missed the first round of the cup with a providential bout of 'flu, the floppy haired blond striker made a sensational impact for the Hammers, scoring twice in the FA Cup quarter final in only his second full game, adding two more in the semi-final and ending a fairy tale season with both goals in the final against Fulham. He also figured in the following season's European Cup Winners Cup Final and appeared in well over 100 senior games for West Ham before moves to a string of other league clubs and stints in the NASL (playing for Vancouver Whitecaps alongside Dale's other export to West Ham and Norwich, Dave Cross). He actually had his best ever goalscoring season while with Burnley in the fourth division, netting 16 times in 1985-86 but ended his FL career back at the top level with a few first division games in a second spell at Norwich.

Paul Brears 1973-76
Born: Oldham A. 25.9.54 5'6" 10st
Midfield
FL Apps/Gls 26+1/0 Total Apps/Gls 30+1/1
Career: Oldham A. am 1971, Dale 7.73 [26+1/-], New Mills 1976. Mount Pleasant c.1982
Honours Manchester County FA Challenge Trophy final 1983

Paul had been a junior at Oldham when Walter Joyce was their youth team coach and made his Dale debut in the new manager' first game in charge. Unlucky enough to be carried off injured after just 25 minutes and require a cartilage operation, he did not play again all season. He figured quite regularly in midfield the following term in Division 4, but he played only twice in 1975-76. He and Phil Mullington (q.v.) played in the same Manchester League Mount Pleasant side, managed by his former Oldham and Dale coach Harold Hulbert.

James Hamilton Laird (Jimmy) Burt
1973-74
Born: Harthill 5.4.50 5'11" 11st6
Right back
FL Apps/Gls 4/0 Total App/Gls 4/0
Career: Whitburn B., Leicester C. 6.67, Aldershot 10.70 [22+2/-], Northampton T. 7.72 [16+5/-], Dale trial 8.73 to 30.10.73 [4/-], Enderby T. 1974. Raunds T. manager 1983-84

Although not making the first team at Leicester, Jimmy had made a number of league appearances, mainly at left back, for Aldershot and Northampton before having a trial at Spotland early in 1973-74. Dale gained a draw in his first game, but his other three matches as stand in for Graham Smith all ended in defeat and he was not considered further. Though a Scot, he then returned to non-league football in the Leicester area.

Michael (Micky) Brennan 1973-75

Born: Salford 17.5.52
5'10" 11st
Forward
FL Apps/Gls 35+2/4 Total Apps/Gls 39+4/4
Career: Manchester C. app 1968, pro 12.69 [1+3/-], Stockport Co. loan 2.72 [18/3], Dale 1.10.73 £5000 [35+2/4], Mossley loan 2.75, Macclesfield T. cs.75, Northwich Victoria 1977-78, Oswestry 1978-79, Witton A. 1979-80 £800, Macclesfield T. 1980-81, Stalybridge Celtic 1981-2, Cleveland Cobras (USA), West Adelaide (Australia) player-coach 1982 and 1983

A promising youngster at Maine Road, where he was the reserves' top scorer in both 1970-71 and 1972-73, Micky made one first division start for City, as stand-in for Francis Lee and appeared twice in the Texaco Cup (alongside Keith Hanvey). Joining Dale for a sizeable fee by their standards after the departure of Bill Atkins and Malcolm Darling, he figured frequently up front though managing only three goals. He went on to have a lengthy career in senior non-league football in the North West, playing 160 games for Northern Premier League Macclesfield in two spells, latterly in defence, before emigrating to Australia.

Donald Joseph (Don) Tobin 1973-76
Born: Huyton 1.11.55 5'7" 10st7
Midfield
FL Apps/Gls 46+2/5 Total Apps/Gls 51+2/6
Career: Everton app 1971-72, Dale pt 3.9.73, pro 3.74 [46+2/5], Crewe A. trial cs.76, Witton Albion 1976-77, Sligo Rovers 1977-78, California Sunshine (USA) 1978 to 1980, California Lightnin' 1981 to 1983, Rochester Flash 1984, Tulsa Tornados 1985, Tampa Bay Rowdies 1988 to 1989, Orlando Lions 1990 to 1993, Dunedin Stirling SC director of coaching 1995, Tampa Bay Extreme manager 2000, Tampa Spartans (University of Tampa) assistant coach 2006*
Indoor League football for Wichita Wings 1978 to 1980, Los Angeles Lazers 1981 to 1983, Canton Invaders player-assistant coach 1983 to 1987, Memphis Rogues player-head coach 1989 to 1991
Honours: Huyton Schools, English Schools Trophy winners, ASL All Star team 1979, 1981, ASL champions 1981, AISA MVP 1986

Don was a member of the Huyton side which won the English Schools Trophy, playing alongside future England international Peter Reid and joined Reid at Everton. His only FL appearances came at Spotland, playing central midfield or on the left flank, and mostly during 1974-75, though he scored four of his five league goals in successive games the following term. However, after emigrating to the US in 1978 he had a 15 year career in the American Soccer League amongst others, being voted into the ASL All Star Teams for 1979 and 1981 and winning the league title with California Lightnin'. Also a top indoor player, he scored 50 goals for LA Lazers and was the American Indoor Soccer Association's Most Valuable Player in 1986, before going into coaching.

Eamon Anthony Kavanagh 1973-74
Born: Manchester 5.1.54   5'9"   10st8
Midfield
FL Apps/Gls 2+2/0   Total Apps/Gls 2+2/0
Career: Manchester C. app 1969-70, pro 6.71, Dale trial 8.73 to 10.12.73 [2+2/-], Bury trial, Workington 1.74 [123+6/11], Scunthorpe U. 8.77 to cs.80 [68+8/3]

Like Hanvey and Brennan a former Manchester City apprentice, Eamon had a short spell at Spotland during Dale's relegation season. He made his debut in midfield against Watford the week that Dale boss Joyce dispensed with the services of experienced trio Renwick, Blant and Kinsella, making him their 23rd player in just 14 games. He later had a lengthy stint as a regular at Workington, ended when they failed to gain re-election, and three seasons with Scunthorpe.

Gary Smethurst Cooper 1973-77

Born: Horwich 12.2.55
5'11"   11st4
Forward
FL Apps/Gls 81+11/14
Total Apps/Gls 89+12/14
Career: Horwich RMI 1970, Everton trial, Bolton W. app 1972-73, Oldham A. trial 2.73, Dale pt 16.7.73, pro 21.12.73 [81+11/14], Southport 11.8.77 [13+7/5], Lancaster C. cs.78, Southport cs.81, Horwich RMI 1.85 to 1986, (USA)
Honours: Lancashire Schools, English Grammar Schools 1972, NPL Cup final 1980

Gary played for Horwich RMI while still at school, when he represented English Grammar Schools, and was offered terms by Dale in the summer of 1973. He made his debut at centre forward in Christmas week, playing six games before, rather oddly, being left out after Dale gained only their second – and last – victory of the season. By 1975-76 he was playing regularly, latterly in midfield, and eventually reached a century of appearances, though managing only 14 goals, remarkably two of them after coming on as substitute in a 5-0 victory over Scunthorpe, a first for Dale. The scorer of Southport's last FL goal he had more success when returning to Haig Avenue in their non-league days, netting 27 times in 1981-82 before a spell in the USA.

Paul Stanley Jones 1973-74
Born: Stockport 10.9.53   5'9"   10st8
Midfield
FL Apps/Gls +0/0   Total Apps/Gls +0/0
Career: Manchester U. app, pro 12.70, Mansfield T. 6.73 [15+5/1], Dale loan 30.11.73 to 27.12.73, Chesterfield cs.74 to 1975

A former Manchester United junior, Paul joined Mansfield in the summer of 1973 but after 10 games was loaned to Dale. He was unused substitute against Blackburn, but by the time of the next league game Dale had added Horne and Grummett to their squad and Paul did not have a further opportunity, returning to Field Mill. He played another 10 games, on the wing or in midfield, but did not appear at all for Chesterfield the following term.

Stanley Frederick (Stan) Horne 1973-76

Born: Clanfield 17.1.2.44
5'10"   12st6
Midfield/central defender
FL Apps/Gls 48/5
Total Apps/Gls 53/5
Career: Aston Villa app 1960, pro 12.61 [6/-], Manchester C. 9.65 [48+2/-], Fulham 2.69 £20,000 [73+6/-], Chester 8.73 £5000 [17+1/-], Dale 19.12.73 £5000 [48/5], Denver Dynamos summer 1974 [20/- NASL], retired injured 9.1.76
Honours: Central League champions 1964, Division 2 champions 1966, Division 1 champions 1968, Division 3 promotion 1971

Signed by his former Villa boss Joe Mercer, Stan played a number of games, at wing half or left back, in the Manchester City side promoted in 1966. He was a regular in their first season in the top flight, but made only four appearances in the league championship winning side. He also won promotion, from Division 3, in four seasons at Fulham, where he partnered Johnny Haynes in midfield. Having been sent off for Chester on the season's opening day, he arrived at Spotland with Jim Grummett in a last effort to rescue Dale's dire 1973-74 campaign. He started the following term in Division 4 playing centre back but suffered a bad knee injury in mid-season and was unable to play again. Prior to his spell at Spotland, Stan had never scored a senior goal in around 150 appearances, but he managed five for Dale including a free kick from the half way line against Barnsley.

James (Jim) Grummett 1973-75

Born: Barnsley 11.7.45
5'10" 12st5
Midfield/defender
FL Apps/Gls 32+1/2   Total Apps/Gls 33+1/2
Career: Ruston Bucyrus, Lincoln C. am 9.62, pro 6.63 [246+4/19], Aldershot 7.71 £4000 [81/6], Chester 6.73 (part exchange) [15+1/-], Dale 19.12.73 £5000, [32+1/2], Denver Dynamos summer 1974 [20/- NASL], Boston U. 30 12.74 £1000
Honours: Lincoln Schools, England youth international 1963 (3 caps)

An England youth international, despite being with fourth division Lincoln, Jim spent eight years in the Imps side, missing only four games in four seasons and totalling 250 league appearances. Although normally a left half, he had a run at centre forward in 1967-68, scoring seven times in eight league games and in a League Cup victory over Newcastle. In fact, he played in every position for the Imps, including replacing the injured keeper in an FA Cup tie. Joining Dale from Chester along with Stan Horne, he figured both as a defensive midfielder and a centre back as Dale slipped into the bottom division. He spent the summer playing, again with Horne, in the North American Soccer League and left Spotland half way through the following term. His father, Jim senior, had also been a Lincoln stalwart wing half just after the war.

Roger William Denton 1973-74
Born: Stretford 6.1.53 5'10" 11st10
Left back
FL Apps/Gls 2/0 Total Apps/Gls 2/0
Career: Manchester U. jnr, Bolton W. 5.71 [3+1/-], Bradford C. 7.72 [25+5/-], Dale loan 14.2.74 to 28.2.74 [2/-], retired cs.74

Roger had made a number of appearances for Bradford City in the fourth division, playing in midfield or at full back, before a loan move to Spotland. Dale conceded eight goals in his two games at left back and he returned to Valley Parade after just a fortnight. He quit the game that summer and had much more success as a professional golfer, becoming captain and later president of the Yorkshire PGA and coaching in Thailand.

Ian Buckley 1973-74
Born: Oldham 8.10.53 5'9" 10st7
Outside left
FL Apps/Gls 6/0   Total Apps/Gls 6/0
Career: Oldham A. app 24.7.69, pro 3.12.71 [5/-], Dale loan 22.2.74 to 21.3.74 [6/-], Stockport Co. 12.8.75 [55+10/2], Durban C. (S. Africa), Cambridge U. 11.11.77 [51+6/2], Newcastle KB (Australia) 1981 to 1983
Honours: Chadderton Schoolboys, England youth international v Spain 1972, Division 3 promotion 1978

Another of Walter Joyce's Oldham youth team, Ian appeared for England at youth level against Spain in 1972 when he also made his FL debut. He was not used again by the Latics, though, and spent a month at Spotland in 1974, Dale managing four draws in his six games on the left flank, one of their better runs of the season. Transformed into a left back by Stockport, he even played in central defence, and later assisted Cambridge to promotion to the second division, as well as playing in South Africa and Australia.

David Andrew (Dave) Seddon 1966-69, 1973-75
Born: Rochdale 13.4.51
Left back
FL Apps/Gls 18+3/0   Total Apps/Gls 21+3/0
Career: Dale am 1966, Madeley College 1969, Stafford Rangers 1970, Dale trial, Nelson, Dale am 1973, pro 7.74 [18+3/-], Mossley loan 1973-74, Stafford Rangers cs.75, Kidderminster Harriers 1978, Hednesford T. 1979-80, Sutton Coldfield T. 1983-84, Willenhall 1985-86, Sutton Coldfield T. coach/assistant manager 1986, Rushall Olympic 1987-88
Honours: British Colleges XI, All England Colleges Cup winners, FA Trophy final 1976, FA XI v British Colleges 1980

Dave played in Dale's reserves while at (rugby union playing) Rochdale Grammar School and when training to be a teacher represented the British Colleges team as well as playing non-league for Stafford Rangers. When he returned to Rochdale he again figured in the reserves and after recovering from a broken leg made his senior bow towards the end of 1973-74, finally turning pro that summer. Surprisingly left out after a decent run in the side in the middle of the following season, he returned for the final game which Dale had to win to avoid the bottom four but was then released. He had a lengthy non-league career, highlighted by a Wembley appearance for Stafford Rangers in the FA Trophy Final, while rising to become a headteacher in Walsall and later Kidderminster.

Matthew David (Dave) Carrick 1973-75

Born: Evenwood 5.12.46
5'8" 11st
Midfield
FL Apps/Gls 25+1/4
Total Apps/Gls 30+1/5
Career: Wolverhampton W. app 1962-63, pro 12.64, Wrexham 7.66 £2500 [20+4/3], Altrincham c.2.68, Port Vale 1.69 [14+2/-], Stalybridge Celtic 1969, Witton Albion, Preston NE £500 11.73 [+2/-], Dale 7.3.74 £1000 [25+1/4], Droylsden cs.75, Altrincham 3.76, Middlewich A., Macclesfield T. 3.78, Droylsden 1979, Oswestry T., New Mills

Originally mainly a left winger, Dave had an in and out career, with three spells in the FL separated by stints in senior non-league football. His brief stint at Preston under Bobby Charlton resulted in them being deducted points, as his registration had not been secured before his debut. Arriving at Spotland when relegation was already certain, he played regularly in midfield for the rest of the campaign and became the only Dale player to score twice in a match all season, when he did so in a 3-3 draw at Cambridge. (His first league goal had been against Dale, for Wrexham in December 1966). After one more season he moved back to non-league football. Sadly, he was diagnosed with MS soon after finishing playing and died at the age of only 42, shortly after Witton Albion played a benefit game for him against Manchester City. Witton fans still consider him one of their finest ever players.

Paul Charles Richard Hallows 1974-80

Born: Chester 22.6.50
5'7" 10st9
Right back
FL Apps/Gls 197/2
Total Apps/Gls 223/2
Career: Bolton W. app, pro 10.67 [44+2/-], Dale 20.5.74 £2000 [197/2], Oswestry 7.80, Mossley 1980-81, Whitworth Valley 8.81
Honours: Chester and Cheshire Schoolboys, Division 3 promotion 1973

Despite a frightening catalogue of injuries, Paul was one of the few successful, long lasting Dale players of the mid to late seventies. At Bolton, he sustained a fractured skull during a match against York, and at various points suffered a detached retina, two ruptured muscles, and long running knee problems which required a cartilage operation in his last year with the Dale. At Spotland he was the undisputed first choice right back after taking over the mantle of the even longer serving Graham Smith in 1974. He missed only one game in his first three seasons and was voted player of the year in 1976. Out of favour in 1979-80 until Bob Stokoe returned as manager, Stokoe not only recalled Paul but made him captain. Sadly he lasted only three games before a final injury ended his league career. Paul had actually played as a goalkeeper at schools level and joined Bolton as a forward. One of his sons, Marcus, played for Sligo and St Patricks in Ireland before having a brief trial at Spotland, while his other son, Paul junior, played for Airbus UK in the Welsh Premier League.

Anthony Michael (Tony) Whelan 1974-77

Born: Salford 20.11.52
6'1" 11st8
Forward/left back
FL Apps/Gls 124/20
Total Apps/Gls 143/21
Career: St Pauls Secondary Modern (Urmston), Manchester U. as 1967, app 7.68, pro 12.69, Manchester City 1.72 [3+3/-], Dale 1.7.74 [124/20], LA Skyhawks (USA) summer 1976, Fort Lauderdale Strikers 3.77 to 1979 [94/5 NASL], Atlanta Chiefs 1980 and 1981 [62/3 NASL], Fort Lauderdale Strikers 1982 to 1983 [17/- NASL], director of youth development 1983, Bolton W. trial c.11.83, Altrincham trial 12.83, Witton Albion 12.83 to 1984. Manchester C. community programme coach 9.87, Manchester U. centre of excellence coach 9.90, academy coach 9.98, director of youth football.
Indoor football: Atlanta Chiefs 1981, Philadelphia Fever 1982
Honours: Stretford Boys, Blue Star Tournament (Zurich) winners 1969, Lancashire Senior Cup final 1972, PFA Division 4 team of the year 1976, American Soccer League champions 1976, NASL Eastern Division champions 1978, American Conference final 1978, NASL and MISL Divisional champions 1981, FA XI 1984

Like Dale teammates Stan Horne and Leo Skeete, Tony was one of the first generation of black British players. He played in Youth Cup semi-finals with Manchester United in 1969 and 1970 and scored in the Lancashire Cup Final in 1971 (having played against the Dale in an earlier round). He also toured Canada, Bermuda and the

USA with the senior team after turning pro but did not make his FL debut until moving to rivals City. He spent three seasons with Dale, playing first at left back, then on the left flank and finally at centre forward, being voted into the PFA fourth division team of the year in 1976 and missing only two games before emigrating to the USA. Having already won the American Soccer League title during a summer in Los Angeles, he became a star of the NASL, playing in the same Fort Lauderdale side as Gordon Banks, George Best and Gerd Muller. Also playing indoor soccer he became involved with youth coaching and was made an honorary citizen of Plantation, Florida for his youth community work. Returning to the UK, he broke his leg playing for Witton Albion and turned to full time coaching, first with City and then back at United, eventually becoming director of youth football. He published a book "The Birth of the Babes; Manchester United Youth Policy 1950-1957" in 2004 and after an Open University degree obtained an MA in sociology at Manchester Metropolitan University. Magazine "The Voice" named him as one of the 30 most influential black people in football, Tony receiving his award in the House of Lords.

Michael Kevin (Mike) Ferguson 1974-76

Born: Blackburn 9.3.43
5'10" 11st7
Outside right/midfield
FL Apps/Gls 68+1/4
Total Apps/Gls 81+1/5
Career: Plymouth A. am 16.3.59, Accrington St. 4.7.60 [23/1, 27/1 expunged], Blackburn R. 15.3.62 £2500 [220/29], Aston Villa 5.68 £55,000 [38/2], Queens Park R. 11.69 £15,000 [68+1/2], Cambridge U. 7.73 [39/4], Dale 1.7.74 [68+1/4], Los Angeles Aztecs loan summer 1975 [22/2 NASL], IA Akrannes (Iceland) manager 3.76, Rossendale U. coach 1976, Halifax T. 12.76 [2/-], Dale caretaker manager 12.9.77, manager 10.77 to 12.78, manager in Sweden, Apoel Nicosia (Cyprus) manager, coach in UAE 1985-86, Enfield manager 1989, Tottenham H. scout 11.89, Evagoras Paphos (Cyprus) manager 1991, England scout 1994 to 1996
Honours: Burnley Schools, FA Youth XI, Devon FA Youth

Mike played in the original Accrington Stanley's last two seasons as a teenage winger, scoring their last FL goal and appearing in their final match at Peel Park against the Dale. (He later became one of the last two Stanley players operating in the league). Blackburn bought his registration from the FL for a knock down fee and he played over 200 times for Rovers in the next six years, scoring twice in their remarkable 8-2 victory at West Ham on Boxing Day 1963. He also figured when they played in the American Soccer League in the summer of 1964. He would have played for England under-23s but was sent off the previous week and suspended. A big money move to Aston Villa only lasted for just over a season and he spent four years in and out of the QPR side before turning up at Spotland in 1974, enabling him to complete his tour of playing on all 92 league grounds. A regular on the right of midfield in his first season, he spent the summer in the NASL and left half way through the following campaign to manage IA Akrannes in Iceland. A year later he returned to Spotland, first as caretaker and then full time manager in succession to Brian Green. Dale were already bottom of the league and never rose above that position all season. When Dale managed just 10 points and 11 goals in the first 20 games of 1978-79, Mike was unsurprisingly sacked and he resumed coaching abroad, later working with former England boss Don Revie in the UAE. Mike also scouted for Spurs, and then for England when Terry Venables became manager.

Neil James Young 1974-75
Born: Manchester 17.2.44 6'1" 12st3
Forward
FL Apps/Gls 8+5/4 Total Apps/Gls 12+5/5
Career: Manchester C. jnr 1959, app 18.7.60, pro 20.2.61 [332+2/86], Preston NE 1.72 £60,000 [67+1/16], Dale 1.7.74 [8+5/4], retired cs.75. Macclesfield T. c.1976
Honours: Division 2 champions 1966, Division 1 champions 1968, FA Cup winners 1969, European Cup Winners Cup winners 1970, England youth international 1962, Anglo-Italian Cup final 1970, Charity Shield winners 1968

Another former top player, Neil had spent over a decade with Manchester City after making his debut as a 17 year old. Very tall for a winger, he was top scorer with 14 goals, including a hat-trick against Orient, as City gained promotion in 1966. After switching to inside forward he was an integral part of the famous attack with Mike Summerbee, Colin Bell and Francis Lee that won the league title two years later, Neil again top scoring with 19. He scored the only goal of the 1969 FA Cup Final against Leicester and the following term netted twice in the Cup Winners Cup semi-final and again in the final. He eventually made 412 appearances for City, netting 108 goals, before a couple of seasons at Preston. Still only 30 when reaching Spotland, he made little impression at fourth division level and when released left the game. He was later inducted into the Manchester City Hall of Fame and published an autobiography 'Catch a Falling Star' in 2004.

Harold John Martin 1974-75
Born: Blackburn 15.3.55 5'9" 10st12
Central defender
FL Apps/Gls 11+2/0 Total Apps/Gls 11+2/0
Career: Blackburn R. as, Bolton W. app 1972, pro 11.73, Dale 1.7.74 [11+2/-], Mossley cs.75, Prestwich Heys 10.75, Nelson, Great Harwood by 1983-84, player-assistant manager 6.85

On the small side for a central defender, Harold was yet another teenager signed up by Walter Joyce. After coming on as substitute on the first day of the 1974-75 season, his first full game was in midfield, but most of his appearances were as stand-in for Keith Hanvey or Dick Mulvaney later in his single league campaign. He was assistant to manager Malcolm Darling at Great Harwood a decade later.

John Leslie Taylor 1974-75
Born: Birmingham 25.6.49 5'11" 11st6
Goalkeeper
FL Apps 3 Total Apps 3
Career: Pwllheli c.1968, Chester 7.70 to 5.75 [70], Dale loan 15.10.74 to 18.11.74 [3], Los Angeles Aztecs summer 1975 [16 NASL], Bangor C. 1975, Stockport Co. 11.75 [1], Worcester C. 1976

John had a relatively short senior career, but at one point managed to play for six clubs in less than two years. Virtually all his league games came with Chester between 1972 and 1974, but his short loan spell at Spotland as cover for Mick Poole was certainly eventful: on his debut, a 3-3 draw with Swansea, he twice saved a penalty only for the referee to order a retake each time. The following summer he played for LA Aztecs with Mike Ferguson but appeared only once more in the FL

Gary Anthony Hulmes 1974-76

Born: Manchester 28.2.57
5'8" 10st7
Forward
FL Apps/Gls 4+6/1
Total Apps/Gls 4+7/1
Career: Manchester U. jnr, Manchester C. jnr, Dale am cs.74, pro 12.74 [4+6/1], Sligo Rovers cs.76, Limerick cs.80, Altrincham 2.81 £5000 [4+1/- Conf], Limerick 1981-82, Sligo Rovers 1986-87
Honours: League of Ireland champions 1977, 1980, League of Ireland v Argentina 1978 and 1980, v Italy, FA of Ireland Cup winners 1982

After netting five for the youth team the week before, Gary scored just three minutes after coming on for his Dale debut as substitute in the 3-3 draw with Swansea in October 1974, while still an amateur, but was given few opportunities after turning pro. However, after crossing to Ireland he played in two title winning sides, appeared in the European Cup against Red Star Belgrade and Real Madrid and the UEFA Cup against Southampton. Scorer of over 100 goals in the League of Ireland, he also played for their representative side against Argentina in a warm up game for the World Cup which the South Americans went on to win.

Richard (Dick) Mulvaney 1974-77

Born: Sunderland 5.8.42
5'11" 12st5
Central defender
FL Apps/Gls 72+1/4 Total Apps/Gls 81+2/4
Career: St. Leonard's School (Silksworth), {Peterlee Juniors?}, Seaham Juniors, Seaham Colliery, Cardiff C. trial, Murton Colliery Welfare, Billingham Synthonia, Blackburn R. am 1962, pro 28.2.64 [135+6/4], Oldham A. 26.8.71 [88+4/2], Dale 21.10.74 [72+1/4], retired 4.10.76. Gateshead pt 10.77, Chester-le-Street player-coach, assistant manager to at least 1987. Ashbrooke Sports Club FC ambassador 2014
Honours: Division 3 champions 1974. As coach; Wearside League champions 1981, Monkwearmouth Cup winners 1981, 1982, Northern League Division 2 champions 1984

A former team mate of Walter Joyce, Dick had progressed from north east non-league football to have a lengthy spell with Blackburn Rovers, mostly in Division 2. Originally a wing half, his early career spanned the introduction of the back four and he could play there or as a defensive midfielder. After three years at Oldham, where he was a reliable member of their third division championship winning side, he moved to Dale and formed a useful central defensive partnership with Keith Hanvey. After two years he quit as he could make a better living working on the docks back on Tyneside, though he later returned to the non-league game. His brother Jim also had a lengthy career in the lower leagues with Hartlepool, Barrow and Stockport. Dick (now Richard snr) was assisting with running Ashbrooke in the Sunderland Sunday League when in his seventies.

George Ernest Townsend 1973-76

Born: Ashton-under-Lyne 29.7.57 5'11" 12st
Left back
FL Apps/Gls 31+1/0
Total Apps/Gls 35+1/0
Career: Huddersfield T. as, Dale app 10.73, pro 7.75 to cs.76 [31+1/-], {Sydney C. (Australia)}, Manley (Australia), Mossley 1983-84, (Australia)
Honours: England youth trial

George was the first Dale player to have trials for the England youth side and became a league regular as a 17 year old apprentice, when he played virtually the whole of the second half of the 1974-75 season at left back, despite his debut ending in a 5-0 defeat at Hartlepool. Replaced by the experienced Tony Lacey the following term, he left to play in Australia. His son Ryan figured in the Australian under-20s World Cup squad and had one game for Burnley while an apprentice.

Robert (Rob) Hutchinson 1974-76
Born: Bolton 9.5.55
Striker
FL Apps/Gls 2/1 Total Apps/Gls 2/1
Career: Blackburn R. app 1973-74, Radcliffe Borough, Dale 12.12.74 to 22.9.75 [2/1], {Macclesfield T. trial ?, Stalybridge Celtic?}

Rob was another youngster given a chance by Walter Joyce, in his efforts to make Dale "the Burnley of the 1970s", making a scoring debut up front in a 2-0 victory over Doncaster on Boxing Day 1974. He also played the following week before the arrival of Bob Mountford consigned him to the reserves and he was released just after the start of the following season.

Robert William (Bob) Mountford 1974-78

Born: Stoke 23.2.52
5'11" 10st10
Striker
FL Apps/Gls 97+1/36
Total Apps/Gls 111+1/40
Career: Brown Edge, Port Vale app 1968, pro 7.70 [64+13/9], Scunthorpe U. loan 10.74 [1+2/-], Crewe A. loan 12.74 [5/-], Dale 1.1.75 £2000 [97+1/36], Huddersfield T. 20.9.77 £10,000 [12+2/4], Halifax T. 3.78 [56+6/11], Newcastle KB United loan summer 1978, Crewe A. 8.80 [3/-], Stockport Co. 11.80 [6+1/3], Newcastle KB United (Australia) player-coach 1.81 to 1983, Brisbane C. (Australia) 1984, Blacktown (Australia), Newcastle Breakers (Australia) assistant coach, Azzuri (Australia) coach, Newcastle-Port Stephen (Australia) junior coach, Edgworth (Australia) under-19 coach, Adamstown Rosebuds manager 2007 (d. 26.8.08)

An iconic figure in the Dale sides of his era (with probably the best Afro sported by any white player!), Bob had been brought up in the famously robust Port Vale sides managed by Gordon Lee. He played on loan for Crewe against Dale in December 1974 and three weeks later signed for them for £2000. He scored twice on his debut and ended the season as joint top scorer with 10 goals in just 18 outings despite twice being sent off and suspended, netting the goal on the final day which beat Swansea and kept Dale out of the bottom four. Always prepared to battle it out with the toughest defenders, he was easily top scorer again in the next two campaigns, netting 14 in the league and three in the FA Cup, including one against first division Norwich, in 1975-76. Early in 1977-78 he was sold to Huddersfield for a useful fee of £10,000 (Dale then going on to finish bottom) and subsequently figured with several other fourth division sides before emigrating to Australia. Also working in the prison service after finishing playing, he was a well known junior coach until his untimely death aged only 56.

Joseph Dougan (Joe) Murty 1974-76

Born: Glasgow 6.11.57
5'10" 11st6
Forward
FL Apps/Gls 15+6/2 Total Apps/Gls 15+7/2
Career: Radcliffe Borough, Oldham A. jnr, Dale app 23.5.74, pro 11.75 [15+6/2], Bury cs.76 [+1/-], Sligo Rovers 1978-79, Prestwich Heys, Buxton 1979-80, Winsford U. 1982, Rossendale U. 2.83, Ashton U. cs.83, Radcliffe Borough 1983-84, Curzon Ashton 1985-86, Mossley 1987-88, Prestwich Heys 1988-89, Oldham T. manager, Buxton manager c.1991, Prestwich Heys manager, Stand Ath. manager, Atherton Collieries manager, Oldham T. manager to 5.98, Curzon Ashton manager 11.98 to 6.00
Honours: Scottish youth trial, North West Counties division 1 champions 1985. As manager; NWC division 2 champions 2000

The second of Walter Joyce's youth players to have an international trial, with Scotland in his case, Joe was one of four players to hit a hat-rick in a staggering 16-1 FA Youth Cup victory over Skelmersdale. He made a number of appearances, mostly from the bench, while still an apprentice, towards the end of the 1974-75 season and had a run of games on the right flank following Mike Ferguson's departure the following term. After a spell with Sligo Rovers alongside Paul Fielding and Gary Hulmes, he had a lengthy career as player and manager in north-west non-league football. His son Steven also played non-league football for the likes of Ashton United, while his cousin Graeme was a Scottish international, playing over 400 games for York and Reading

William G. (Billy) Bell 1974-75
Born: Manchester 16.6.53
Midfield
FL Apps/Gls 5+1/0 Total Apps/Goals 5+1/0
Career: Ancoats Lads, Manchester C. jnr 1969, Oldham A. jnr, Ashton U., Droylsden 1971, Hyde U. 1973, New Cross Labour Club, Dale am 9.74 [5+1/-], Mossley 22.9.75, Buxton, Prestwich Heys
Honours: Northern Premier League cup final 1976

The final debutant of 1974-75, Billy had temporarily quit the senior game and been playing for a pub team when he was offered a trial at Spotland by his former Droylsden boss Derek Partridge, who was running Dale's third team. A tough tackling midfielder, he earned a call up to the first team and after coming off the bench at Brentford had a run of five games in place of Paul Brears. Though retained for the following term he soon moved to Mossley where he played regularly at fullback and gained a reputation as a 'hard man'; indeed, he was sacked for being sent off in the NPL cup final.

William Charles (Bill) Summerscales

1975-77
Born: Stoke 4.1.49
6'1" 11st
Centre half
FL Apps/Gls 87/4 Total Apps/Gls 100/4
Career: North Staffordshire College of Technology, Leek T., Port Vale am 1969, pro 2.70 £400 [126+3/4], Dale 1.7.75 [87/4], Stafford Rangers 7.77, Newcastle KB (Australia) 1978 to 1980, Marquis FC. Stoke C. under-15s coach, Redgate U. committee
Honours: Division 4 promotion 1970

Bill only turned pro when he was 21 and it was 1971-72 before he gained a regular place in Port Vale's third division side, a run ended when he broke his neck in a game against York in January 1974. He recovered to play the following season and then joined Dale along with team mate Tony Lacey. The regular centre half for two years, he missed only a handful of games before being released. He spent some time in Australia before returning to his home town to coach Stoke City's under-15s, again teaming up with Lacey.

Anthony John (Tony) Lacey 1975-77

Born: Leek 18.3.44
5'8" 10st2
Left back
FL Apps/Gls 83/0
Total Apps/Gls 96/0
Career: Leek CSOB, St Luke's (Exeter), Stoke C. 10.65 [2+2/-], Port Vale loan 2.70, signed 4.70 £2500 [193+7/9], Dale 1.7.75 [83/-], Stafford Rangers cs.77, Stoke C. youth coach, reserve coach, acting manager 4.85 to 5.85, youth development officer, Wolverhampton W. youth coach 1997, head of youth recruitment to 17.6.09
Honours: Division 4 promotion 1970

Like long time team mate Bill Summerscales, Tony was a late comer to the professional game after completing his degree at St Luke's. He was only on the fringe of the first team at Stoke but helped Port Vale to promotion in his first season and appeared exactly 200 times in the league for them, figuring in midfield, on the wing or at full back. Signed by Dale to provide much needed experience, he was briefly used in midfield before settling into the left back slot. Like Summerscales surprisingly released by Brian Green (possibly for financial reasons) in 1977, he returned to Stoke as coach and was briefly acting manager a few years later (losing all eight games) before running their youth development programme. He spent twelve years at Wolves in a similar capacity.

Andrew (Andy) Sweeney 1975-76

Born: Oldham 15.10.51
5'6" 10st7
Outside left
FL Apps/Gls 12+5/0
Total Apps/Gls 15+5/0
Career: Our Lady's School (Royton), Oldham A. am 2.11.70, pro 9.2.71 [37+5/2], Bury loan 8.3.73 [2/-], Dale 3.7.75 [12+5/-], Mossley cs.76, Witton Albion, Droylsden, Uppermill, Glossop 9.80
Honours: Chadderton Schoolboys, Lancashire Senior Cup final 1971, Division 4 promotion 1971, Division 3 promotion 1974

Andy was another member of Walter Joyce's Oldham youth team to arrive at Spotland. A "box of tricks" winger, he played a few times when Oldham won promotion to the third division in his first season, also appearing in the Lancashire Cup Final defeat by the Dale, but when they were promoted again managed just one substitute appearance. He started the first 11 games of 1975-76 on Dale's left wing but thereafter was mostly restricted to the bench.

Christopher Paul (Chris) Duffey 1975-76
Born: Kirby 8.1.52 5'8" 9st10
Forward
FL Apps/Gls 2/0 Total Apps/Gls 2/0
Career: Bolton W. app 1969, pro 4.70 [8/-], Crewe A. loan 9.72 [6/3], Crewe A. 7.73 [54+3/12], Bury 10.74 [17+4/8], Shrewsbury 5.75 to 2.76 [4+4/1], Dale loan 27.11.75 to 17.12.75 [2/-]. Southport 12.79 to 2.81

Chris joined Crewe in 1973 after a successful loan the previous term and netted 10 goals in his first full season, missing only one game on the left flank. Transferred to Bury, he was used as a striker and scored all their goals in a 4-1 win against Halifax on Boxing Day 1974, but was unable to cement a regular place. Joining Dale on loan from Shrewsbury, he appeared just twice, the second in the 3-0 defeat at Brentford when Mick Poole and two Bees players were sent off. He later reappeared at Southport, playing regularly for a couple of seasons.

Brian Charles Oliver 1974-76
Born: Liverpool 6.3.57 5'11" 12st10
Goalkeeper
FL Apps 3 Total Apps 4
Career: Everton jnr, Burnley jnr, Coventry C. jnr 8.72, Peterborough U. app 25.11.72, Bury app 2.74, Dale 11.7.74, pro 3.75 to 10.75, re-signed 11.75 [3], Southport loan 17.12.75 [2], Morecambe cs.76, New Mills 1976, Ashton U. 1977-78, Caernarfon 1977-78, Pwllheli c.1979. Stork c.1983, Salbreck Rangers (Sunday League)
Honours: Liverpool Schoolboys, Welsh Intermediate Cup winners 1978, Welsh League champions 1978

Brian had the odd experience of making his senior debut after being released, when he was quickly recalled to play in an FA Cup tie against Gateshead when Mick Poole was suspended. (He had previously played against his own side, when Darlington goalkeeper Ogley had to go off injured in a friendly against the Dale at the start of that season). Despite various problems, including a ruptured spleen, he had a successful time in the Welsh League with Caernarfon and after three seasons out with cartilage trouble returned to minor football on Merseyside.

Philip Thomas (Phil) Mullington 1975-77, 1978-79

Born: Oldham 25.9.56
5'10" 11st10
Midfield
FL Apps/Gls 67+8/6
Total Apps/Gls 76+8/7
Career: Oldham A. as 11.5.71, app 1972, n/c 7.75, Dale n/c 19.12.75, pro 1.76 [59+7/6], Northwich Victoria 7.77, Mossley 10.77, Ashton U. 11.77, Crewe A. 1.78 [1/-], Winsford U. 1978, Dale trial 8.78 to 10.78 [8+1/-], Carolina Hills (Hong Kong) 1.79

Yet another former Oldham junior, Phil joined Dale on non-contract terms in December 1975 and in only his third game on the left of midfield sensationally scored in Dale's FA Cup draw against first division Norwich. After 18 months as a regular he left for non-league football – with a very brief interlude at Crewe – but reappeared at Spotland at the start of the 1978-79 season. However Dale picked up just four points in the first 11 games of the season during his two month trial and he headed off to play in Hong Kong.

William (Billy) Boslem 1975-78

Born: Middleton 11.1.58
6'0" 11st6
Defender
FL Apps/Gls 42+3/1
Total Apps/Gls 46+5/1
Career: Dale jnr 1974, am 10.75, pro 28.9.76 [42+3/1], Mossley loan 1975, Buxton cs.78 to at least 1980
Honours: NPL cup final 1976

A junior at Spotland, Billy made his debut at centre back just after his 18th birthday and made a number of appearances at the end of the 1975-76 season, some of them in midfield. Dale were so short of players, that though still an amateur, Billy began the first match of the following term on the bench, turning pro shortly afterwards and playing a number of further games over the next two years, sometimes at full back, as Dale continued to struggle near the foot of the league. Oddly, Billy's only games for Mossley were the two legs of the NPL Cup Final.

22

David (Dave) Ainsworth   1974-76

Born: Bolton 28.1.58
Forward
FL Apps/Gls +2/0
Total Apps/Gls +2/0
Career: Dale am 1973, app 7.74, pro 1.76 [+2/-], Mossley cs.76, Radcliffe Borough 1.77, Macclesfield T.

Dave was another 18 year old drafted into the side towards the end of 1975-76 prior to Walter Joyce's departure, appearing twice from the bench, in a 3-0 defeat at Watford and a 0-0 draw with Barnsley. He was then one of the large number of ex-Dale players to turn out for Mossley in the 'seventies, albeit briefly in his case.

David (Dave) Helliwell   1976-77

Born: Blackburn 28.3.48
5'8"   9st12
Midfield
FL Apps/Gls 20+11/3
Total Apps/Gls 23+11/4
Career: Blackburn R. app 1965, pro 5.66 [15/1], Lincoln C. 5.69 £4000 [11+2/1], Workington 7.70 [184+13/20], Dale 7.76 [20+11/3], Morecambe 7.77, retired 1978

Dave had made a number of second division appearances for Blackburn but really made his mark in a long stint at Workington, where he played over 200 senior games on the wing. One of Brian Green's first signings for Dale, he spent the first half of the campaign mainly on the bench, but after getting into the side in midfield after Christmas he become something of a crowd favourite at Spotland, nicknamed 'Smokin' Joe'. He scored in two of only four Dale victories in the second half of the season, but they still finished with twice as many points as his previous club who lost their league place at the end of the season.

Nigel O'Loughlin   1976-82

Born: Rochdale 19.1.54
5'8"   10st10
Midfield/left back
FL Apps/Gls 242+3/18
Total Apps/Gls 267+3/20
Career: Rhyl, Shrewsbury T. 8.72 [23+10/7], Dale 7.76 [242+3/18], Ashton U. 7.82, Whitworth Valley 1983-84, manager 1987-88, Castleton Gabriels 1987-88 (+ Tim Bobbin c.1983, Dicken Green c.1989, Free Trade 1990-91; Sunday League)
Honours: Wales Schools, Division 4 promotion 1975, Rochdale Sunday League XI 1983 to 1989, Greater Manchester Knockout Cup winners 1987

Born in Rochdale but brought up in North Wales (hence playing for Wales Schools), Nigel scored seven times in only 13 starts on the left wing during Shrewsbury's promotion run in 1975. Arriving at Spotland a year later, he was a stalwart of some of the toughest times in Dale's history, accumulating 270 apearances in six seasons during which Dale twice finished bottom before reviving under Peter Madden. Primarily a midfielder, Nigel also appeared quite often at full back and was the side's penalty taker for a spell. After leaving Spotland when only offered part time terms, he was involved in minor football around Rochdale for many years. Also a coach driver in his spare time, he reputedly once drove the Dale team bus to Torquay and then had to play when one of his team mates was unable to turn out.

Alan David Tarbuck   1976-78

Born: Liverpool 10.10.48
5'6"   10st
Winger
FL Apps/Gls 48/1
Total Apps/Gls 56/3
Career: Everton app 1964-65, pro 8.66, Crewe A. 6.67 [80+5/18], Chester 10.69 [70/22], Preston NE 9.71 £5500 [42+6/17], Shrewsbury T. 3.73 £17,000 [107+17/17], Dale 7.76 [48/1], Bangor C 7.78
Honours: Division 4 promotion 1968, 1975, Welsh Cup final 1970

Arriving from Shrewsbury at the same time as Nigel O'Loughlin (indeed O'Loughlin was his understudy for the Shrews at one point), Alan accumulated nearly 400 career games despite terrible luck with injuries. He made his mark in the lower leagues with Crewe, scoring 10 times when they won promotion in his first season at Gresty Road. A broken leg in 1969 cost him a transfer to Sheffield United but he eventually moved to second division Preston before a longer stint at Shrewsbury where he won a second promotion. The fourth of Brian Green's signings in the summer of 1976, he was first choice on the left wing in each of his two seasons with Dale, but had the misfortune to break his leg half way through each of them.

Ian Bannon 1976-80, 1980-81

Born: Bury 3.9.59
Defender 6'0" 12st9
FL Apps/Gls 112+10/0
Total Apps/Gls 125+10/0
Career: Clarence FC (Bury), Dale as 1974, app 1.9.76, pro 9.77 [112+10/-], Oswestry T. cs.80, Dale n/c 1980-81, (Australia), Newcastle Rosebuds (Australia) 1986
Honours: England youth trial

Coming through Dale's junior ranks, Ian became an apprentice in 1976 and was called up for a trial with the England youth team. He made his FL debut when 17 and 3 months – Dale only had 14 professionals to call on - and became Bill Summerscales' centre back partner for the rest of the 1976-77 season. Still an apprentice when the following season started, he was an automatic choice in the side, missing only three matches. Not used until the closing stages of the following term, his return, at centre half alongside Brian Taylor, coincided with Dale's amazing run of seven wins in the last eight games to avoid the re-election places. Released after well over 100 games when Dale finished bottom in 1980, when he was still only 20, he returned as a non-contract player in the reserves before emigrating to Australia where, like former Dale teammate Bob Mountford, he worked for the prison service.

Stuart James Mason 1976-77

Born: Whitchurch, Shropshire 2.6.48
5'8" 10st9
Midfield
FL Apps/Gls 2/0
Total Apps/Gls 2/0
Career: Whitchurch Alport, Wrexham am 11.64, app 1965, pro 7.66 [28/-], Liverpool 10.66, Doncaster R. loan 11.67 [1/-], Wrexham 6.68 [144+13/3], Chester 6.73 [132+5/7], Dale loan 12.76 to 1.77 [2/-], Crewe A. loan 10.77 [4/1], Bangor C. player-manager 12.77, Rhyl, Oswestry T. manager. Coedpath manager, Wrexham commercial manager 1980s
Cricket for Shropshire
Honours: England youth international 1966 (3 caps), Division 4 promotion 1970, 1975, Welsh Cup winners 1972, final 1971, 1978, Debenham's Cup winners 1977

Liverpool spotted Stuart when he appeared regularly for Wrexham as a 17 year old apprentice and played for the England youth team, and soon after he turned pro they stepped in to sign him. He never made it past their Central League side, though, and a couple of years later he returned to the Racecourse where he was a regular for the next five years, appearing in the European Cup Winners Cup in 1972-73 after Wrexham won the Welsh Cup. He also played well over 100 games for Chester, adding another promotion to the one gained at Wrexham. After losing his place he spent a month on loan at Spotland but played only twice. As player-manager of Bangor, he guided his side to his third Welsh Cup Final and during the 'eighties returned to Wrexham as commercial manager, also running a sports shop. He was also a cricketer good enough to play for Shropshire in the Minor Counties championship. A great friend of Bob Scott (q.v.), sadly Stuart died when he was only 57.

George William Hamstead 1976-77
Born: Rotherham 24.1.46 5'7" 10st10
Forward
FL Apps/Gls 3+1/0 Total Apps/Goals 3+1/0
Career: Rotherham U. am 1963, York C. 9.64 [32+3/1], Barnsley 7.66 [147+2/22], Bury 7.71 to cs.79 [189+7/29], Dale loan 24.1.77 to 21.2.77 [3+1/-], Bury reserve team coach
Honours: Division 4 promotion 1965, 1967, 1974, Lancashire Senior Cup final 1973

George was another experienced player brought in for a brief loan period during 1976-77. Starting out with York when they were promoted in 1964-65, he also played around 150 games for Barnsley, again gaining promotion. He went on to make over 200 appearances for Bury, scoring in the Lancashire Cup Final and being everpresent on the left wing and top scoring with 12 goals when they won promotion in 1974. He played some further games after his spell with Dale and stayed at Gigg Lane until 1979, later being the reserve team coach. He also ran Bury Angling Centre.

John Henry Dungworth 1976-77

Born: Rotherham 30.3.55
6'0" 10st7
Striker
FL Apps/Gls 14/3
Total Apps/Gls 14/3
Career: Huddersfield T. jnr 1969, app 28.7.70, pro 4.4.72 [18+5/1], Barnsley loan 12.10.74 [2+1/-], Oldham A. 10.5.75 [2+2/-], Dale loan 10.3.77 to 15.5.77 [14/3], Aldershot 2.7.77 [105/58], Shrewsbury T. 1.11.79 £100,000 [81+5/17], Hereford U. loan 9.10.81 [7/3], Mansfield T.

10.8.82 [50+6/16], Rotherham U. 8.2.84, player-coach 1986 [177+11/16], Frickley Ath. 1988-89, Glasshoughton Welfare 1993-94, Boston U. 1994-95, Sheffield U. coach, Leeds U. academy manager, Huddersfield T. reserve team coach, first team coach 12.06 to 4.08, Sheffield Wednesday reserve team coach 1.09 to 12.09, Chesterfield development coach to 4.13, Sheffield U. academy coach 9.13*
Honours: Welsh Cup final 1980, Division 4 Adidas Golden Boot 1979

John had relatively little first team experience when Dale borrowed him from Oldham in 1977, though he had made a number of second division appearances for Huddersfield back in 1972-73. He did well playing up front with Bob Mountford in a two month spell and Brian Green would have liked to sign him permanently but could not afford the fee. This proved Aldershot's gain as he missed only one game and scored 29 league goals in the next two years, winning the Division 4 'golden boot' in the second. When he netted nine more in 14 games at the start to 1979-80, second division Shrewsbury came in to sign him for £100,000. He continued to score goals at a good rate and eventually signed for Rotherham where he made the best part of 200 appearances, latterly as player-coach playing at full back or centre half. He played non-league until he was 40 and has since become a well-known coach, working for both Sheffield United and Sheffield Wednesday, among others.

James (Jimmy) Mullen 1976-77
Born: Oxford 16.3.47   5'8"   10st10
Outside left
FL Apps/Gls 6+2/1   FL Apps/Gls 6+2/1
Career: Oxford C., Reading 11.66 [7/1], Charlton A. 11.67 [7/-], Rotherham U. 2.69 [173+3/24], Blackburn R. 8.74 £8000 [6+4/-], Bury 6.76 [2+2/-], Dale loan 9.3.77 to 15.5.77 [6+2/1], (USA summer 1977), Great Harwood T. 1977-78

Dale's fourth loan signing in the second half of 1976-77, Jimmy had had a varied career yet only really been a league regular during his five years at Rotherham. Indeed his eight appearances for Dale almost matched that at any of his other four league clubs. At Bury he was in competition for the number 11 shirt with George Hamstead but in the event both lost out to another future Dale man, Peter Farrell, and Jimmy followed Hamstead in spending time on loan at Spotland.

Christopher (Chris) Shyne 1976-79
Born: Rochdale 10.12.50   5'11"   11st
Goalkeeper
FL Apps 20   Total Apps 21

Career: {Sacred Heart}, Castle 1975, Dyers Arms, Dale am 1976, pro 4.77 [20], Wigan A. 8.79 to 10.79 [10], Whitworth Valley 1981, Castleton Gabriels c.1984, {Ashton U. 1985-86?}, Whitworth Valley joint manager 1987-88 Castleton Gabriels manager 1987-88, Milton 1988-89, Sacred Heart 1990-91, Whitworth Valley 1992-93, Castleton Gabriels 9.93 to at least 1994-95 (+ Tim Bobbin 1979-80, Plough 1980, Wheatsheaf 1989, Free Trade 1990, Dicken Green 1991-92, St Johns Tavern 1994 to 1996 Sudden Websters 1999-00; Sunday League) (d. 2.04)
Honours: Rochdale Sunday League XI (over 50 representative games) 1975 to 1996, Greater Manchester Inter League Trophy winners 1981, Greater Manchester Knockout Cup winners 1987, Rowe League Cup winners 1990, final 1995, Rochdale SL division 1 winners 1991, F.J. Williams Shield 1993, North West Sunday League Champion of Champions 1993, Rochdale SL under-21s v Bradford SL 1995-96, British Millerain Challenge Cup final 2000

A remarkable servant of local football in Rochdale, 26 year old Chris had been plying his trade at this level for several years when given the chance to replace Mike Poole in Dale's league side for the last two games of 1976-77, when the latter headed off for a summer in the States. Chris played further games over the next two years and also played in the league for Wigan before figuring with Whitworth Valley and Castleton Gabriels, amongst others over the next 15 years. Also a stalwart of the Rochdale Sunday League, he figured with many of the top local sides like Tim Bobbin and Dicken Green over the years, often alongside other ex-Dale players such as Neil Mills and Jason Smart, as when helping Dicken Green win the North West champion of champions cup when he was 43. He amazingly represented the Sunday League's representative side over a 22 year span helping them win numerous trophies – he saved three penalties in the shoot-out to claim the Greater Manchester Cup in 1993 - and continued to play until he was 50. Sadly Chris was struck down by serious illness and died only a couple of years later, the RSL naming one of their cup competitions in his memory.

Anthony John (Tony) Morrin 1977-79
Born: Swinton 31.7.46
5'8"   11st3
Midfield
FL Apps/Gls 29+1/0   Total Apps/Gls 33+1/0
Career: Bury app 1962, pro 10.63 [3/-], Burnley 7.65, Doncaster R. 8.66, Stockport Co. 10.66 [27+5/2], Barrow 3.69 [97+3/6], Exeter C. 7.71 [180+2/15], Stockport Co. 3.77 [13/1], Dale 7.77 to 5.79 [29+1/-], Bangor C. loan 1978-79
Honours: Division 4 champions 1967, Lancashire Senior Cup final 1970

One of the four signings that Rochdale could afford in the summer of 1977, Tony had been a pro for 14 years. Signed by first division Burnley as one for the future after just three games for Bury, he played a number of games for Stockport when they were promoted in 1967, but his career did not really take off until joining Barrow two years later. Everpresent in their midfield in 1969-70 when they surprisingly reached the Lancashire Cup Final despite being relegated from Division 3, he played 100 games for them before signing for Exeter, where he had an even longer stint. Tony played fairly regularly in his first Dale season but appeared just once the following term.

Robert William (Bob) Scott 1977-79

Born: Liverpool 22.2.53
6'3" 13st4
Centre half
FL Apps/Gls 71/3
Total Apps/Gls 78/3
Career: Wrexham jnr, pro 7.71 [15+4/-], Reading loan 1.75 [5/-], Hartlepool 7.76 [37/-], Dale 15.7.77 [71/3], Crewe A. 8.79 [238+1/15], coach 1985, commercial manager, Northwich Victoria 1985, caretaker player-manager, Wrexham 1.86 [2+1/-]
Honours: Welsh Cup winners 1975, Cheshire Cup final 1986

A massive central defender, with a style to match, Bob had had one season as a regular for Hartlepool before joining Dale. An automatic choice in his first season despite Dale finishing bottom by a considerable margin and Bob being suspended twice for a sending off at Halifax (the second for bringing the game into disrepute by swearing at the ref on his way off!). He also played regularly the following term, scoring winning goals in two home victories as Dale revived in the second half of the season. Moving to Crewe, he took over as captain and accumulated an impressive tally of fourth division appearances, missing only five games in five years before becoming coach and commercial manager. After a brief FL comeback at Wrexham, he later owned Scott's night club in the town.

Ian Wright Seddon 1977-78

Born: Prestbury 14.10.50 5'8" 10st
Midfield
FL Apps/Gls 30+1/3 Total Apps/Gls 33+1/3
Career: Wardley GS, Bolton W. app, pro 6.69 [51+13/4], Chester 9.73 [62+11/7], Stockport Co. loan 11.75 [4/-], Chesterfield loan 1.76 [2/-], Cambridge U. 2.76 [34+3/3], Dale 7.77 [30+1/3], Wigan A. 7.78 [1/-], Macclesfield T. 10.78, Runcorn cs.79, Newcastle KB (Australia) 1979, Bulova (Hong Kong) 12.80, {Stalybridge Celtic?}, Chorley 1985-86, Atherton Collieries manager
Cricket in Bolton League
Honours: Division 4 promotion 1975, champions 1977

Ian made a number of second division appearances in midfield for Bolton early in his career, but his most productive season was when he won promotion with Chester in 1974-75. Never really an automatic choice after that, though he figured in another promotion side at Cambridge, he arrived at Spotland two years later and played regularly apart from when sidelined through injury in the middle of the season. He later spent some time playing in Australia and Hong Kong and, interestingly, published a biography 'Ah'm Tellin' Thee', of Bolton Wanderers' legend Tommy Banks in 2012.

Edward David (Dave) Esser 1977-82

Born: Bowden, Cheshire 20.6.57
5'6" 10st2
Forward/midfield
FL Apps/Gls 169+11/24
Total Apps/Gls 186+14/27
Career: Everton jnr 1972, app 1974, pro 5.75, Dale 15.7.77 [169+11/24], Apoel Nicosia (Cyprus) 7.82, Karlskrona (Sweden), Altrincham 1983-84 [9+3/- Conf], Hyde U. loan 9.83, Witton Albion 2.84, Northwich Victoria 1.85 [13/1 Conf], Witton Albion, Macclesfield T. 1.86 [1+4/2 Conf], Witton Albion 1987-88, Stalybridge Celtic 1989, Winsford U. 1989-90, Ashton U. 1990 to 1992
Honours: Stockport Schools, Cheshire Schools, Northern Premier League champions 1987, North West Counties League champions 1992

Dave made Rochdale club history when he was their first player to be sent off on his debut for 55 years, when dismissed in the season's opener against Halifax in the League Cup, though he then scored the winner in the second leg. He went on to make exactly 200 senior appearances over the next five years, mostly in a struggling side (he had the dubious honour of scoring Dale's only goal in a run of 15 games in 1980), initially playing up front despite his diminutive stature, but later in midfield or out wide. When freed in 1982 he joined one of his former managers, Mike Ferguson, at Apoel Nicosia and also played in Sweden before a lengthy stint in the non-league game around the Cheshire area, winning the NPL with Macclesfield in 1987.

Edmund A. (Ted) Oliver 1977-81

Born: Manchester 16.3.61
5'6" 9st6
Full back/midfield
FL Apps/Gls 19+3/1
Total Apps/Gls 20+3/1
Career: Dale jnr 1976, app 16.3.77, pro 3.79 to cs.81 [19+3/1], Stockport Co. 1981-82

With Dale possessing only 11 professionals plus one apprentice with some league experience, when they lost Esser and Mountford to suspension for the first league game of 1977-78, Ted was drafted in at right back at the age of just 16 years and 156 days, Dale's youngest ever player. Indeed, when Hallows was sent off in the next game, Ted also had to appear in the League Cup tie against the might of Leeds United a week later, a tiny figure against the likes of Joe Jordan. He played several further games later in the season, but had a more remarkable run in the side when he played in midfield in the last seven games of the following term, Dale winning six of them to escape the bottom four. He appeared only a couple of times after that, though, and was released when still only 20, figuring once for Stockport County reserves.

Paul Cuddy 1977-79
Born: Kendal 21.2.59
5'11" 12st6
Defender
FL Apps/Gls +1/0 Total Apps/Gls +1/0
Career: Dale jnr 1976, am 1977 to 1978-79 [+1/-], Huddersfield T. trial 1978, Bolton W. trial, Prestwich Heys, Chorley, Altrincham c.3.82 [238+17/1 Conf], Witton Albion 1991-92 [12+1/- Conf], Chorley, Barrow cs.93 [14+1/- Conf], Horwich RMI, Mossley 3.95, coach cs.95, Fleetwood 10.95, Ramsbottom U., Nantwich T. manager, Abbey Hey assistant manager
Honours: England semi-pro international (3 caps) v Italy, Holland, Scotland 1986-87, reserve v Wales 1987-88, FA XI v UAU 1983-84, Cheshire Senior Cup winners 1982, final 1987, FA Trophy finalists 1982, winners 1986

With Dale unable to field a complete professional side even for the first league game of the 1977-78 season, Paul, an 18 year old amateur, was handed a place on the bench, coming on to replace Billy Boslem in the 4-0 defeat at Barnsley. Though this proved to be his only taste of league action, he later became a top player at Conference level, appearing in a total of 344 games for Altrincham, including two FA Trophy Finals at Wembley, and winning three caps for the England semi-professional side.

Leslie Terence (Terry) Owen 1977-79

Born: Liverpool 11.9.49
5'7" 11st1
Striker
FL Apps/Gls 80+3/21
Total Apps/Gls 84+3/23
Career: Everton app 1965, pro 12.66 [2/-], Bradford C. 6.70 [41+11/6], Chester 6.72 £1000 [161+15/40], Cambridge U. 8.77 [1/-], Dale 8.9.77 [80+3/21], Port Vale 7.79 [14+4/3], Northwich Victoria cs.80 [6+2/2 Conf], Oswestry T. 1981, Colwyn Bay, Caernarfon T. 1983, Prestatyn T. 1984
Honours: Division 4 promotion 1975

Terry was an experienced lower league striker who signed for Dale after just one game for Cambridge in 1977. He had previously spent five seasons with Chester, top scoring with 14 goals when they won promotion and reached the League Cup semi-final in 1975. Signed by Brian Green, who had been his coach at Chester, just before Green quit as Dale boss, Terry missed only one game in the rest of the season and was easily top scorer with 12 goals, also being voted player of the season. Again top scorer the following term, he scored twice in the amazing 3-0 victory away to promotion favourites Barnsley which inspired the late season escape from the foot of the table. However, he was freed by Doug Collins, his third manager in just over a year, for refusing to move home nearer to Rochdale. (He had missed a potentially crucial game when his car broke down). Though an Evertonian himself, Terry later became more famous as the father of Liverpool and England star Michael. His other son Andrew was a non-league player with Holywell T. and his son-in-law Ritchie Partridge appeared for Liverpool and Chester amongst others.

Robert Henry (Bobby) Scaife 1977-80

Born: Northallerton 12.10.55
6'0" 12st4
Midfield
FL Apps/Gls 95+3/9
Total Apps/Gls 101+5/11
Career: Middlesbrough app, pro 10.72, Halifax loan 1.75 [5+1/1], Hartlepool 9.75 [77+3/10], York C. trial cs.77, Dale 4.10.77 [95+3/2], Whitby T. 7.80, Scarborough, Guisborough T., South Bank 2.81, Blyth Spartans 1982-83, South Bank 1985-86, Newcastle Blue

27

Star 1985-86, Whitby T. 1986-87, Guisborough T. 1988-89, Whitby T. player-manager 1990, manager to 1995, Pickering 1996-97, Dunston Federation Brewery manager 8.97, Billingham Synthonia manager 6.07, Whitby T. assistant manager 2009, caretaker manager to 18.10.10
Honours: FA XI v Northern League 1983-84, Middlesex Wanderers tour to Indonesia 1984, Northern League division 2 champions 1986. As manager: Northern League champions 2004, 2005, Northern League Cup winners 1998, 1999, 2000, 2004, 2005, final 2006

Bobby had a couple of seasons as a regular at Hartlepool but was without a club when signed up by new Dale boss Mike Ferguson in October 1977. He played regularly in midfield for the rest of the season, scoring twice in the 3-0 defeat of Wimbledon, but could not steer Dale away from the bottom of the table. Injured for the latter part of the following term, he was in and out of the side in 1979-80 but, as Dale's PFA representative, was in the thick of the players' dispute with Bob Stokoe following the manager's attempt to fine them for lack of effort. Moving into non-league football, he figured in the Blue Star side which amazingly won 36 and drew one of their 38 games in their first season in the Northern League. Later, his long career saw him play an FA Cup tie against a side including his teenage son Nicky (who also played at Halifax and York), possibly a unique occurrence. In a decade as boss of Dunston Federation Brewery he won two league titles and five cups and also managed the Northern League's representative team. He is reckoned to have participated in over 1,000 Northern League matches as player or manager. Bobby's father Bob snr was chairman of Whitby Town.

Steven (Steve) Shaw 1977-79
Born: Manchester 10.8.60 5'6" 10st2
Midfield
FL Apps/Gls 6/0 Total Apps/Gls 7/0
Career: Dale jnr 1976, app 7.77 [6/-], Buxton 9.78, Middleton

Another 17 year old apprentice to get his chance as Dale struggled on the playing front as well as the financial one, Steve played seven games, generally on the left of midfield, in 1977-78, unfortunately all of them defeats. At the end of his apprenticeship he joined Buxton along with Billy Boslem.

Adrian (Adie) Green 1977-78
Born: Leicester 22.10.57 6'0" 10st9
Left back
FL Apps/Gls 7/0 Total Apps/Gls 7/0
Career: Leicester C. app 1974, pro 6.76, Dale loan 8.12.77 to 9.1.78 [7/-], Aldershot 7.78 [7+14/-], Woking, Basingstoke 1980 to 1986

A young professional at Leicester, Adie spent a month on loan at Spotland over the Christmas period in 1977, figuring mostly at left back. Unfortunately, apart from a surprising 3-0 defeat of Wimbledon, Dale - with four other teenagers in the side - had nothing to show for them. At Aldershot he figured more from the bench than from the start but he later had a long spell with non-league Basingstoke.

Robert (Bobby) Hoy 1977-81

Born: Halifax 10.1.50
5'7" 10st
Winger
FL Apps/Gls
61+5/12
Total Apps/Gls
64+5/12
Career: Huddersfield T. jnr 4.65, app 1.66, pro 11.67 [140+4/20], Blackburn R. 3.75 (part exchange for B. Endean) [13+6/-], Halifax T. 6.76 [30/7], York C. 8.77 [10+4/1], Dale 14.12.77, retired 3.78, re-signed 8.78 [61+5/12], Macclesfield T. 3.81, Burnley trial 1983, Bradford C. trial 8.83
Honours: England youth international 1968, Division 2 champions 1970, Division 3 champions 1975

Bobby scored on his debut as a 17 year old at Huddersfield, where he was considered their best prospect since Dennis Law. He figured quite regularly on their right flank in 1969-70 when Huddersfield won the second division title, but by the time he left for Blackburn after 144 league games, the Terriers were down in Division 3, though he immediately helped Rovers go the other way. He joined Dale late in 1977 – one of only two permanent signings Ferguson was able to make during the season - but played only a few games on the left wing before retiring to concentrate on his other career as a folk singer. He returned for the following campaign, though, and had the most productive season of his whole career, playing 41 times and scoring 10 goals. These included two in the remarkable 4-0 away success at Scunthorpe in December 1978 that kick started Dale's revival in the second half of the season, first under caretaker boss Peter Madden and then Doug Collins. However, his remaining time at Spotland was blighted by injury before he finally moved on in 1981.

Brian Patrick Hart 1977-80, 1981-82
Born: Farnworth 14.7.59 6'0" 11st7
Defender
FL Apps/Gls 73+5/0 Total Apps/Gls 81+5/2
Career: Radcliffe Borough, Bolton app 1975, Dale am 12.77, pro 3.78 [73+5/-], Bangor C. cs.80 player-commercial manager [36/3 Conf], Dale n/c 1981-82, Horwich RMI, Glossop, Northwich Victoria 1982-83, Southport 8.83, Bangor C. 1983-84 [3/- Conf], Hyde U. 1983-84, Mossley 1984-85, Horwich RMI 1985-86, secretary c.1992
Honours: NPL Cup final 1984, GMAC Cup winners 1988

Along with Ian Bannon, the most successful of the young defenders thrust into the Dale team at the time, Brian was unused substitute several times before playing the last eight games of 1977-78 at left back. He spent the next two seasons as a regular in the side mostly in central defence or at right back and though never scoring a league goal, netted goals that took Dale through to round 3 of the cup in 1979-80. Taking up the unusual dual role of player and commercial manager at Bangor, he spent part of 1981-82 back at Spotland as a non-contract player in the reserves before doing the rounds of non-league sides in the north west and playing in a couple of cup finals. Horwich RMI's captain, and twice player of the year, he actually spent most of the 1988 GMAC cup success against Weymouth between the posts when the 'keeper was injured. He was subsequently their club secretary.

Andrew (Andy) Slack 1977-80
Born: Heywood 9.6.59 5'9" 11st7
Goalkeeper
FL Apps 15 Total Apps 17
Career: Blackpool jnr, Bolton W. app 1975, Dale am 1977, pro 21.1.78 [15], retired injured 5.80

A sorter in a Heywood tannery while an amateur in Dale's reserves, Andy was handed his league debut in January 1978, when Poole left for the USA. Given that Dale were already entrenched at the bottom of the league and collected only 24 points all season, this was a pretty thankless task, but Andy looked to be a fine prospect, playing a blinder in a 1-0 defeat at leaders Watford. Sadly, though, he was injured after just three games the following term and despite several attempted comebacks had to retire from the game.

Mark Hilditch 1977-83, 1990-92

Born: Middleton 20.8.60
6'1" 11st8
Forward
FL Apps/Gls 196+17/42 Total Apps/Gls 221+21/47
Career: Crompton House School (Shaw), Shawside, Dale am 1976-77, pro 11.78 [184+13/40], Tranmere R. cs.83 [47+2/12], Altrincham trial 8.86 [1+1/- Conf], Wigan A. c.9.86 [89+14/26], Dale cs.90 [12+4/2], Buxton 12.91, Bacup Borough 1992-93, Manchester County FA Schools coach from 1992-93, Fleetwood, Mossley assistant player-manager 7.93, Morecambe, Oldham A. coach 5.97, coach in Japan, Oldham A. Centre of Excellence coach, safeguarding officer*
Cricket for Heyside
Honours: Lancashire Senior Cup final 1987-88

Yet another 17 year old amateur given their chance in the league side, Mark proved to be by far the longest surviving of them. He scored the only goal on his full debut in April 1978 to earn a rare victory, but despite frequent outings at number 9 did not score again until the following May. However, the three goals he then scored in successive games clinched Dale's escape from the bottom four. He missed only two games the following year when Dale did finish bottom, yet again netted only three league goals. The mustachioed striker came good under Peter Madden, netting 26 times in partnership with Barry Wellings over the next two seasons. Released in 1983 he spent several seasons at Tranmere, despite long injury lay-offs, and with Wigan in Division 3, often figuring in midfield or defence, though he netted his only career hat-trick on New Year's Day 1990, before returning to Spotland. Limited by injury he made only a few appearances before retiring from league football in November 1991, but did set a record in playing for Dale across 15 seasons. Briefly assistant to Steve Taylor at Mossley, he worked as a PTI at Wakefield jail and coached Manchester Schools before a long stint on Oldham's coaching staff. He was also a useful club cricketer and keen golfer

John Price 1977-79
Born: Nantwich 28.4.60.
Midfield
FL Apps/Gls 10+2/0 Total App/Gls 11+2/0
Career: Middlewich Athletic, Dale am 11.77, pro 1.78 [10+2/-], Macclesfield T. cs.79

John made his debut in the penultimate game of 1977-78, as a substitute against Torquay the day after his 18th birthday. He made his full debut in the following game and made several further appearances in midfield the following term, though he was only on the winning side once.

Robert (Bobby) Finc 1977-78
Born: Rochdale 13.2.59
Defender
FL Apps/Gls +1/0 Total Apps/Gls +1/0
Career: St Wilfrid's School, Milton 1974-75, York C. trial, Dale am 1976, n/c 1.78 [+1/-] (+ Tim Bobbin 1983, Milton 1988-89, Free Trade 1990-91; Sunday League)
Honours: Rochdale Schools Cup final 1970, Lancashire Amateur Shield winners 1975, Rochdale Sunday League XI 1983, Lancashire Sunday Cup winners 1988

Having played cricket for Rochdale Schools and won the Lancashire Amateur Shield with local side Milton, Bobby played in Dale's reserves as an amateur before signing non-contract terms. His one senior appearance was as substitute in the final game of 1977-78, a goalless draw with Aldershot, when he came on for Paul Hallows. He played Sunday League football for Tim Bobbin along with several other ex-Dale men including Chris Shyne and Nigel O'Loughlin, winning the Lancashire Sunday Cup. He also figured for the RSL representative side with future England international Geoff Thomas. He became a PE teacher at Oulder Hill School and also coached Manchester Giants basketball team.

Philip Anthony (Phil) Ashworth 1978-80
Born: Burnley 14.4.53 6'0" 12st
Forward
FL Apps/Gls 9+2/0 Total Apps 11+2/1
Career: Accrington St. 1973, Burnley U. 1973, Nelson 1974, Blackburn R. 9.1.75, Bournemouth loan 20.9.75, signed 16.10.75 [30+1/2], Workington 22.7.76 [38+1/7], Hartlepool trial 8.77, Southport 11.8.77 [22+2/9], Dale 7.7.78 [9+2/-], Portsmouth 29.9.79 [3+1/4], Scunthorpe U. 6.7.80 [14+9/3], GAIS (Sweden) 6.81, Cambridge C. 10.81, Devonport C. (Tasmania) 2.85, Brigg T. 1985-86, Burnley commercial manager, Rossendale U. 1986, Clitheroe 1986, Bottesford T. 1987, Brigg T. 1988, Bottesford T. player-manager 1989 to 1994
Honours: Division 4 promotion 1980

Phil had the rather unfortunate record of being with both Workington and Southport when they were voted out of the league in successive seasons (despite Phil scoring in each of his first seven games for the latter). He was signed by Mike Ferguson – himself with Accrington when they went out of business – but failed to net a league goal and could easily have suffered an unprecedented treble but for Dale's late season rally that took them out of the bottom four. Despite not having appeared in the first team in the second half of 1978-79 due to a hernia operation, he was signed by Portsmouth as cover for their strikers early the following term and remarkably scored twice in each of his first two games as Pompey topped the table. After a year at Scunthorpe, his sixth league club in as many seasons he played in Sweden and Australia before a long non-league career and a spell back in his home town as Burnley's commercial manager.

Eric Snookes 1978-83

Born: Smethwick 6.3.55
5'7" 10st
Left back
FL Apps/Gls 183/1
Total Apps/Gls 208/1
Career: Aston Villa as, Preston NE app 1971, pro 3.73 [20/-], Crewe A. 7.74 [33+1/-], Southport 7.75 [106+4/2], Dale 7.7.78 [183/1], Bolton cs.83 [6/-], Macclesfield T. 7.84, Workington 1985-86, Barrow 1985-86 [8/- Conf], Formby cs.88, Hesketh Bank player-coach. Preston NE Football in the Community
Honours: Smethwick & Worcester Schools

Eric made a number of second division appearances at Preston but was best known for long stints in the bottom division with Southport and Dale totalling almost 300 league games. Like Phil Ashworth he arrived at Spotland following Southport's FL demise and was the Dale's regular left back for five seasons. Notable for his flowing red hair and sometimes rather wild tackling, Eric played just over 200 games for Dale – it would have been more but for the fairly regular suspensions! At one point he reportedly drew a bid of £60,000 from Carlisle which was turned down as Dale wanted an unlikely £90,000. He eventually departed on a free and after a brief spell up in Division 3 with Bolton played non-league football. He was with the Community Programme in Football at Preston and after gaining a GNVQ in tourism and leisure taught the YTS players at North End.

David Wynne (Dave) Felgate

1978-79, 1979-80
Born: Bleanau Ffestiniog 4.3.60
6'2" 13st10
Goalkeeper
FL Apps 47 Total Apps 47
Career: Blaenau Ffestiniog, Bolton W. app 1976, pro 1.8.78, Dale loan 4.10.78 to 5.79 [35], Bradford C. loan 7.79, Crewe A. loan 27.9.79 [14], Dale loan 9.3.80 to 7.5.80 [12], Lincoln C. loan 5.9.80, signed 12.80 £25,000 [198], Cardiff C. loan 12.84 [4], Grimsby T. loan 23.2.85 [12], Grimsby T. 7.85 £27,500 [24], Bolton W. loan 14.2.86 [15], Rotherham U. loan 12.86, Bolton W. 17.2.87 £16,000 [223], Bury 17.7.93, Wolverhampton W. n/c 12.8.93, Chester 1.10.93 [71+1], Wigan A. 4.7.95 to 1996 [3]. Leigh RMI 1998 [30+2 Conf], Hyde U. loan 2001-02, Radcliffe Borough 2002, coach 2003, Bacup Borough 2003-04, Chorley 1.04, Bacup Borough 8.04, Manchester C. academy coach, Rossendale U. assistant manager 11.05, Stockport Co. goalkeeping coach 2006, Manchester C. academy goalkeeping coach 1.09*
Honours: Wales Schools, Wales v Romania 1983, Division 4 promotion 1981, 1988, Division 3 play-off final 1991, Division 3+ promotion 1994, Football League Trophy final 1983, Sherpa Van Trophy winners 1989, Lancashire Senior Cup winners 1988-89, 1990-91, final 1995-96, NPL Division 1 promotion 2003

A hefty goalkeeper in the same mould as his Welsh compatriot Neville Southall, Dave had an incredibly lengthy career given that in four seasons he did not make a single appearance in his first spell at Bolton. He spent two loan periods at Spotland over an eighteen month period, aiding their great escape from the foot of the league in 1979. Joining Lincoln, his brilliant form following promotion saw him voted third division goalkeeper of the year and earn a place in the Wales squad in 1981. He eventually won a full cap as substitute for Southall against Romania two years later. He played his first game for Bolton while on loan, ten years after first signing for them and subsequently appeared well over 200 times for them, being everpresent in their 1988 promotion side and winning the Sherpa Van Trophy and the Lancashire Cup twice. After a third promotion, at Chester, his FL career was ended after in excess of 600 games by an injury sustained in a pre-match kick-in in August 1995 though he played for Wigan Reserves against Dale the following spring and had one last great day in the cup for Leigh RMI against Fulham when he was 40. He played on at lower levels for another four years before entering coaching, working with the Manchester City academy.

Geoffrey Patrick (Geoff) Forster   1978-79
Born: Middlesbrough 3.8.54
Forward
FL Apps/Gls +1/0 Total Apps/Gls +1/0
Career: Winnybanks, South Bank, Berwick R. trial, Dale trial 12.78 [+1/-], South Bank, Stockport Co. trial, Darlington trial, Whitby T. 1979, Hartlepool U. 5.80 [10+4/4], Guisborough T. 1983-84, South Bank, Whitby T. 1985-86

A striker from the Northern League, Geoff was offered a trial at Spotland in December 1978, but had the misfortune to arrive just as Mike Ferguson was leaving. Though appearing as substitute in a 3-0 defeat to Barnsley he was left somewhat in limbo as first Peter Madden and then Doug Collins took over, and he returned to South Bank. He also had trials at Stockport and Darlington and later had a season with Hartlepool, managing four goals in only 10 starts.

Peter Anthony Creamer   1978-79

Born: Hartlepool 20.9.53
5'11" 11st4
Defender
FL Apps/Gls 18+2/0
Total Apps/Gls 18+2/0
Career: Manchester U. jnr, Middlesbrough app 1969, pro 10.70 [9/-], Dallas Tornado summer 1975 [12/1 NASL], York C. loan 11.75 [4/-], Doncaster R. 12.75 [31+1/-], Hartlepool 10.76 £4000 [63/3], {Millwall trial?}, Gateshead 1978, Dale n/c 12.78 to 5.79 [18+2/-], (Australia), Gateshead 1981, Whitby T., Bishop Auckland, Willington 1985-86, Whitby T. manager 1986 to 1988, Evenwood T. manager, Postchaise FC
Honours: Hartlepool Schools, Durham County Schools, England Schools international (2 caps) 1969, Division 2 champions 1974

Though a schoolboy international (at football and cricket), Peter had few opportunities during five years in the professional ranks at Middlesbrough, where he was an understudy to regular full backs Craggs and Spraggon, but did appear a few times in their promotion to the first division. The majority of his league games came with Doncaster and Hartlepool but he was playing for Gateshead when recruited by new Dale caretaker-manager Peter Madden, along with former Middlesbrough colleague Brian Taylor, to shore up a shaky defence. Released at the end of the season, he played in Australia as well as in non-league football back in the north east. He also managed at non-league level and was still playing in the Spennymoor and District League in the 1990s. His son Chris was on the books of Middlesbrough and Hartlepool, but didn't appear in the FL.

Brian Taylor 1978-83

Born Hodthorpe 12.2.54
5'11" 11st9
Central defender
FL Apps/Gls 152+2/10
Total Apps/Gls 166+2/10
Career: Middlesbrough app, pro 7.71 [14+4/1], Doncaster R. 12.75 £12,000 [118+1/12], Dale 12.78 [152+2/10], Whitworth Valley cs.83, {Bolton St. Thomas?}, Dale reserve team coach 8.85, acting manager 11.86, stadium manager, Whitworth Valley player-coach cs.87 (+ Cock & Magpie 1984 to 1989; Sunday League). Lancashire FA district coach 2.88, Burnley junior coach 1989, Halifax T. assistant manager 1989-90 to 10.91, Burnley Football in the Community, Halifax T. Football in the Community
Honours: Division 2 champions 1974, Rochdale Sunday League XI 1984, Lancashire FA Shield 1987, Rochdale Sunday League champions and cup winners 1989

A nephew of Gordon Harris of Burnley, Brian made a few appearances at centre back for Middlesbrough either side of their promotion to the top flight in 1974, making his debut in place of former England hero Nobby Stiles. He moved to Doncaster along with Peter Creamer in 1975 for a sizeable fee, and played well over a hundred games before teaming up with Creamer once more at Spotland. Initially playing left back, he soon became a fixture at centre back as Dale made their amazing escape from the bottom four. He remained a regular, netting six times when Peter Madden returned to guide Dale to the relative heights of 15th in 1980-81, until breaking his leg in the last game of the following season. He gave up league football the following year but returned to Rochdale as reserve team coach and was acting manager briefly when Vic Halom was sacked. Also working as stadium manager at Spotland while doubling as a Sunday footballer with the successful Cock & Magpie side, he subsequently had a variety of jobs coaching juniors and working for the Community Football programme.

Christopher Martin Nigel (Chris) Jones 1978-80

Born: Altrincham 19.11.45 5'10" 12st3
Centre forward
FL Apps/Gls 51+5/19
Total Apps/Gls 54+7/21
Career: Manchester C. jnr, pro 27.5.64 [6+1/2], Swindon T. 30.7.68 £15,000 [49+19/18], Oldham A. loan 21.1.72 [3/1], Walsall 16.2.72 £6000 [54+5/14], York C. 9.6.73 £7800 [94+1/33], Huddersfield T. 31.8.76 [9+5/2], Doncaster R. 7.7.77 [14+6/4], Darlington loan 14.1.78 [14+2/3], Dale 13.12.78 [51+5/19], Le Havre (France) 7.80, Bridlington T. 9.80, Frickley Ath. manager 2.81, Rowntree Mackintosh (York)
Honours: Cheshire Boys, Division 1 champions 1968, Division 3 promotion 1969, 1974, Anglo-Italian Cup winners 1969

Chris played in the Manchester City team that reached the semi-final of the Youth Cup in 1964 and was the reserves' top scorer for three seasons in a row but managed just two appearances when they won the league title in 1968. He had useful spells at Swindon, winning promotion in his first season, and Walsall, but really made his mark at York where his goals as part of a strike partnership with Jimmy Seal (q.v.) fired them into Division 2 for the first time. In December 1978 he was one of the three former Doncaster players, with Brian Taylor and Peter Creamer, signed by caretaker boss Peter Madden to try and rescue Dale's dire season. Dale had scored just 11 goals in 21 league games but Chris netted in a remarkable 4-0 win away at Scunthorpe and ended the season with 10 goals as Dale escaped the bottom four. The following year Dale did finish bottom, but Chris was easily top scorer, hitting a hat-trick against Northampton, Dale's first for eight years, and was voted the supporters' player of the year despite having been freed by Bob Stokoe. He later worked as a PE teacher at Tadcaster GS and was chairman of York coaches association, also becoming a Radio York football commentator. His autobiography "A Tale of Two Great Cities" was published in 2015.

John Douglas (Doug) Collins 1978-80

Born: Newton, Yorkshire 28.8.45
5'8" 10st6
Midfield
FL Apps/Gls 6+2/0
Total Apps/Gls 6+2/0
Career: Rotherham U. app, Grimsby T. am 3.63, pro 6.63 [94+6/11], Burnley 9.68 £27,000 [172+14/18], Plymouth A. 5.76 [22+2/1], Sunderland 3.77 [4+2/-], Tulsa Roughnecks 1978 [5/- NASL], Derby Co. coach, Dale player-manager 1.79 to 11.79 [6+2/-]. Sydney Olympic (Australia) coach 6.81 to 8.82, Marconi (Australia) coach 1983, Canberra Arrows (Australia) coach 1984. Wollongong City (Australia) coach 1989. South Coast Wolves (Australia) coach 1995-96
Honours: Division 2 champions 1973, Charity Shield 1973, Lancashire Senior Cup winners 1970, 1972, Texaco Cup final 1974

Doug made his mark as a youngster with Grimsby with 100 league games, mainly as a winger, before a sizeable fee took him to first division Burnley. Spending eight years at Turf Moor, he was a regular in their midfield when, following relegation, they won the second division title in 1973. He had just one further season in the league after leaving Burnley before playing in the NASL and moving into coaching. However in January 1979 he was appointed as player-manager at Spotland and engineered their amazing escape from the foot of the table as they won nine out of 10 home games and seven of the last eight games of the season. However, despite pre-season optimism, the following term again started disastrously and with the player-manager reluctant to play himself, the board dispensed with his services after just 10 months. He subsequently emigrated permanently to Australia, coaching a number of National Soccer League sides.

Michael (Mike) Milne 1978-79
Born: Aberdeen 17.8.59 5'9" 11st
Defender
FL Apps/Gls 1+1/0 Total Apps/Gls 1+1/0
Career: Sunderland app, pro 5.77, Dale 2.79 [1+1/-], Montrose cs.79 [77+7/2 ScL], Keith 1982

Mike had been at Sunderland when Doug Collins had a brief spell there and he became Collins' only signing in his first term as Dale boss. He was only on the fringe of the side, though, starting just one game in place of the Eric Snookes at left back in April 1979, before heading back to his native Scotland and becoming a regular for Montrose.

Ian Watson 1979-80

Born: North Shields 5.2.60
6'0" 12st
Goalkeeper
FL Apps 33
Total Apps 40
Career: Sunderland app 1977, pro 2.78 [1], Dale loan 8.79 to 3.80 [33], Newport Co. cs.81, Gloucester C. loan 1982-83, Berwick R. cs.83 to 1986 and 1987-88 [87/1 ScL]

Another Sunderland player recruited by Doug Collins, Ian was drafted in on a long term loan at the start of 1979-80 and played every match until March, despite Dale long being marooned at the foot of the table. Moving to Newport, he missed most of 1981-82 and all of 1982-83 through injury and was unable to add to his tally of FL games, though he subsequently played regularly for Berwick Rangers, even scoring a goal against Stranraer in 1985.

Alan Weir 1979-83

Born: South Shields 1.9.59
5'9" 10st
Defender/midfield
FL Apps/Gls 96+10/3
Total Apps/Gls 113+10/3
Career: Horsley Hill School, Sunderland app 1975, pro 5.77 [1/-], Dale 7.79 £11,000 [96+10/3], Hartlepool U. 8.83 [9+1/-], Eppleton CW cs.84, Whitley Bay 1986-87, North Shields 1987. South Shields assistant manager to 1.04
Honours: England youth international v Uruguay, Hungary, France 1977-78

Like Milne and Watson a former Sunderland apprentice, Alan had also captained the England youth side after turning pro. Primarily a central defender, though he also played as a defensive midfielder, he was signed by Dale for a record fee of £11,000 in the summer of 1979. He scored in the 7-2 friendly victory over Dutch side Den Bosch and after eight games Alan was top scorer in the league, too, with three of the Dale's meagre tally of just five goals. A regular in his first year, he was less used when Peter Madden took over, subsequently playing mainly at full back, but did pass a hundred games before he faded from the scene in 1982-83 and had a brief stint with Hartlepool.

John Dennis Wann 1979-81

Born: Blackpool 17.11.50
5'8" 10st11
Midfield
FL Apps/Gls 66+1/7
Total Apps/Gls 75+1/7
Career: Blackpool app 1966, pro 7.67 [11+6/-], York C. 1.72 £7000 [65+1/7], Southend U. loan 12.74, Chesterfield loan 11.75 [3/-], Hartlepool loan 1.76 [2/-], Darlington 7.76 [119+2/13], Dale 7.79 £8000 [66+1/7], Blackpool 8.81 to 3.82 [13+6/-], York C. trial 4.82, Bury 8.82, Morecambe, Workington 1982-83, Chester n/c 10.83 [2+1/-], Workington 1983-84, Runcorn 1984-85 [1/- Conf], Fleetwood 1984-85, Wren Rovers coach
Honours: Division 2 promotion 1970, Division 3 promotion 1974, (Lancashire Senior Cup winners 1982-83), Anglo-Italian Cup winners 1971

A second expensive signing (by Dale standards) in the summer of 1979, Dennis had started his career at Blackpool, making a couple of substitute appearances when they gained promotion in 1970. He also played a few first division games as well as the Anglo-Italian Cup Final against Bologna. He was at York with Chris Jones, recovering from a broken leg on Boxing Day 1972 to appear in their promotion side the following season, and played over 100 times for Darlington. Dennis was sent off on his Dale debut in the League Cup against Blackpool, but was a frequent performer in midfield in both his seasons at Spotland. He had a brief spell back at Blackpool and while at Bury was unused substitute in the Lancashire Cup Final, though not appearing in their league side.

Edward (Eddie) Cliff 1979-81

Born: South Liverpool 30.9.51
5'10" 11st5
Right back
FL Apps/Gls 25+1/0
Total Apps/Gls 25+1/0
Career: Burnley app 1967, pro 10.68 [21/-], Notts Co. 7.73 [5/-], Lincoln C. loan 10.74 [3/-], Chicago Sting summer 1975 and 1976 [16/- NASL], Tranmere R. 9.76 [44+6/4], Dale 9.79 to 5.81 [25+1/-]
Honours: Youth Cup winners 1968, Lancashire Senior Cup winners 1970, 1972, Division 2 champions 1973, Atlantic Conference Northern Division champions 1976

A teammate of manager Doug Collins at Burnley, Eddie played in their Youth Cup winning side and in two Lancashire Cup Finals, but only managed 21 FL appearances in five years, understudying Mick Docherty when Burnley won the second division title in 1973. Injuries at Notts County further restricted his career, though he spent a successful summer in the NASL when Chicago Sting won their divisional championship, Eddie figuring when they defeated a New York Cosmos side which contained the legendary Pele. His best return was at Tranmere, but continuing injuries meant that he had only two short spells in the first team at Spotland, mostly at right back, spending virtually all of 1980-81 skippering the reserves before retiring.

John Charles McDermott 1979-80
Born: Manchester 14.10.59 5'10" 11st2
Forward
FL Apps/Gls 5+3/1 Total Apps/Gls 5+3/1
Career: Manchester U. app, pro 10.76, Wigan A. n/c cs.79, Dale 24.9.79 to 1.80 [5+3/1]

John was recruited in September 1979 and had a short run of games, mostly on the left flank, after scoring on his full debut in a 3-2 defeat at York. Oddly his last start came in the 3-2 victory over Northampton, Dale's first win in 13 games, Mark Hilditch subsequently being switched to No. 11 following the signing of Jimmy Seal.

Laurence Courtney (Larry) Milligan 1979-80
Born: Liverpool 20.4.58 5'7" 12st
Defender
FL Apps/Gls 8+1/0 Total Apps/Gls 8+1/0
Career: Blackpool app, pro 4.76 [19/-], Portsmouth loan 3.79 [7/-], Aldershot trial cs.79, Barrow 9.79, Dale 10.79 [8+1/-], (USA c.5.80), Morecambe c.1980, Fleetwood 1984-85, player-manager 1986-87, Morecambe c.1989 (+ Dayton House 1986-87; Blackpool Sunday League)
Honours: FA Vase final 1985, Gledhill Trophy final 1987

Larry had gained some FL experience at Blackpool but was playing in the Northern Premier League when given his chance by Dale. He played four games at left back soon after signing and figured a few times in central defence towards the end of the season, playing in three of Dale's total of just seven league victories. After playing in the FA Vase Final at Wembley for Fleetwood, he subsequently became their player manager when only 28.

Colin Waldron 1979-80

Born: Bristol 22.6.48
6'0" 13st13
Centre half
FL Apps/Gls 19/0
Total Apps/Gls 22/0
Career: Bury app 1965, pro 8.66 [20/-], Chelsea 7.67 [9/-], Burnley 10.67 [308/16], Manchester U. 5.76 [3/-], Sunderland 2.77 [20/1], Tulsa Roughnecks 1978 [11/1 NASL], Philadelphia Fury 6.78 [17/1 NASL], Mossley 9.78, Atlanta Chiefs 1979 [14/- NASL], Dale 10.79 to 5.80 [19/-]
Honours: Division 2 champions 1973, Charity Shield 1973, Lancashire Senior Cup winners 1970, Texaco Cup final 1974

With Dale gaining just one win in the first 15 games of 1979-80, Doug Collins turned to his long time Burnley colleague Colin to try and stiffen the defence. He had been a promising youngster at Bury before signing for Chelsea, but quickly moved on to Burnley when Tommy Docherty quit as Chelsea boss. He completed over 300 games as a dominant centre half in nine seasons with the Clarets, being everpresent when they were second division champions in 1973 (and scoring the goal that guaranteed the title), before a short lived move to Manchester United where Docherty was now manager. He teamed up again with Doug Collins at Sunderland and the pair then figured with Tulsa Roughnecks in the NASL. Colin was unable to improve Dale's fortunes and missed the end of the season through injury before retiring. His brother Alan was with Bolton, Blackpool and Bury and Colin himself was in the restaurant business with former Manchester City hero Colin Bell.

James (Jimmy) Seal 1979-81

Born: Pontefract 9.12.50
5'10" 11st8
Striker/midfield
FL Apps/Gls 44+9/5
Total Apps/Gls 49+10/5
Career: Upton Robins, Wolverhampton W. app, pro 3.68 [1/-], Walsall loan 1.70 [17/8], Walsall loan 12.70 [24/6], Barnsley £6000 5.71 [43/12], York C. 7.72 (p/e for K. McMahon) [152+9/43], Darlington £7500 11.76 [115+7/19], Dale 1.11.79 £5000 [44+9/5], Gainsborough Trinity cs.81, Goole T. 1983-84, Bridlington Trinity, Wiggington, Haxby T., York C. scout 7.93
Honours: Division 3 promotion 1974

Jimmy was originally with Wolves but made his mark as a goalscorer while on loan at Walsall. After 12 goals in his first full season at Barnsley, he had great success at York, partnering Chris Jones (q.v.) up front in the side which gained promotion to the second division in 1974. A well built striker, he was top scorer the following term and netted in a memorable 1-1 draw at Arsenal in the FA Cup. The Quakers' record signing, he made over a hundred appearances for Darlington and was a seasoned campaigner in the lower leagues before signing for Dale. Unfortunately he found himself in a terminally struggling side – his debut was a 4-0 defeat – and after Doug Collins was sacked, though scoring in three successive games, he was unable to prevent Bob Stokoe's side later enduring a record breaking (and soul destroying) run in which they scored one goal in 15 games. Losing his place the following term, he reappeared in a midfield role before heading for the non-league game and later scouting for York.

Neil Colbourne 1979-81
Born: Swinton 25.8.56
Goalkeeper
FL Apps 1 Total Apps 1
Career: Manchester C. jnr, {Bethesda Ath. 1976?}, Hyde U. 1977-78, Halifax T. n/c, Dale n/c 1.80 [1], Huddersfield T. loan 1980-81, Hyde U. 10.80, Irlam T. 1981, Droylsden 1984-85, {Oldham T. 1990-91?}

With just one NPL game for Hyde at the start of that season behind him, Neil was a non-contract player in Dale reserves when called upon to replace the on-loan Dave Felgate against Huddersfield in April 1980, the club not possessing a professional goalkeeper of their own. He again figured with the reserves the following term and though Dale had lost his sole senior game 2-0, he must have impressed the opposition, at least, as they took him on loan.

John {D.} Cohen 1979-80
Born: {Salford AMJ.62?}
Defender?
FL Apps/Gls +0/0 Total Apps/Gls +0/0
Career: Dale 1979 to 5.80

John was unused substitute in the last game of the 1979-80 season, bizarrely selected in the squad for the first time the day after Bob Stokoe had decided not to retain him.

Christopher Leslie (Chris) Pearce 1980-81, 1982-83

Born: Newport 7.8.61
6'0" 11st4
Goalkeeper
FL Apps 41
Total Apps 50
Career: Wolverhampton W. app 1977, Blackburn R. 10.79, Dale loan 8.80 to 9.80 [5], Barnsley loan 8.81, Dale 7.82 [36], Port Vale 6.83 [48], Wrexham 7.86 [25], Burnley 7.87 [181], Bradford C. 7.92 [9], retired injured. Chorley, Fleetwood, Accrington St., Rossendale U. 1995
Honours: Wales Schools, Wales youth international, Sherpa Van Trophy final 1988, Division 4 promotion 1986, champions 1992

After former Southport 'keeper John Coates and young reserve Ian Senior had played in the pre-season games, Dale borrowed Welsh youth international Chris from Blackburn in time for the first serious game of 1980-81. After the dire previous campaign, Dale got off to a highly promising start with two wins and two draws in Chris's five league games. Two years later he was signed on a permanent deal and was the first choice for a year before moving on. His most productive spell was at Burnley where he played almost 200 times including in the Sherpa Van Trophy Final and a few games when they were fourth division champions. His brother Dave was a well known British boxing champion, but while at Burnley Chris proved less successful as a pugilist, suffering a broken nose in a fight with a teammate during training. A dressing room character, Chris was known as the "clown prince" at Spotland, and was well known for his comic impersonations, including Norman Wisdom.

Alan Jones 1980-81

Born: Grimethorpe 21.1.51 5'6" 10st11
Right back
FL Apps/Gls 40+4/5
Total Apps/Gls 43+4/6
Career: Huddersfield T. app, pro 12.68 [30+2/-], Halifax T. 8.73 £4500 [109/6], Chesterfield 9.76 £9000 [39/6], Lincoln C. 11.77 £11,000 [24+2/4], Columbus Magic loan summer 1979, Bradford C. 9.79 [16+3/1], Dale 7.80 [40+4/5], Frickley Ath. cs.81 [+2/- Conf]

One of several Yorkshire based players signed up by Peter Madden when he took over as manager at Spotland in the summer of 1980, Alan had made a number of first division appearances at right back for Huddersfield at the start of his career. However, he accumulated much of his FL experience in just over three seasons on the right wing at Halifax. Again used at full back by Bradford City, he operated almost exclusively in this role at Spotland, missing only two games. He notched six goals, becoming the first Dale full back to score twice in a game in a 2-0 victory over Crewe. His son Gary followed him in appearing for Halifax, at the end of a ten year league career, most notably at Notts County.

Peter Burke 1980-82

Born: Rotherham 26.4.57
6'0" 11st10
Centre half
FL Apps/Gls 68/2
Total Apps/Gls 73+1/3
Career: Barnsley app 1972-73, pro 8.75 [35/1], Halifax T. 3.78 [77+6/9], Dale 7.80 [68/2], Colne Dynamos 1982, Newcastle KB U. (Australia) 1983 to 1984, Canberra C. (Australia) 1984 to 1986

The second of the signings who became known as 'Madden's Mercenaries', like Alan Jones, Peter had acquired most of his first team experience at Halifax. Still only 23 when he arrived at Spotland, he had two seasons as the first choice centre half but was injured for the latter part of his second term, before being freed. He later had several succesful seasons in Australia, figuring in the National Soccer League's best defence with Newcastle in 1983.

Barry Wellings 1980-83

Born: Liverpool 10.6.58
5'7" 11st1
Striker
FL Apps/Gls 111+5/31
Total Apps/Gls 128+5/36
Career: Everton app 1974, pro 6.76, York C. 6.78 [40+7/9], Dale 7.80 [111+5/31], Tranmere R. 2.83 [16/3], Northwich Victoria cs.83 [17/1 Conf], Tranmere R. 12.83 [9/-], Oswestry 3.84, Swansea C. n/c 10.84 [5/3], Academica de Coimbre (Portugal) 1985 to cs.89, Southport 11.90, Runcorn cs.91 [9+7/1 Conf], Droylsden 1992-93

Despite his Liverpudlian origin, Barry was also playing in Yorkshire when signed by Peter Madden. The diminutive blond haired striker immediately struck up a successful partnership with Mark Hilditch up front and top scored with 14 goals as Dale finished 15th, their best season since relegation. The side's penalty taker, he was top scorer again the following campaign and was everpresent each time. Indeed, he completed an impressive run of 128 consecutive games, 111 of them in the league, before losing his place and moving to Tranmere. Still only 24, he moved in and out of the league scene for a couple of years before a lengthy stint in the Portugese Primeira Divisao with Academica. He subsequently returned to the north west non-league scene, playing for Southport with much later Dale striker Steve Whitehall. After finishing in football, Barry concentrated on his golf.

Eugene (Eui) Martinez 1980-83

Born: Chelmsford 6.7.57
5'8" 10st10
Winger
FL Apps/Gls 110+6/16
Total Apps/Gls 121+9/17
Career: Harrogate T., Bradford C. n/c, pro 7.77 [38+14/5], Dale 6.80 [110+6/16], Newport Co. trial 8.83, signed 11.83 [18+2/1], Northampton T. loan 2.84 [12/2], Guiseley

Frequently jeered by opposition supporters during the Falklands War, as they thought he must be an Argentinian, Eui was actually brought up in Yorkshire! Though a popular player with the fans at Valley Parade he was never able to establish a regular place in their side, but at Spotland he was an instant success as well as a crowd favourite with his wing skills. An automatic choice on the left wing for two seasons, he also netted nine goals in 1981-82. Dale had earlier turned down substantial bids for his services, but after he lost his regular place he moved to third division Newport on a free.

Peter Graeme Crawford 1980-83

Born: Falkirk 7.8.47
6'2" 13st
Goalkeeper
FL Apps 70
Total Apps 74
Career: Bo'ness U., East Stirlingshire 1967 [3 ScL], Sheffield U. 9.68 [2], Mansfield T. loan 7.71 [2], York C. 10.71 [235], Scunthorpe U. 8.77 £3500 [104], York C. 1.80 (exchange for J. Neenan) [17], Dale 9.80 £2000 [70], n/c 1.83 to 5.83, Northallerton loan 1982-83, Scarborough 8.83 to 12.85 [93 Conf], Goole T. 1989, Copmanthorpe
Honours: Division 2 promotion 1971, Division 3 promotion 1974, Alliance Premier League Cup winners 1984

Graeme was a hugely experienced, physically commanding goalkeeper whose best work was done while accumulating over 250 appearances for York. Between September and December 1973 he went unbeaten for a record 11 games – Aldershot's former Dale striker Jack Howarth being the man to score at either end of the run, 17 hours and 19 minutes of playing time apart. Graeme became Dale's first professional goalkeeper of their own for two seasons when bought for £2000 just after the start of 1980-81 and helped them to regain mid-table respectability. He had to share goalkeeping duties with the returning Mick Poole the following year, but made a return as a non-contract player late in 1982-83. He played in the Conference until he was 38, made a comeback with Goole in the FA Cup when he was 42 and subsequently played on even longer with Copmanthorpe in the York and District League.

Robert James (Bob) Higgins 1980-81

Born: Bolsover 23.12.58
6'2" 13st6
Centre half
FL Apps/Gls 4+1/0
Total Apps/Gls 5+1/0
Career: Burnley app, pro 7.76 [3/-], Hartlepool U. loan 11.79 [2/-], Dale trial 8.80, pro 10.80 [4+1/-], Morecambe cs.81, Burnley U. 1981-82

A tall defender, Bob had made his league bow with Burnley in Division 2 but did not make further progress at Turf Moor and signed for Dale as defensive cover after a trial. He had a brief run of games in mid-season 1980-81 in the absence of regular centre backs Burke and Taylor. His brother Andy played for Dale a couple of years later.

Terence (Terry) Cooper 1981-82

Born: Croesyceiliog 11.3.50
5'9" 11st
Defender
FL Apps/Gls 35/2
Total Apps/Gls 41/3
Career: Newport Co. jnr, pro 7.68 [64+4/1], Notts Co. 7.70 [3+6/-], Lincoln C. loan 12.71 [3/-], Lincoln C. 8.72 £5000 [265+2/12], Scunthorpe U. loan 11.77 [4/-], Bradford C. 6.79 £10,000 [47+1/2], Dale 7.81 [35/2], retired 5.82
Honours: Wales youth international, (Division 3 promotion 1973), Division 4 champions 1976, PFA Division 4 team of the year 1976

Terry started out as a junior with Newport County, making his FL debut at right back a week after his 18th birthday, and captained the Welsh youth team. Signed as a midfielder but later used mainly as a central defender, he had considerable success in a long stint at Lincoln, playing in the side which won the fourth division title with a record number of points, and was one of five of their players selected for the PFA's divisional team of the year. After seven years, during which he was twice the Imps player of the season, and nearly 300 games, he was sold to Bradford City and in 1981 was one of several experienced lower league players to join the Dale, including Bantams' team-mate Terry Dolan. He was a regular at centre back or right back for a season but retired on being released and later became a prison PTI back in Wales.

Terence Peter (Terry) Dolan 1981-82

Born: Bradford 11.6.50
6'1" 11st3
Midfield
FL Apps/Gls 42+1/1
Total Apps/Gls 47+1/2
Career: Eccleshill U., Bradford C. jnr 1966, am 6.67, Bradford PA am 12.68, pro 4.69 [46+2/-], Huddersfield T. 10.70 [157+5/14], Bradford C. 8.76 [191+4/43], Dale 7.81 [42+1/1], Thackley cs.82, East Bowling Unity coach, Harrogate T. 1983-84, player-coach 1984-85, Bradford C. youth coach 1.85, coach 8.86, manager 1.87 to 1.89, Dale manager 4.89, Hull C. manager 1.91, Huddersfield T. assistant manager 8.97, York C. manager 2.00 to 2003, Guiseley manager 10.06 to 1.07. RIASA coach*
Honours: Division 4 promotion 1977

Despite attending a rugby union playing school, Terry joined his local club Bradford City when he was 16 but subsequently made his FL debut for the other Bradford team in 1969, playing as a centre half. Soon after they failed to be re-elected he joined first division Huddersfield but played in all four divisions with the Terriers in just six years. Due to an injury to the Town 'keeper, he also had to play in goal in an FA Cup quarter final game against Birmingham. He then spent five years back at Bradford City as an automatic choice in their midfield, gaining promotion in 1977. He also notched an impressive tally of 43 league goals, many from the penalty spot or powerfully struck free kicks. He spent one season at Spotland, missing just three games, and completed his round of all 92 league grounds in what turned out to be his final FL game before he was released in the summer of 1982. He then came out with the immortal quote "When a club like Rochdale gives you a free transfer, you have to seriously question your future in the game"! (This was the seventh time in his 14 year career that his side had been relegated or finished in the re-election places). In fact, he subsequently went into coaching and worked his way through the ranks in another spell at Valley Parade, becoming the City manager in 1987 and guiding them to the play-offs in his only full season in charge. He then returned to Spotland as boss and after building a new side almost from scratch – only four of Danny Bergara's side stayed at the club – managed to steer them into the top half of the table for the first time since their relegation 16 years earlier and to the fifth round of the FA Cup. The following year he played in Dale's 'A' team at the age of 40 due to an injury crisis and also had to drive the team bus to save money. Despite his side briefly holding second place in the table, he became increasing unpopular with Dale fans for his team selections and in January was tempted away by a better deal at Hull, Dale subsequently receiving £40,000 in compensation. He also managed York and later worked for the US Richmond University coaching school in the UK, whose products include Nahki Wells who has played for Terry's old clubs Bradford City and Huddersfield.

David (Dave) Goodwin 1981-82
Born: Nantwich 15.10.54 5'11" 11st7
Forward
FL Apps/Gls 34+5/6 Total Apps/Gls 37+5/6
Career: Stoke C. app, pro 6.72 [22+4/3], Workington loan 10.76 [7/-], Mansfield T. 11.77 [42+4/5], Bury 9.80 [2+2/-], Dale 7.81 [34+5/6], Crewe A. cs.82 [4+3/-], Stafford Rangers, Macclesfield T. 1.83, Witton Albion, Nantwich T. cs.85, Macclesfield T. 10.85
Honours: Cheshire Senior Cup winners 1983

Dave had made a number of appearances for Stoke in the first division and for Mansfield in the lower leagues, but easily the most productive of the eleven seasons he spent as a league player was his single one at Spotland when he made 39 FL appearances. Although he could play as a striker and scored the winner on his debut as substitute against Hartlepool, he was generally used on the flanks by Dale as Wellings and Hilditch continued as the regular central strikers. He made nearly 100 appearances for Macclesfield in their Northern Premier League days.

Neville Roy Hamilton 1981-84

Born: Leicester 19.4.60 5'8" 10st
Midfield
FL Apps/Gls 72+2/5 Total Apps/Gls 87+6/5
Career: Leicester C. app, pro 11.77 [4/-], Mansfield T. 1.79 £25,000 [84+5/4], Dale 7.81 [72+2/5], Wolverhampton W. cs.84, retired 1985. FA coach, coach in USA, Leicester C. community development officer 1988, Football in the Community by 1994, Leicester schools coach, Leicester C. academy assistant director, Chesterfield director of football 11.02, Rushden & Diamonds coach, Notts Co. coach 7.04, Rushden & Diamonds assistant manager 1.05 to 1.06 (d.9.2.09)

Although playing only four times for Leicester, Neville did make his debut against Manchester United. Bought by Mansfield for a sizeable fee he was a regular in their midfield for a couple of years, sometimes figuring alongside Dave Goodwin and joining Dale with him in 1981. A popular figure, it was only in his third season that he really became a regular, making 39 league appearances. This earned him a chance with second division Wolves, but sadly he suffered a heart attack in pre-season training at Molyneux and had to retire from the game. After a stint coaching in the USA he joined Leicester's community football programme and also ran his own coaching school. He was later Leicester's academy director and held several other coaching positions before his heart problems recurred and Neville died at the tragically early age of just 48.

Stephen William (Steve) Warriner 1981-83
Born: Liverpool 18.12.58 5'7" 10st
Right back
FL Apps/Gls 11+1/1 Total Apps/Gls 16+1/1
Career: Liverpool as, app 12.74, pro 12.76, Newport Co. 7.78 [28+8/2], Dale 7.81 [11+1/-], Tranmere R. 1.83 to cs.83 [5+4/-]
Honours: Lancashire Schools, Division 4 promotion 1980

Steve did not progress beyond the Central League side at Anfield but was at Newport for three years. After winning promotion, though only generally on the fringe of the side, he figured for them when, as Welsh Cup winners, they amazingly reached the quarter finals of the European Cup Winners Cup in 1981. He joined Dale that summer, but didn't make his first start until the following April, figuring in the remaining games at right back. Suffering with cartilage problems, he moved on to Tranmere after a few games the following year.

William Raymond (Bill) Williams 1980-85, 1994-95
Born: Littleborough 7.10.60 5'10" 12st7
Defender
FL Apps/Gls 89+6/2 Total Apps/Gls 105+8/2
Career: Ashe Labs, Dale am 1980-81, pt 8.82 [89+6/2], Stockport Co. cs.85 [104/1], Manchester C. 7.10.88 £85,000 [+1/-], Stockport Co. 2.12.88 £30,000 to cs.94 [153+3/7], Dale am 10.94, Littleborough 1995, manager 1998-99 to c.2003
Cricket for Littleborough
Honours: Division 4 promotion 1991, Division 3 play-off final 1992, Division 2+ play-off final 1994, Autoglass Trophy final 1992, 1993, Rochdale Sunday League XI 1980-81, 1995-96, 1997-98, 1999-2000, Greater Manchester Inter League Trophy winners 1981, Lancashire Sunday League Trophy winners 1996-97, Butterworth Cup

winners 1997, final 2002, Champion of Champions Cup winners 1996-97, FJ Williams Shield 2002

Bill was a star local amateur footballer – his father Frank was president of the Rochdale Amateur League - when given a trial in Dale reserves in 1980-81. He made his FL debut in midfield towards the end of the following term and then signed part-time terms for 1982-83. Switching largely to central defence though he still sometimes figured in midfield or at right back, he was a regular for three seasons before signing for Stockport. After a century of appearances there, too, he earned an apparent dream move to Manchester City, but he played only once as substitute before deciding to quit the big time and return to Edgeley Park after just two months. He took his overall Stockport tally to well over 300 games over the next six years. Their rise up the league saw them regular visitors to Wembley and Bill's final game as a professional came in the 1994 Division 2 play-off final. Dale could have re-signed him in 1990 but couldn't come up with the £30,000 that County wanted, and in 1994-95 he played briefly in the reserves but decided against a comeback at league level instead returning to his amateur roots with the successful Littleborough side in Sunday football. Also a useful club cricketer, throughout his career Bill worked in the family decorating business and his son Bill jnr also became a part time footballer with Barnoldswick Town as well as figuring for Littleborough.

David Stephen (Dave) Thompson 1979-86, 1994-97

Born: Manchester 27.5.62
5'9" 11st6
Winger
FL Apps/Gls 237+29/24
Total Apps/Gls 288+34/27
Career: St. Wilfrid's School, Bishop Henshaw School, North Withington, Dale jnr 1979, am 1980, pt 8.82, pro 5.84 [147+8/13], Brighton & HA trial 8.85, Manchester U. loan 8.85, Notts Co. 22.8.86 (exchange for A. Young) [52+3/7], Wigan A. 20.10.87 £35,000 [107+1/14], Preston NE 1.8.90 £75,000 [39+7/4], Chester C. 14.8.92 [70+10/9], Dale 8.8.94 £6000 [90+21/11], Southport 6.97 [53+24/4 Conf], Marine 6.99, player-coach to 2004
Honours: Lancashire Senior Cup final 1991-92, Division 3+ promotion 1994, FA Trophy final 1998

Dave joined Dale while at school, figuring in the youth team in 1979-80 and the reserves the following season. He then went to college in Leeds but made his FL debut for Dale in the last two games in May 1982, Dale beating Northampton 5-3 on his full debut. Remarkably 'Thommo' was everpresent the following year, making 55 consecutive league appearances from his debut, and made over 150 appearances in four years as a hard running right winger. Chosen as the Division 4 player of the year in the People in 1984-85, he had trials at Brighton and, a keen Manchester United fan, spent a month with United, unfortunately not being able to impress due to injury. Valued at £30,000, he was traded to Notts County in exchange for Alan Young and later cost £75,000 when moving to Preston. Never a prolific scorer, he netted his one career hat-trick for Chester against Scarborough in 1994 during their surprise run to promotion. He reappeared at Spotland when he was 32 and added another hundred appearances, finally totalling 266 in the league for the Dale and an impressive 322 in all senior games, placing him fourth in the all time list. He then played at non-league level until he was 42, playing at Wembley in the FA Trophy Final for Southport (one of a remarkable tally of 36 cup ties in just two seasons).

Jack Trainer 1982-83
Born: Glasgow 14.7.52   6'2"   12st5
Centre half
FL Apps/Gls 7/0   Total Apps/Gls 12/0
Career: Cork Hibernian 1975-76, Halifax T. 8.76 [101+4/5], Hong Kong Rangers 1979, Bury 9.80 [1/1], Kokkolan Pallo-Veikot (Finland) 1981, Waterford 1981, {Morecambe?}, Dale 8.82 to 9.82 [7/-], {Bury trial?}, Morecambe 11.82 to 1984. Bolton W. coach education manager 2007

Jack had a varied career, hailing from Scotland but figuring with clubs in Ireland as well as playing in Hong Kong and Finland. The vast majority of his FL appearances came as Halifax's regular centre half for three seasons – he was everpresent in his debut season - before a stay at Bury where he became surely one of very few defenders to score in their only league appearance for a club, spending the rest of the season out injured. With Dale down to the bare bones of a squad, he signed a short term contract at the start of the 1982-83 season and played in the first 12 games, Dale winning only two of them. In later years he worked in Bolton's coaching school.

Michael John (Micky) French 1982-83

Born: Eastbourne 7.5.55
6'0" 12st4
Centre forward
FL Apps/Gls 35+1/11
Total Apps/Gls 42+1/12
Career: Eastbourne U., Queens Park R. app, pro 8.74, Brentford 2.75 [56+9/16], Swindon T. 2.77 [5+5/1], Doncaster R. 7.78 [36/5], Aldershot 5.79 [70+4/16], Dale 7.82 [35+1/11], Lewes cs.83, Worthing c.1985, Horsham coach 1986, Hailsham 1987. Eastbourne U. manager 1997-98. Eastbourne T. coach c.2008
Honours: England youth international 1971

An England youth cap while still with Eastbourne United, Micky also ended his career in his native Sussex and played for a number of southern FL clubs. He also had single season spells with Doncaster and Rochdale. In terms of goals, his year at Spotland, when he top scored with 11 in the league, was his most productive. Playing up-front as target man, he scored a hat-trick against Hereford in Jimmy Greenhoff's first game in charge in March 1983 but was still released at the end of the season. Following serious knee problems which required lengthy hospital treatment the following year, he moved into non-league coaching and management.

Andrew (Andy) Stafford 1982-83

Born: Littleborough 28.10.60   6'1" 11st12
Forward
FL Apps/Gls 1/1 Total Apps/Gls 3/1
Career: Dale jnr 1974, Manchester C. as, Blackburn R. app 1977, n/c 1978, Halifax T. 1.79 [33+8/1], Stockport Co. cs.81 [21+4/-], Dale trial 8.82 to 9.82 [1/1], Runcorn, Mossley 1982-83, Chorley, Horwich RMI 1984, Daisy Hill c.1986 to at least 1988
Honours: Rochdale Schoolboys, Greater Manchester Schools

A local schoolboy star, Andy had been on Dale's books as a junior but was signed as an apprentice by Blackburn. He made his FL bow after signing for Halifax and set up the only goal in their remarkable FA Cup victory over Manchester City in 1980. He had a brief trial back at Spotland at the start of 1982-83, playing on the left flank in the first two Lancashire Cup games and then joining the ranks of players to score in their only FL game for the Dale when he did so against Hartlepool.

Peter Farrell 1982-85

Born: Liverpool 10.1.57
5'7" 10st9
Midfield
FL Apps/Gls 71+2/16
Total Apps/Gls 86+2/18
Career: Ormskirk, Bury 9.75 [49+5/9], Port Vale 11.78 £40,000 [85+4/10], Doncaster R. loan 8.81, Shrewsbury T. loan 10.81, Dale 8.82 [71+2/16], Crewe A. 10.84 [7+1/1], IFC Goteburg (Sweden), Vastra Frolunda (Sweden), Crewe A. 11.85 [19+1/1], IFK Goteburg (Sweden) 1986-87, Hamilton Ac. 1986-87 [3/- ScL], IBK Keflavik (Iceland) 1987-88, Apoel Nicosia (Cyprus), Barrow cs.89 [44+10/8 Conf], coach 1991, Blackpool coach by 1998, Bolton W. coaching school by 2008, Brentford coach cs.11*
Honours: Liverpool Boys, Lancashire Schools, FA Trophy winners 1990

One of Peter Madden's three major signings in the summer of 1982, Peter had already played around 150 games for Bury and Port Vale. A schoolboy star with the always highly rated Liverpool Boys and Lancashire Schools sides, prior to losing a year due to a knee operation he had been in line for a move from Gigg Lane to the first division. He missed only three league games for Dale in 1982-83 and was second top scorer with eight goals from midfield, latterly partnering new boss Jimmy Greenhoff. Taking over penalty duties, he netted 10 times in the first half of the following season but missed most of the remainder due to injury (though he remained the joint top scorer) and was in dispute over his contract during the summer. Eventually joining Crewe, he also played in Sweden, Scotland, Iceland and Cyprus, as well as appearing in the FA Trophy Final for Barrow. Moving onto their coaching staff, he subsequently moved up to FL level and while at Blackpool was responsible for Rickie Lambert joining them as a junior. Peter's son Tom had trials with his original club, Bury.

Gerald Patrick. (Gerry) Keenan 1982-83, 1983-84

Born: Liverpool 25.7.54
5'9" 11st
Full back
FL Apps/Gls 35/1
Total Apps/Gls 38/1
Career: Liverpool jnr, Skelmersdale, Bury 8.75 [69+2/3], Port Vale 9.78 £15,000 [105+1/7], Dale 9.82 [30/1], Ashton U. cs.83, Dale 10.83, Curzon Ashton cs.83, Dale 9.83 to 11.83 [5/-], {Accrington St., Ashton U.?}, Rossendale U. 1985-86, {Bacup

Borough?}, Accrington St. player-manager 1986-87, Ashton U. assistant player-manager, player-manager, Rossendale U. player-manager, Bacup Borough player-manager 10.87 to 10.88, {Rossendale U manager?}, Bacup Borough 1989-90, joint manager 1990-91, Castleton Gabriels, Bacup Borough manager 12.92, St Josephs (Rossendale)

Gerry had been a team-mate of Peter Farrell at both Bury and Port Vale and when Ronnie Blair decided to cancel his contract at Spotland, Peter Madden moved to team them up again. Although already suffering with knee problems when he signed, Gerry managed 30 games in his first season, almost all at right back. Released in the summer, he was again called upon to fill a gap the following October before recurrence of his injury and the return of Brian Greenhoff ended his involvement. He subsequently had a long (and torturous) tour of nearby non-league clubs Ashton United, Accrington Stanley, Rossendale United and Bacup Borough, frequently as player-manager. Indeed he played in Dale scout Tom Nichol's testimonial game in 1993-94 when he was nearly 40.

Paul Thomas Comstive 1982-83

Born: Southport 25.11.61
6'1" 12st7
Midfield/left back
FL Apps/Gls 9/2
Total Apps/Gls 10/2
Career: Blackburn R. jnr 1978, pro 10.79 [3+3/-], Dale loan 9.82 to 10.82 [6/2] and 2.83 to 3.83 [3/-], Wigan A. 8.83 [35/2], Wrexham 11.84 [95+4/8], Burnley 7.87 £8000 [81+1/17], Bolton W. 9.89 £37,000 [42+7/3], Chester 11.91 £10,000 [55+2/6], Southport cs.93 [52+9/11 Conf], Morecambe cs.95 [21+7/1 Conf], Chorley 1996, Southport assistant manager 11.99, Burscough coach to 7.05. Fleetwood Hesketh manager 2008
Honours: Lancashire Senior Cup (final 1982-83), winners 1984-85, Welsh Cup winners 1986, Sherpa Van Trophy final 1988, Division 3 play-off final 1991

Paul had two spells on loan to Dale in the same season while in Blackburn's reserves, netting on his debut at left back and then figuring in midfield. Subsequently making fairly regular moves around the league, his best spells were at Wrexham, where he played around a hundred games and figured in their Welsh Cup winning side, and Burnley, for whom he appeared in the Sherpa Van Trophy Final. While at Wrexham he was sent off in successive games but for Burnley he once scored two goals direct from corners in the same game. He also scored the first goal at Chester's new Deva Stadium and later moved into non-league coaching and management, latterly with Fleetwood Hesketh, before his untimely death from a heart attack when he was only 52.

William (Willie) Garner 1982-83
Born: Stirling 24.7.55 6'0"
Centre half
FL Apps/Gls 4/0 Total Apps/Gls 5/0
Career: Campsie Black Watch, Aberdeen 1975 [112+1/1 ScL], Celtic 1981 £50,000 [1/- ScL], Alloa Ath. loan 8.82 [7/1 ScL], Dale loan 9.82 to 10.82 [4/-], Alloa Ath player-manager 10.82 [48/6 ScL], Aberdeen assistant manager 2.84, Cove Rangers 1986-87, Rosslyn Sports 1987-88, Keith player-manager 1988-89, Stoneywood 1989-90, Berwick R. 1990 [47/1 ScL], Craigroyston player-manager 1992, Newtongrange Star player-manager 1995, manager 1997 to 1999, Harthill Royal manager 2000 to 2002, Glenrothes manager 2005 to 2006, Tayport manager 2008 to 2011, Ballingry Rovers manager 2014*
Honours: Scottish League Cup winners 1977, final 1980, Scottish Cup final 1978, Scottish Premier Division champions 1980, 1982

Willie made his mark with well over a century of appearances for Aberdeen in the late seventies when they finished 3rd and then 2nd before finally winning the Premier Division title in 1980. He also played in their side which beat Celtic in the Scottish League Cup final but had a somewhat less successful time after joining Celtic, scoring an own goal (or two, according to some accounts) on his debut as the perennial winners failed to get past the initial group stages of the League Cup. After a loan spell at Alloa, Willie joined Dale on the same terms and looked to be exactly the dominant central defender that they had long been seeking. Unfortunately Alloa thought the same, and offered him the position of player-manager. Remarkably scoring a hat-trick from centre half against Morton in the League Cup, he subsequently became assistant manager back at Aberdeen, when still only 28, but after a couple of years lost his job as No. 2 to Alex Ferguson. Willie then returned to playing and later, after a six year gap playing non-league football, appeared in nearly 50 further games in the Scottish League with Berwick Rangers. He subsequently embarked on a lengthy tour of the Scottish junior leagues as player-manager (turning out until he was 42) and then manager.

Geoffrey Robert (Geoff) Thomas 1981-84

Born: Manchester 5.8.64
5'10" 10st7
Midfield
FL Apps/Gls 10+1/1 Total Apps/Gls 10+2/1
Career: Littleborough Parish 1980-81, Dale jnr 1981-82, Ashe Labs 1982, Dale n/c 13.8.82 [10+1/1], Crewe A. 22.3.84 [120+5/21], Crystal Palace 8.6.87 £80,000 [192+3/26], Wolverhampton W. 1.8.93 £800,000 [36+10/8], Nottingham F. 18.7.97 [18+7/4], Barnsley 7.99 [14+24/4], Notts Co. 3.01 [8/1], Crewe A. 8.01 [8+6/2], retired 2002
Cricket for Littleborough
Honours: England (9 caps) 1991 to 1992, England 'B' (3 caps) 1990, Rochdale Sunday League Youth XI, Manchester County Inter-league Cup winners 1983, Rochdale Sunday League XI 1982-83, North of England Amateur Youth v FA Youth 1983, Division 2 promotion 1989, Division 1+ champions 1998, FA Cup Final 1990, Full Members Cup winners 1991

The most successful player ever to come out of the Rochdale Sunday League, Geoff was playing football (and cricket) in Littleborough while working as an electrician and came to notice when the league's youth XI won the County Cup, Geoff scoring twice in a 9-0 win in one game and twice more in the final against the Salford SL. Already associated with the Dale's youth set-up, he was selected for the North of England amateur youth team and then made his league debut, as substitute at Hereford in October 1982. After one other isolated appearance a year later, he finally managed an extended run in the side after scoring against Crewe in January 1984. However, with Dale unable to afford to offer him a full professional contract, it was Crewe who signed him up. After three years as a regular in their midfield, he was sold to Crystal Palace for £80,000 and went on to star in their run to the FA Cup Final (beating Dale along the way) in 1990. He won his first England 'B' cap the same year and went on to win nine full caps. After over 200 games for Palace he moved to Wolves for £800,000 but was beset with injuries, missing almost two years. After short spells elsewhere, including helping Forest to the first division title in 1998, he returned to Crewe (by now also in Division 1) but retired in 2002. He was diagnosed with leukaemia and after battling the condition, started a charitable foundation to support research in the area, most notably by riding the full Tour de France course to raise funds.

Carl Swan 1982-83
Born: Sheffield 12.12.57 6'2" 11st10
Central defender
FL Apps/Gls 3/0 Total Apps/Gls 4/0
Career: Matlock T., Worksop T., Buxton 1979-80, Burton A. £2250, Doncaster R. 12.80 £7000 [14+1/1], Dale loan 10.82 to 11.82 [3/-], Grantham 2.83, Chesterfield cs.83, Goole T., Buxton 1983-84, Mossley 1984-85, Belper T., Goole T. 1985-86, Matlock T., Buxton 1986-87
Honours: Division 4 promotion 1981

The son of Peter Swan, the former Sheffield Wednesday player, Carl figured alongside his father when the latter was player-manager at Matlock and Worksop after his lifetime ban following the 1963 betting scandal was lifted. Carl's first involvement at FL level came at Doncaster, winning promotion in his first season. A broken leg impeded his progress and he had played only a dozen or so games before a short loan spell at Spotland. Although his three league games resulted in one win, one draw and one defeat, he also figured in the FA Cup defeat by Altrincham and Dale boss Peter Madden brought in Gerry McElhinney on a long term loan from Bolton instead.

Roy Greaves 1982-83
Born: Farnworth 4.4.47 5'11" 11st12
Midfield
FL Apps/Gls 19+2/0 Total Apps/Gls 20+2/0
Career: Bolton W. jnr 1963, pro 1.65 [487+7/66], Seattle Sounders summers 1980 to 1982 [92/5 NASL], Dale player-coach 10.82 [19+2/-], Bolton St. Thomas cs.83, player-manager 4.84
Honours: Division 3 champions 1973, Division 2 champions 1978, NASL national western division champions 1980, 1982

A tremendous stalwart at Bolton, Roy had already been a junior at Burnden Park prior to a 15 year professional career which saw him play just short of 500 league games plus another 80 in the FA Cup and League Cup. He also netted the impressive total of 85 league and cup goals, including two hat-tricks, mostly while playing in midfield, though he could play up-front. He was top league goalscorer for the Trotters in 1967-68 and 1968-69 and frequently wore the No. 9 shirt when in midfield. During this period Bolton were relegated from Division 2 but then won the third division title and five years later gained promotion to the top flight. Roy spent three summers in the

NASL with Seattle Sounders and then in October 1982 was recruited by Peter Madden as player-coach to try and turn round the Dale's fortunes after only two wins in the first 13 games. With Roy in their midfield, Dale did improve somewhat, but then slid back down the table precipitating Madden's sacking. The board decided not to promote Roy to the top job and instead brought in Jimmy Greenhoff as the new manager, and after a handful of further games (at full back), Roy left the club.

Francis Gerard (Gerry) McElhinney 1982-83
Born: Londonderry 19.9.56 6'2" 13st
Centre half
FL Apps/Gls 20/1 Total Apps/Gls 20/1
Career: Derry C., Limavady U., Dungiven Celtic, Celtic, Finn Harps loan, FC Berne (USA) 1978, Distillery 1978-79, Chicago Sting (USA) loan summer 1979, Bolton W. 9.80 £25,000 [107+2/2], Dale loan 11.82 to 4.83 [20/1], Plymouth A. 1.85 £30,000 [90+1/2], Peterborough U. cs.88 £15,000 [87/1], coach 1991, Corby T. joint manager 1993-94. Graham Street Pimms manager cs.02 to 12.06
Gaelic football for St. Mary's Banagher, Derry, Cavan (Philadelphia), Connemara Gaels (Chicago), Sligo (New York)
Honours: N. Ireland (6 caps), Division 3 promotion 1986, Division 4 promotion 1991

A late comer to the English game at the age of 24, Gerry joined Dale on loan from Bolton in the autumn of 1982 and proved a great success at centre half, despite the side's struggles in the lower regions of the table. However, this was nothing compared to his rise after returning to Burnden Park. He had already played a number of games at left back or centre back over the previous two years, but he now established himself at centre half in place of the long serving Paul Jones (q.v.) and won the first of his six Irish caps in November 1983. However, he lost his place the following term and subsequently had lengthy spells at Plymouth, missing only two games when they were promoted to Division 2, and Peterborough, before becoming the latter's coach. His brother was also on Plymouth's books at the same time as Gerry, but didn't make the senior side. Gerry had started as a Gaelic footballer, winning two Ulster championships with Derry and a GAA All-star award in 1975 and even played the game while in the USA. He was also a notable amateur boxer, winning Mid-Ulster titles at middleweight and light-heavyweight.

Peter Nicholson 1982-83
Born: Cleator Moor 12.1.51 6'0" 12st
Defender
FL Apps/Gls 7/0 Total Apps/Gls 7/0
Career: Carlisle U. app, Blackpool 8.69 [3+3/-], Bolton W. 6.71 [303+15/12], Lytham St. Annes cs.82, Dale n/c 11.82 [7/-], Lytham St. Annes 1.83, Carlisle U. n/c 3.83 [+1/-], Lytham St Annes 1983-84, Carlisle U. n/c 5.84 [1+1/-], Chorley 1984-85, Barrow 1985-86 [5/- Conf]
Honours: Division 3 champions 1973, Division 2 champions 1978

Though with Carlisle and Blackpool as a teenager, playing a few games for the latter in Division 1, Peter made his mark after joining Bolton in 1971. Immediately becoming a regular in midfield, over the next eleven years he accumulated over 300 appearances, also appearing all across the back four and in fact playing in every outfield position bar centre forward. After two promotions, he played regularly in Bolton's two seasons in the top flight at the end of the seventies but was released in 1982. Joining Lytham St. Annes, he was recruited as a non-contract player at Spotland following the appointment of his long time team-mate Roy Greaves as player-coach (the pair had between them played 945 senior games for the Trotters). Peter played right, left and centre back in the course of his seven games before returning to St. Annes, though he did twice later reappear for odd games with second division Carlisle. In later years he was a matchday host at Bolton when they reached the Premier League.

Stuart Christopher Thompson 1981-84

Born: Littleborough 2.9.64
6'0" 12st
Forward
FL Apps/Gls 23+8/8
Total Apps/Gls 24+8/8
Career: Blackburn R. app 1980, Dale app 7.81, pro c.9.82 [23+8/8], Runcorn loan, FC Bruges (Belgium) trial cs.84, Chorley 7.84, Horwich RMI 1985, Eintracht Aalter (Belgium) 6.85, Bacup Borough 1987-88, Glossop NE, Buxton, Southport loan, Rossendale U., Curzon Ashton, (+ Cock & Magpie 1984 to 1995; Sunday League), Whitworth Valley 1995, player-manager 1997-98, reverted to player 2000, Nelson player-assistant manager, coach to 2009-10 (also Dale assistant youth coach 7.04, Preston NE academy coach 7.06), Manchester C. academy scout 7.10*
Honours: Rochdale Schools, Greater Manchester Schools, England Schools 1980

The first Rochdale schoolboy to play for England Schools, Stuart was actually on Blackburn's books at that point but transferred his apprenticeship to Dale in 1981. Overtaken for a first team place by amateur namesake Dave at the end of that season, Stuart made his first appearance, as substitute, in December 1982 and played his first full game the week Peter Madden was sacked. He scored in the first two games of Jimmy Greenhoff's reign but never became a regular up front, sharing squad duties with fellow youngster Malcolm O'Connor. In fact, his finest goalscoring moments were two strikes in a 3-3 draw with Doncaster when playing out of position in midfield. After a spell in Belgium he had a long career in non-league and Sunday football around the north west. Still Nelson's player-assistant manager when he was 45, he doubled up as an academy coach, first with Dale but most recently at the Etihad.

James (Jimmy) Greenhoff   1982-84

Born: Barnsley 19.6.46
5'9" 12st
Midfield
FL Apps/Gls 16/0 Total Apps/Gls 18/0
Career: Leeds U. app 6.61, pro 8.63 [90+6/19], Birmingham 8.68 £75,000 [31/14], Stoke C. 8.69 £100,000 [274/76], Manchester U. 11.76 £120,000 [94+3/26], Crewe A. 12.80 [11/4], Toronto Blizzard summer 1981 [24/6 NASL], Port Vale player-coach 8.81 [44+4/5], Dale player-manager 8.3.83 [16/-], Port Vale coach 3.84
Honours: Barnsley Boys, English Schools Trophy winners 1961, Yorkshire Schools, England u-23 (5 caps), England 'B', Football League v Scottish League 1976, Division 2 champions 1964, (Division 1 champions 1969), European Fairs Cup final 1967, winners 1968, FA Cup winners 1977, final 1979, FL Cup winners 1968, 1972, Watney Cup winners 1973, Charity Shield 1977

Often talked of as the best player of his generation never to play for England, Jimmy did play for England 'B', the Under-23s and for the Football League as a classy inside forward. At Leeds he made his FL debut at 16, the year before they were promoted to the top flight, and after being losing semi-finalists and finalists in the previous two years he was in one of the first British sides to win European honours when they took the 1968 Fairs Cup – though oddly he was transferred to Birmingham between the two legs (which were played at the start of the 1968-69 season). He was also in Leeds' League Cup winning side the same year and repeated this four years later while at Stoke, where he played the bulk of his FL games and netted 76 league goals. A move to Old Trafford when he was 30 gave him the chance to win further honours and he appeared alongside younger brother Brian in the United side which beat Liverpool in the 1977 FA Cup Final, deflecting Lou Macari's shot past Ray Clemence for the winner. After a spell in the bottom division with Crewe and a summer in the USA, he became player-coach at Port Vale and played a notable part when Vale came back from 3-0 down to draw with the Dale early in 1983. Shortly afterwards he succeeded Peter Madden in the Spotland hot seat, playing most of the remaining games in the centre of midfield, also recruiting brother Brian as player-coach. Although Dale just scraped clear of re-election, with Jimmy not playing significantly due to injury, the following term showed no sign of improvement and he resigned after exactly one year in charge. He subsequently returned to Port Vale and ran soccer schools, including one at Butlin's.

Brian Greenhoff   1982-84
Born: Barnsley 28.4.53 5'10" 12st2
Right back
FL Apps/Gls 15+1/0 Total Apps/Gls 18+1/0
Career: Manchester U. app 8.68, pro 6.70 [218+3/13], Leeds U. 24.8.79 £350,000 [68+2/3], Wits University (S. Africa), Rovaniemen Palloseura (Finland) 1982, Bulova (Hong Kong) 1982-83, Dale player-coach 9.3.83 to 5.83, re-signed n/c 24.11.83, assistant manager 16.12.83 to 3.84 [15+1/-]. Chadderton, Whitworth Valley manager 8.91 to 8.93, Chadderton coach 11.94
Cricket for Robinsons, Norden
Honours: Yorkshire Schoolboys, England (18 full caps) 1976 to1980, England u-23 (4 caps), England 'B', Division 2 champions 1975, FA Cup winners 1977, final 1976, (1979), Lancashire Senior Cup final 1972

Brian came through the ranks at Old Trafford to make his debut in 1973 and played a total of 270 games for United in all competitions. Initially a midfield player, he helped United regain their place in the top flight in 1975, switching to central defence by the time they won the FA Cup in 1977 thanks to brother Jimmy's deflected winner. He was non-playing substitute in the 1979 final against Arsenal and was then transferred to Leeds where he suffered from a number of injuries. He had won several under-23 caps and made his full England debut in 1976, eventually playing 18 times for his country as a solid, unspectacular defender, despite them missing out on the 1978 World Cup finals. After playing abroad, and already living locally, in Bamford, he was recruited by his brother as his number two at Spotland. He played a number of games in midfield or at right back, leaving when Jimmy resigned as manager a year later. Brian also played cricket in the Lancashire leagues (as did his son Brian jnr), appearing for Norden 2nd XI in the Burton Cup Final and once hitting six sixes in succession in an 18 ball half-century. His other son Paul played for Dale's youth sides and appeared in the reserves in 1992-93, as well as turning out in local football and figuring alongside his father when Brian made a playing comeback for Whitworth Valley at the age of 40. Brian wrote an autobiography "Greenhoff!" in 2012 but died at his home in Norden only a year later.

Everton Dale Carr 1982-83
Born: Antigua 11.1.61
5'7" 11st6
Full back
FL Apps/Gls 9/0 Total Apps/Gls 9/0
Career: Leicester C. app, pro 1.79 [11+1/-], Halifax T. 8.81 [49+4/-], Dale 24.3.83 [9/-], Nuneaton Borough cs.83 [113+3/- Conf], Weymouth cs.87 [3+1/- Conf], Bath C. 10.87 [6/- Conf], Barnet 11.87 [1+5/- Conf], Nuneaton Borough 1987-88, Oadby T.

Everton (presumably named after the West Indian cricketer Everton Weekes rather than the football club) had an appropriate middle name for his stint at Spotland. He had earlier played a few games for Leicester in the same side as Gary Lineker and was a regular for Halifax for a season before his brief switch to Rochdale, where he replaced the injured Eric Snookes. He had a long stint with Nuneaton Borough in the Conference and during a second spell played against the Dale in the FA Cup. His cousin Winston White figured even more briefly for Dale in 1986.

Andrew Martin (Andy) Higgins 1982-84

Born: Bolsover 12.2.60
6'3" 12st4
Centre half/forward
FL Apps/Gls 31+2/6
Total Apps/Gls 38+2/8
Career: Belper T., Chesterfield app, pro 2.78 [1/-], Port Vale 2.81 [11+3/-], King's Lynn, Hartlepool 9.82 [3+1/1], King's Lynn 12.82, Dale 24.3.83 [31+2/6], Chester 7.84 [16+3/1], Hellenic (South Africa) cs.85, Heidelberg U. (South Africa)

Even taller than his brother Bob, who had played for Dale a couple of years earlier, Andy had accumulated less than 20 FL appearances for his three clubs and had been playing for King's Lynn when recruited by Jimmy Greenhoff, who had been his coach at Port Vale. He scored on his Dale debut at centre forward, but played thereafter at centre half when Gerry McElhinney's loan ended. A similar pattern was followed the following term, and after a pre-season hat-trick Andy managed six league and cup goals in his dual roles, though he also netted own goals in successive games. After netting in a victory over Darlington at the end of February – only Dale's second in 19 league games – he missed the rest of the campaign through injury and after a season at Chester tried his luck in South Africa

Malcolm Joseph O'Connor 1982-84
Born: Ashton 25.4.65 6'1" 13st
Forward
FL Apps/Goals 12+4/3 Total Apps/Goals 14+5/4
Career: Curzon Ashton, (Nottingham F. trial), Dale n/c 1982, pro 9.83 [12+4/3], Curzon Ashton cs.84, Hyde U. 1985-86, Northwich Victoria cs.88 £12,000 [240+16/97 Conf], Curzon Ashton cs.95
Honours: Northern Premier League v FA XI 1987-88, England semi-professional squad 1987-88, Drinkwise Cup winners 1993, Northern Premier League Cup winners 1986, Mid Cheshire Senior Cup, FA XI v Combined Services 1994-95

Signed originally on non-contract terms from Curzon Ashton, Malcolm made his debut as substitute just before his 18th birthday and turned pro that summer. He scored on his full debut in the first game of the 1983-84 season, in the Lancashire Cup, but had to wait until November for his next taste of action. He figured in the squad fairly regularly for the rest of the season but was not retained and returned to Curzon. His development into one of the top non-league strikers came when he joined Hyde United, winning their player of the year and netting a remarkable 55 goals in 66 games in 1986-87. He netted another 34 when they were runners up in the Northern Premier League the following term and totalled 105 goals in all at Hyde. After figuring in the England semi-pro squad, a big fee at non-league level took him to Northwich Victoria. He again netted over 100 goals for his new club, including one of the quickest ever goals, in just 9 seconds against Cheltenham in the FA Trophy in 1991-92. He totalled well over 250 games in the Conference for the Vics, also earning representative honours in an FA XI. Back at Curzon, he showed he had not lost his goal touch, netting 32 in his first season.

Steven Harold (Steve) Conroy 1983-85

Born: Chesterfield 19.12.56
6'0" 12st2
Goalkeeper
FL Apps 49 Total Apps 64
Career: Sheffield U. jnr 1972, app 10.73, pro 6.74 [104], Leeds U. loan 8.81, {Kettering T. loan 1982-83 [3 Conf]?}, Rotherham U. n/c 3.83 [5], Dale 6.83 [49], Rotherham U. 30.1.85, retired injured 12.85.

Sheffield U. coach
Honours: Chesterfield Schools, North East Derbyshire Schools, England Schools, Division 4 champions 1982

A schoolboy international, Steve signed for Sheffield United prior to his 17th birthday and went on to play over 100 games in goal for the Blades between 1977 and 1982. In 1979-80, they topped the third division table until Christmas, when Steve was injured, but by the time he returned a year later they were on their way down to the bottom division and he played only once as they bounced back the following year (spending time on loan to first division Leeds). Arriving at Spotland in the summer of 1983, he was everpresent in his first season, making a total of 54 league and cup appearances, keeping twelve clean sheets despite Dale finishing in the bottom four. Also winning the player of the year award, he was unfortunately injured in September 1984 and did not play in the league again, even after returning to Rotherham. One odd event in his Dale career saw Steve nearly arrested for fighting with a Crewe fan who tried to steal his spare gloves from the back of his goal at half time.

Robert Anthony (Bob) Oates 1983-84

Born: Leeds 26.7.56
5'11" 11st7
Defender
FL Apps/Gls 42/1
Total Apps/Gls 49+1/1
Career: Leeds Ashley Road, Scunthorpe U. 8.74 [306+9/15], Dale 8.83 [42/1], Walton U. cs.84. Burnley Football in the Community by 1994
Honours: England youth international v N. Ireland 1974, Division 4 promotion 1983

A one-time England youth international – he was the last non-league player selected for England until 2011 - Bob was a highly experienced lower league performer, having made well over 300 appearances for Scunthorpe before moving to Spotland. In one spell of just over five years, he missed just five games, originally playing in midfield but later moving into the defence. Still only 27 when signed by Jimmy Greenhoff, after helping the Iron to promotion in his final season, he was virtually everpresent in his single season with Dale, alternately figuring at right back or in the centre of the defence, but when released dropped into non-league football. In the 1990s he worked with Football in the Community at Burnley and in 2004 became operations director at Sunderland.

Leslie (Les) Chapman 1983-85

Born: Oldham 27.9.48
5'7" 10st4
Left back/midfield
FL Apps/Gls 87+1/0 Total Apps/Gls 105+1/1
Career: Huddersfield T. am 1965, High Barn, Oldham A. trial 9.66, signed 1.2.67 [75+1/9], Huddersfield T. 25.9.69 (exchange for D. Shaw) [120+3/8], Oldham A. 5.12.74 (part exchange for C. Garwood) [186+1/11], San Jose Earthquakes summer 1978 [20/2 NASL], Stockport Co 17.5.79 [32/1], Bradford C. 29.2.80 £10,000 [137+2/3], Dale 6.6.83 [87+1/-], caretaker player-manager 3.84, player-assistant manager 6.84, Stockport Co. 7.7.85 [38/3], player-manager 10.85, Preston NE 6.8.86 [50+3/1], player-assistant manager, manager 2.90 to 9.92, Manchester C. youth team coach 1.93, Huddersfield T. youth coach 7.96, Manchester C. kitman 10.97*
Honours: Chadderton Boys, Division 2 champions 1970, Division 4 promotion 1982, 1987, Lancashire Senior Cup winners 1967

Les was originally a trainee accountant in local government, but a trial with Oldham when he was 18 led to a more than forty year involvement with the professional game. A tricky winger in his earlier days, he had two productive spells with his home town club, totalling 289 games, either side of a century of appearances for Huddersfield. While with the Terriers he played in their Division 2 title winning side and won the BBC's 'goal of the month' for a strike against Arsenal. Converting to a midfield man, and later a left back, he also played well over a hundred times for Bradford City and, including cup ties, did so again with Dale. The regular left back in 1983-84, as senior pro he was made caretaker manager when Jimmy Greenhoff resigned, but after just failing to edge Dale out of the bottom four reverted to a player for a further season as assistant to former Latics' team-mate Vic Halom, alternating between left back and midfield. Moving to Stockport, he soon became player-manager for a spell. He next joined Preston as a player, before being promoted to player-assistant manager, gaining promotion with his third different club and extending his FL career into his 40th year, when he and former Oldham and Huddersfield colleague Frank Worthington were the two longest serving players in the game. Indeed, Les remained registered as a player for two further seasons and over the years played around 860 senior games, including 745 in the FL.

In 1990 he took over as North End manager, but a poor start to the 1992-93 season saw him dismissed. He was subsequently on the coaching and backroom staff at Manchester City, latterly as long serving kit-man.

Michael (Mike) Doyle   1983-84

Born: Manchester 25.11.46
6'0"   12st2
Central defender
FL Apps/Gls 24/1
Total Apps/Gls 32/1
Career: Manchester C. jnr 1962, pro 5.64 [441+7/32], Stoke C. 6.78 £50,000 [115/5], Bolton W. 1.82 £10,000 [40/2], Dale 7.83 to cs.84 [24/1]
Honours: Stockport Boys, England (5 full caps) 1976 to 1977, England under-23s (8 caps) 1968 to 1969, Young England v England XI 1968, Football League v Scottish League 1972, 1976, Division 2 champions 1966, promotion 1979, Division 1 champions 1968, FA Cup winners 1969, FL Cup winners 1970, 1976, final 1974, European Cup Winners Cup winners 1970, Anglo-Italian Cup final 1970-71, Charity Shield 1968, 1969, 1972, 1973

Mike was a true legend at Manchester City, accumulating the huge total of 558 appearances in major competitions over a 14 season career, ten of them as an automatic choice, first as an old fashioned wing half and then in midfield or central defence. Over that time, he played in their second division title winning side and the famous team which secured the league championship under Joe Mercer and Malcolm Allison two years later. City also won the FA Cup once and the League Cup twice with him in their ranks, Mike netting the winner against West Brom in the 1970 final, as well as triumphing in the European Cup Winners' Cup. In such a talented squad, Mike was the hard man who would 'sort out' any opponent who tried to disrupt City's flowing game, famously being sent off by Clive Thomas, along with Manchester United's Lou Macari, in 1973-74 and initially refusing to leave the pitch. Mike also played for England under-23s and for the Football League before winning five full caps. He had a further three seasons at Stoke, helping them to promotion, and eighteen months at Bolton before arriving at Spotland. Unable to help keep Dale out of the bottom four, he faded from the scene due to injury in the second half of the campaign, finishing with 627 FL appearances in total. Mike had earlier written an autobiography describing his time at City and a second book 'Blue Blood' appeared in 2003.

Ian James Griffiths   1983-85
Born: Birkenhead 17.4.60   5'6"   10st2
Midfield
FL Apps/Gls 40+2/5   Total Apps/Gls 47+3/6
Career: Tranmere R. jnr, pro 2.79 [110+6/5], Dale 7.83 [40+2/5], Port Vale 10.84 [9+3/-], Wigan A. cs.85 [73+9/7], Fujita (Japan) c.1988, Mazda Hiroshima (Japan), Bolton W. trial 1989-90, Wigan A. 8.90 [6+5/-], Wrexham 3.91 (exchange for G. Worthington) [14/-], Rhyl 1992
Honours: Lancashire Senior Cup final 1986-87, Welsh Cup final 1991, Japanese division 2 west champions 1989

Ian played over a hundred games on the left flank for his local club Tranmere before being one of seven new signings at Spotland in 1983. He took over from manager Greenhoff on the left of midfield after the first three league games and played the majority of matches for the rest of the season. In dispute over his contract in the summer, he soon moved to Port Vale but saw more league action at Wigan. He was also one of the first British professionals to play in Japan.

Vernon Allatt   1983-84

Born: Cannock 28.5.59
5'11"   11st8
Forward
FL Apps/Gls 40/8
Total Apps/Gls 48+1/10
Career: Hednesford T. cs.76, Walsall trial 1978, Halifax T. 11.79 [66+4/7], Bolton W. cs.82, Halifax T. 11.82 £2000 [27+1/7], Dale 8.83 £2000 [40/8], Crewe A. 6.84 £2000 [36+3/6], Preston NE 11.85 [17+2/3], Stockport Co. 18.10.86 [23+1/10], Hercules (Holland), Hednesford T. cs.87, Crewe A. 12.87 [4+1/2], Hednesford T. 1988

Working down a pit before turning pro, Vernon played around 100 games in two spells at Halifax before Dale signed him for a small fee. Initially the foil to the more muscular Steve Johnson up front, he missed only a handful of games, even filling in as an unlikely centre back at one point, and was one of three players to reach 10 goals in the season, two of his coming in the season's best win, 4-1 against Reading. He was sold on to Crewe and continued to move around the lower leagues for a further four seasons, with stints in Holland and with his original club Hednesford mixed in. At Crewe he figured in the same side as Bob Scott (q.v.), with whom he had become firm friends after having the temerity to kick the huge defender back in an earlier encounter! His non-league playing career was ended by a near fatal car accident.

Stephen Anthony (Steve) Johnson 1983-84, 1985-86, 1989-91

Born: Liverpool 23.6.57
6'0" 12st9
Centre forward
FL Apps/Gls 40+9/12
Total Apps/Gls 51+11/17
Career: South Liverpool, Bangor C. 1975, Altrincham 1977, Bury 11.77 [139+15/52], Dale 8.83 £13,500 [17+2/7], Wigan A. 2.84 £25,000 [50+1/18], Bristol C. 27.3.85 £35,000 [14+7/3], Dale loan 12.85 to 1.86 [3+3/1], Chester loan 3.86 [10/6], Scunthorpe U. 7.86 £20,000 [59+13/20], Chester 8.88 [35+3/10], Husqvana IF (Sweden) 1989, Dale 10.89 [20+4/4], Cork C. 8.90, Limerick, Northwich Victoria 10.90 [1+2/1 Conf], Bacup Borough 1991, Radcliffe Borough, Castleton Gabriels 12.92, Caernarvon T. cs.93, Haslingden, Ramsbottom U. 1995
Honours: (Division 4 promotion 1986)

Memorably described as "a brick outhouse of a centre forward" in a radio match report, Steve had three separate spells at Spotland. He had scored 50 goals in 150 games at Bury — three of them against Rochdale in 1981 - when Dale spent a record £13,500 on him, a fee set by a tribunal after Bury had asked for £60,000. He scored ten times by December including both goals in Dale's surprise FA Cup victory at runaway leaders York, the first after just 14 seconds, but was then sold to Wigan to ease the financial pressure. He next reappeared with Dale when they borrowed him from Bristol City two years later, appearing in the famous FA Cup tie at Manchester United. Bought by Scunthorpe in 1986 after assisting Chester to promotion while on loan, he netted 16 goals in his first season with them but Dale obtained his signature for a third time when he returned from a spell in Sweden in 1989. He figured in the run to the FA Cup fifth round, thus appearing the only three times that Dale reached round three between 1980 and 1996. (Indeed, in his Bury days, he had also played when they beat Dale in round three and went out at Liverpool in the fifth round). He left for Ireland at the start of the next campaign but later reappeared in the Rochdale area with the likes of Castleton Gabs.

Ian McMahon 1983-87

Born: Wells 7.10.64
6'0" 12st
Defender/midfield
FL Apps/Gls 89+2/8
Total Apps/Gls 105+5/8
Career: Thornham Middle School, Oldham A. as 16.10.80, app 27.7.81, pro 12.10.82 [2/-], Dale 1.84 [89+2/8], retired injured 1986-87. Oldham T. manager 11.88, Rochdale Hornets secretary-general manager 8.92, Oldham A. marketing executive 12.93, (Royals manager 1995-96; Sunday League), Hull C. chief executive 1997-98, Doncaster R. chief executive 1998-99, Des Moines Menace (USA) youth coach, West Michigan Edge junior coach, West Michigan Fire Juniors technical director 2005-06, West Michigan Firewomen head coach, Fort Wayne Fever chief executive officer, Women's League Soccer commissioner 2011, American Youth Soccer Organisation national executive director 10.14*

Ian had his promising career curtailed at the age of just 21, but has subsequently had an eclectic career in the sports business. He had made just a couple of appearances for Oldham when joining Dale, initially on loan, half way through 1983-84: a sending off in only his second game at centre half meant that he had the unusual experience of signing a permanent deal while suspended. Also used at left back, the following season he secured a regular place in midfield and won the supporters' young player of the year award as Dale recovered from a poor start to finish 17th. However, an injury in March 1986 required two cartilage operations and sadly Ian was forced to give up the game. He became manager of local league club Oldham Town when only 24 and took a degree in sports law, also gaining an MBA. He returned to the other half of Spotland in 1992 as secretary and general manager of Hornets and then became marketing executive back at Oldham, also running Sunday league side Royals. He was next the chief executive at Hull City before taking a similar role at Doncaster in the doomed regime that ended with the chairman accused of trying to burn down Belle Vue for the insurance money. Perhaps unsurprisingly, Ian was able to write a book 'The Only Way is Up', about this part of his career! He subsequently moved to the USA, acting in numerous coaching and executive capacities including commissioner of the Women's League. He also spent a year as head of the Hong Kong Rugby Football Union.

Shaun Reid   1983-89, 1992-95

Born: Huyton 13.10.65
5'8" 11st10
Midfield
FL Apps/Gls 232+8/14 Total Apps/Gls 304+10/22
Career: Everton as, Bolton W. jnr, Manchester C. jnr, Dale yts 8.83, pro 5.84 [126+7/4], Preston NE loan 12.12.85 [3/-], York C. 23.12.88 £32,500 [100+2/7], Dale 16.8.92 [106+1/10], Bury 5.7.95 £25,000 [20+1/-], Chester C. 11.96 [53+9/2], coach 8.99, Leigh RMI 8.00 [+1/- Conf], Swindon T. coach to 8.01. Sunderland scout, Plymouth A. assistant coach 7.11, Prescot Cables manager 1.12, Warrington T. manager 3.12*
Honours: Division 3 promotion 1996, Peter Swales (Unibond) Challenge Shield winners 2000

Younger brother of Everton's England star Peter, Shaun was one of the first batch of YTS lads ever recruited by the Dale, brought in by Roy Greaves who had known him when he was a junior at Bolton. He made his FL debut, in the same match as Ian McMahon, in the wake of Dale's FA Cup demise at Telford in January 1984, and played regularly thereafter, despite six bookings in only 13 games earning him the first of many suspensions during his career. The following season the combative midfielder was a regular until being simultaneously sent off and carried off following a crunching tackle in a defeat at Scunthorpe. Again this set the pattern for future years as Shaun battled a catalogue of injuries, including three broken legs, broken ribs, achilles and ankle ligament damage and the removal of all his cartilages. Nevertheless he totalled 240 league appearances for Dale in two spells separated by four years at York, who paid a sizeable £32,500 for his services. Passing 300 games in total, he was sold again in 1995, joining Bury where he was sent off in only his second game but gained the sole promotion of his career. He ended his career at Chester (after 432 FL appearances, all of them in the fourth tier), coming back briefly after missing the whole of 1997-98 with cruciate problems, and then taking a coaching position. He later scouted for Sunderland when his brother was their manager and subsequently acted as a players' agent. He also assisted his brother as coach at Plymouth and then turned to non-league management, gaining notice as the boss of FA Cup giant-killers Warrington in 2014.

Mark R. Ennis   1982-85
Born: Salford 20.11.65
Right back
FL Apps/Gls 1/0 Total Apps/Gls 1/0
Career: (Salford junior football), Joiners Libs, Dale jnr 1982-83, pro 11.83 [1/-], Salford C. 1985
Honours: Greater Manchester Youth

After playing for the Greater Manchester youth team and in local football, Mark played in Dale's 'A' team in 1982-83. Following a number of games in the reserves, he got his first team chance in a friendly against Barrow in January 1984 and then replaced the injured Brian Greenhoff at right back against Swindon the following week, the game ending 3-3. Though remaining with the club the following term this proved to be his only senior action.

James Bernard (Jimmy) Blake   1983-85
Born: Manchester 5.5.66
Right back
FL Apps/Gls 2/0 Total Apps/Gls 2/0
Career: Dale n/c 9.83 to 1984-85

A second young full back to earn a first team try out early in 1984, 17 year old Jimmy also figured in the Barrow friendly and then appeared in successive games in place of the younger Greenhoff just before he and his brother left the Spotland scene. Like Mark Ennis, Jimmy played in the reserves the following season but was not selected for the first team again.

Paul John Heaton   1983-84, 1984-86

Born: Hyde 24.1.61
5'10" 11st5
Midfield/full back
FL Apps/Gls 85+4/9
Total Apps/Gls 103+5/10
Career: Manchester C. jnr, Oldham A. as 17.11.76, app 14.6.77, pro 18.1.79 [124+12/28], Dale loan 22.3.84 to 20.4.84 [2+3/-], Dale 7.84 [83+1/9], Rovaniemi PS (Finland) 7.86, Kuusysi Lahti (Finland) 9.87, Kajaanin Palloilijat (Finland) 1988 to 1990 and 1994 to 1996, Kajaanin Haka (Finland) 1997 to 2000, FC Tarmo 2001, coach 2005
Honours: Finnish Cup Winners 1987

With Dale short of experienced players in the wake of the Greenhoffs' departures, caretaker boss Les Chapman brought in his former Oldham team-mate Paul on loan. He had previously accumulated almost 150 games for the Latics since his debut in 1978, despite suffering two broken legs, playing mostly in a wide midfield role, though his most recent games had been at left back. In the event he started only two games during his loan spell, being otherwise on the bench, but he signed permanently for Dale the following summer. This time he was virtually everpresent, not being in the squad only five times in his two years at Spotland, playing interchangeably on either wing and at right back and in fact playing everywhere except centre forward and central defence. In April 1985, against Hereford, he had the honour of scoring Dale's first winning goal in a match south of Crewe for eight and a half years. Leaving the English game when still only 25, he tried his luck in Finland, subsequently marrying a local girl and playing on until he was 41. He also figured in the European Cup Winners Cup for Rovaniemi.

John Stephen Humphreys 1983-84

Born: Farnworth 18.7.64
5'9" 10st2
Forward
FL Apps/Gls 6/0
Total Apps/Gls 6/0
Career: Oldham A. app 4.6.80, pro 26.7.82 to cs.84 [7+6/-], Dale loan 23.3.84 to 5.84 [6/-], Horwich RMI 10.84

Recruited along with Paul Heaton, John had started just seven games for the Latics, though he had scored against Rochdale in the Lancashire Cup at the start of 1982-83. He figured in six games at Spotland, either on the right wing or up front when Dave Thompson and Vernon Allatt were unavailable.

James Alexander Joseph (Jim) McCluskie 1983-86

Born: Rawtenstall 29.9.96
Forward
FL Apps/Gls 14+5/0
Total Apps/Gls 15+6/0
Career: Dale yts 8.83, pro 5.84 [14+5/-], St Peters (Jersey) cs.86, Mossley 10.87, Hyde U. 12.89 £8000, Witton Albion 1991-92 £10,000 [20+13/9 Confl], Barrow 1992-93, Mossley 1992-93, Accrington St. 1992-93, Morecambe 8.93 £2000 [28+35/17 Conf], (assistant manager 10.95 to 2.96), Accrington St. 1997, manager 2.98 to 3.98, Rossendale U. 1998, manager 1999, Bacup Borough manager 9.00, Rossendale U. manager 2001 to 11.02, Rossendale U. assistant manager 9.03, manager 1.04 to 5.04. Preston NE head of youth scouting

Honours: FA Trophy final 1992, NPL champions 1991, 1995, NPL Cup winners 1989, Manchester Premier Cup winners 1989, Reporter Floodlit Cup winners 1989; As manager: North West Counties League champions 2001

Jim was a YTS player in Dale's reserves when first included in the first team squad. He scored twice in a friendly against Barrow in January 1984 and again in one against Finnish side Pallo Iirot and subsequently got his chance up front in the last five league games of the season, when still only 17. Apart from being non-playing substitute in the Associate Members Cup, he did not figure again until 1985-86, eventually starting seven successive games on the left wing towards the end of that season. Like Malcolm O'Conner, who he had succeeded as the reserves main striker, he went on to a highly productive non-league career, netting 77 times in 123 games for Mossley and 99 in four years with Morecambe, 39 of them when they gained promotion to the Conference. He was a player of the year with both clubs and also played in the Trophy Final with Witton Albion, later moving into management before working as a youth scout for Preston. His brother Steve also assisted Mossley and Bacup.

Andrew Geoffrey (Andy) Dean 1983-85

Born: Salford 27.11.66
Full back
FL Apps/Gls 1/0 Total Apps/Gls 1/0
Career: Blackburn R. jnr, Burnley as, Dale yts 7.83, pro 11.83 [1/-], Salford C. 1985-86

The third of the reserve full backs given a chance in 1983-84, Andy replaced suspended caretaker manager Les Chapman for the penultimate game of the season, which Dale lost 3-0 away to promoted Doncaster. Still only 17, he again figured in the reserves the following term, but like Mark Ennis he then joined Salford City without making any further first team appearances.

Stephen Gerald (Steve) Edwards 1984-85

Born: Birkenhead 11.1.58
5'9" 11st
Right back
FL Apps/Gls 4/0
Total Apps/Gls 10/0
Career: Oldham A. as 4.10.73, app 4.6.74, pro 13.1.76 [77+3/-], Crewe A. 5.2.83 [57+1/1], Dale 10.7.84 [4/-], Tranmere R. 10.10.84 [72/6], Oswestry T. 1986-87, Bangor C. 1987-88, Fleetwood 1987-88, Mossley 1989-90, Vauxhall Motors
Honours: Ellesmere Port Schoolboys

Another former Oldham player and teammate of new Dale boss Vic Halom, Steve had been at Boundary Park for 10 years as an associated schoolboy, apprentice and professional, making 80 league appearances nearly all at full back, though he had originally been a midfielder. He figured regularly in just over a year at Crewe, in central defence and both full back positions. His stay at Spotland was much less productive, just four league games and six early season cup matches. He moved on to Tranmere after only three months and was their skipper the following season. Steve's grandfather Ernie Marsh was on Stoke's books in the 1930s.

Joseph (Joe) Cooke 1984-86

Born: Dominica, Leeward Islands 15.2.55
6'1" 13st
Centre half
FL Apps/Gls 75/4
Total Apps/Gls 90/5
Career: Bradford C. as 7.70, app 1971, pro 5.72 [184+20/62], Peterborough U. 1.79 £45,000 [18/5], Oxford U. 8.79 £50,000 [71+1/13], Exeter C. 6.81 £25,000 [17/3], Bradford C. loan 1.82, signed 2.82 £10,000 [61+1/6], Dale 7.84 [75/4], Wrexham 7.86 £11,000 [49+2/4], retired cs.88, Liversedge
Honours: Bradford Boys, Division 4 promotion 1977, 1982

A huge favourite with the fans at Bradford City and Dale for his massive physical presence and power in the air, Joe made his debut for the Bantams in September 1971 when only 16 and signed his first professional contract the following summer. Starting out at centre half, he played some games up front in 1974-75 and became a full time centre forward in the following campaign, netting 24 goals, and added 18 more when City were promoted. After shorter spells elsewhere, and having reverted to central defence, he returned to Bradford in 1982 during another promotion campaign, taking his overall tally of matches for them past 300, despite some injury problems. A key signing by Vic Halom, Joe skippered Dale for two seasons, netting the goal against Mansfield at the end of 1984-85 that guaranteed their escape from the re-election zone. Sold to Wrexham as Dale trimmed their budget, he skippered them in the European Cup Winners Cup, but had to retire through persistent cartilage problems. Joe subsequently opened a health club, and ran a gym in Cleckheaton.

Gerard Anthony (Ged) Keegan 1984-85
Born: Little Horton, Bradford 3.10.55
5'6" 10st9
Midfield
FL Apps/Goals 2/0 Total Apps/Goals 7/0
Career: Manchester C. app 6.8.71, pro 2.3.73 [32+5/2], Oldham A. 8.2.79 £25,000 [139+5/5], Mansfield T. 1.10.83 [18/1], Dale 26.7.84 [2/-], Altrincham 9.84
Honours: England under-21 v Wales 1976, Football League Cup winners 1976, Lancashire Senior Cup winners 1974

Ged was spotted by Malcolm Allison as an 11 year old and came through the junior ranks at City, winning the Lancashire Cup while in the reserves, to make his FL debut in 1975. A slightly built midfielder notable for his flame-coloured hair, City also used him as, essentially, a wing back at times, Ged playing right back in the 1976 League Cup Final after scoring in the semi-final from midfield. The Wembley success came after just eight FL starts and he was selected for the England under-21s the same year, but was unable to gain a regular first team place and was transferred to Oldham for a small fee. He figured around 150 times for the Latics, again playing either at right back or as an energetic midfielder and missed only three second division games in two years. He had a brief spell at Mansfield before joining the ex-Oldham contingent at Spotland under Vic Halom and Les Chapman. However, he played only twice in the league before being quickly moved on to non-league Altrincham. He was a keen golfer, competing in local tournaments.

Leslie Oliver (Les) Lawrence 1984-85
Born: Rowley Regis 18.5.57 6'0" 13st5
Striker
FL Apps/Gls 15/4 Total Apps/Gls 21/5
Career: Stourbridge, Shrewsbury T. 2.75 [10+4/2], Telford U. loan 1976-77, Torquay 7.77 [170+19/45], Weymouth, Port Vale 8.82 [5+3/-], Aldershot 7.83 [39/23], Dale 8.84 £15,000 [15/4], Burnley 19.11.84 £20,000 [22+9/8], Peterborough U. 7.86 [28+5/9], Cambridge U. 2.88 [11+2/-], Kettering T. cs.88 [4+4/1 Conf], Aylesbury c.12.88 £12,000 [18+1/1 Conf], Corby T. 8.90
Honours: Welsh Cup winners 1977, Division 4 promotion 1983

Big striker Les was the new manager's one expensive buy in the summer of 1984. Costing a record £15,000 from Aldershot, he had just completed by far his best goalscoring season, with 25 in all competitions, including four against Chester. He had earlier played in the Welsh Cup Final with Shrewsbury and spent five seasons as a solid performer for Torquay netting nearly 50 times in 200 games, 19 of them in 1978-79 with a hat-trick against Barnsley. He had managed just five for Dale, who endured a difficult start to the season, when Burnley came in with a bid that saw Dale make a slight profit after just three months. Hampered by injuries over the next two or three years, he still scored about a goal every three games but dropped into non-league football in 1988.

Barry Diamond 1984-86

Born: Dumbarton 20.2.60
5'7" 11st5
Striker
FL Apps/Gls 50+2/16 Total Apps/Gls 64+3/19
Career: Gillingham, Dumbarton, Barrow 3.78 [3/- Conf], Workington £2500 9.79, Oulon Pallesuro (Finland), Workington, Manchester C. trial, Cambridge U. trial, Barrow 3.83 [12/1 Conf], Dale £2000 7.84 [50+2/16], Stockport Co. loan 12.85 [6/-], Barrow n/c 2.86 [5/- Conf], Halifax T. 2.86 [17+5/3], Wrexham loan 1.87 [2+2/-], Morecambe cs.87, Gainsborough Trinity 1987-88, Colne Dynamos 1987-88, Mossley 1988-89, Stalybridge Celtic (+Tophams; Sunday League), Hyde U. 1988-89, (South Africa 3.89), Altrincham 1989 [7+1/2 Conf], Chorley 1989-90 [7/3 Conf], Stalybridge Celtic 1991-92, Curzon Ashton, Rossendale U., Mossley 1993-94, Horwich RMI 1993-94, Castleton Gabriels
Honours: NPL champions 1984, NPL Challenge Shield winners 1984, FA Vase winners 1988

Barry had an extremely varied and well travelled career at different levels of the game, first obtaining first team football while at Barrow in 1978. Sold to Workington he also had a spell in Finland and trials with league clubs before finding his way back to Barrow. In 1983-84 when they won the Northern Premier League title under Vic Halom, Barry notched a remarkable 41 goals in 57 outings. Having been a Dale target before, he was immediately signed by Halom when the latter took over at Spotland. The tough little Scottish striker was a big success in his first season, netting 18 times in all and latterly forming a prolific partnership with Steve Taylor. The following term he lost out to Ronnie Moore as Taylor's partner and played a few games on the wing before an ill starred loan move to Stockport that saw him turn from Dale hero to villain when central to the award of two County penalties and the sending-off of Dale skipper Joe Cooke when the two sides met. After two further brief spells in the FL, he resumed his tour of non-league football, figuring in the brief upsurge of Colne Dynamos where he netted the goal that took them to the FA Vase Final at Wembley. Maintaining his goalscoring touch, he scored 18 goals in 25 games after signing for Horwich in 1993.

Gary Haworth 1984-85
Born: Bury 25.4.59
Striker
FL Apps/Gls 1/0 Total Apps/Gls 1+1/0
Career: {Rossendale U. 1979-80?}, Radcliffe Borough, Dale trial 7.84, signed 8.84 [1/-], Radcliffe Borough 1985 to at least 1988
Honours: North West Counties League division 2 champions 1983, division 1 champions 1985

Gary had been playing in the lower levels of non-league football for some time when he came to notice with 35 goals in 43 games for Radcliffe Borough in 1983-84. Signed up by Dale at the age of 25, he was a substitute in one of the pre-season Lancashire Cup games and made his FL bow in place of Les Lawrence for the game against Wrexham in September 1984. These proved to be his only senior appearances and he soon returned to Radcliffe where he became the club's record goalscorer.

Simon John Holden 1984-86, 1986-88

Born: Littleborough 9.3.68
5'9" 10st7
Midfield
FL Apps/Gls 35+14/4
Total Apps/Gls 39+17/4
Career: Balderstone School, Dale as 8.83, yts 1984, pro 7.85, Wheatsheaf, Dale 3.11.86 [35+14/4], Gillingham trial 8.88, Mossley 8.88, Wheatsheaf 11.88 (Sunday League), Castleton Gabriels 1990 to 1992
Honours: Rochdale Schoolboys 1982, 1983, Greater Manchester Schools, Rochdale Sunday League XI 1989

A star in local schoolboy football, Simon was selected as substitute in the Lancashire Cup tie against Blackpool at the start of the 1984-85 season when aged 16 years and 5 months, missing Ted Oliver's record for Dale's youngest ever first team player by just six days. He was also included in the 14-man squad for a league game in October but then drifted into local league football with Wheatsheaf. However, he was re-signed in 1986 and was handed a start in the FA Cup tie against Wrexham by caretaker boss Brian Taylor who had also been playing local football. Gaining a regular spot in midfield, he helped Dale escape relegation in the last week of the season with a crucial goal in the remarkable 5-3 win against Halifax after being 2-1 down. He also figured regularly the following term when the cash strapped Dale fielded a number of very young teams (Simon was still only 19) before a short stint at Mossley under Keith Hicks (q.v.) and a return to Sunday League football.

Paul Anthony Malcolm 1984-85

Born: Heworth 11.12.64
6'4" 13st10
Goalkeeper
FL Apps 24 Total Apps 27
Career: Newcastle U. app, pro 12.82, Durham C. cs.83, Dale trial 8.84, signed 9.84 [24], Shrewsbury T. 7.85, Barnsley 8.86 [3], Weymouth loan 2.88 [5 Conf], Doncaster R. 7.88 [34], retired injured 1989-90. Whitley Bay c.1991

When Dale lost Steve Conroy to injury just after the start of the 1984-85 season, they drafted in Paul, Durham City's player of the year, to make his FL debut. The massive 'keeper, still only 19, played his part in earning Dale's first points of the season at the fourth attempt and played every match until the following February when Dave Redfern came in on loan. He had somewhat restricted chances with his other league clubs, playing only in the Full Members Cup for the Shrews and being sent off on his Doncaster debut, a fractured leg subsequently ending his career. He then worked as a goalkeeping coach back in Newcastle

John L. Cavanah 1984-85
Born: Salford 4.8.61
Full back
FL Apps/Gls 14+3/0 Total Apps/Gls 17+4/0
Career: Sunderland jnr, Blackburn R. jnr, Preston NE am c.1977, Altrincham am 1979, pro 1981 [12+6/- Conf], Bangor C. 1982 [45/- Conf], Barrow 8.84 [4/- Conf], Dale n/c 9.84 [14+3/-], Newcastle KB (Australia) 1985, Newcastle Rosebuds (Australia) 1986
Honours: FA Trophy final 1984

John had several years' experience at Conference level, including an appearance for Bangor in the FA Trophy Final, when he became the second non-league player signed up by Dale to make their debuts against Hartlepool in September 1984, the match providing their first success of the season. A part-timer, working for Salford Council, he figured fairly regularly at right back until a defeat by Blackpool on Boxing Day, but was largely restricted to the bench thereafter. Heading to Australia, he remained there after his playing career. [NB. Usually cited as Cavanagh, the correct spelling of his surname is as above.]

Thomas Steven (Tommy) English 1984-85
Born: Cirencester 18.10.61 5'9" 11st6
Striker
FL Apps/Gls 3/1 Total Apps/Gls 3/1
Career: Coventry C. app 1978, pro 6.79 [62+4/17], Leicester C. 9.82 [29+15/3], (Germany, Holland), Dale trial 12.9.84 [3/1], Plymouth A. n/c 24.9.84 [+4/1], Colchester U. 1984-85 [1/-], Canberra City (Australia) summer 1985, Colchester U. 11.85 [34+13/17], Wealdstone cs.87 [21+3/10 Conf], Bishops Stortford cs.88, Colchester U. 10.89 [12+1/3], Happy Valley (Hong Kong) 1990, Crawley T. 1990, Wivenhoe T., Cornard U. 1994, Sudbury T., Harwich & Parkeston to 1999
Honours: England youth international, Division 2 promotion 1983

The third debutant against Hartlepool, Tommy had a rather different pedigree. A former youth international, he had considerable initial success as a striker at Coventry, scoring 10 times in 30 games in his first season as an eighteen year old. He also assisted Leicester in their promotion back to the first division, actually playing half the season at centre back. After trials on the continent, he scored on his debut for Dale, but soon decided to try his luck at Plymouth. He came on for his debut when they were 2-1 down to Preston and netted the equaliser before Argyle amazingly ran out 6-4 winners. He then joined his brother Tony at Colchester, reappearing the following season after a stint in Australia and sharing in a remarkable family double when both he and Tony were sent off in the same game, against Crewe. At non-league level, he hit 26 goals in a season for Bishop Stortford before a final spell at Colchester. His son, also Tom, was on the books of Norwich and Arsenal as a junior.

John Matthew Pemberton 1983-85

Born: Oldham 18.11.64
5'11" 12st3
Right back
FL Apps/Gls 1/0
Total Apps/Gls 1/0
Career: Chadderton, Manchester U. trial, Dale am 1983-84, n/c 26.9.84 [1/-], Crewe A. n/c 29.3.85, pro cs.85 £1000 [116+5/1], Crystal Palace 24.3.88 £80,000 [76+2/2], Sheffield U. 27.7.90 £300,000 [67+1/-], Leeds U. 12.1.93 £250,000 [44+9/-], Crewe A. player-coach 8.8.97 [1/-], Nottingham F. reserve team coach 1999 to cs.09 (caretaker manager 12.08), Crystal Palace coach 2.10, Sheffield U. academy manager 5.10, Nottingham F. coach 10.12, Bristol C. coach 5.13 (caretaker manager 12.13), assistant manager*
Honours: Division 2 play-off winners 1989, FA Cup final 1990, League Cup final 1996: As coach; Central League champions 2008, FA Youth Cup final 2011, League 1 champions 2015

John spent some time on Dale's books as an amateur and non-contract player, but played just once in the first team, replacing John Cavanah in a 2-1 home defeat by Aldershot in October 1984. Towards the end of the season, like Geoff Thomas, he moved to Crewe and turned professional, the Alex paying a nominal £1000 for him. Becoming a regular at full back he appeared over a hundred times before following Thomas to Palace and sharing in the promotion and FA Cup Final appearance. He also figured in a bizarre game of five penalties against Brighton in March 1989, missing one of the four awarded to Palace, as did the famous pair of Wright and Bright. Big money transfers took him to Sheffield United (where he ended up in goal on his debut) and Leeds, playing in another Final, this time in the League Cup, but he missed the whole of 1996-97 through injury. He wound up his career with a move back to Crewe as player-coach but was injured in only his second match and forced to retire. He subsequently coached Forest's reserves for ten years, leading them to the 2008 Central League title, and was briefly caretaker manager the following season, Forest winning both his games in charge. While Academy coach back at Bramall Lane, he was suggested as a possible Dale boss before Steve Eyre was appointed. He was Bristol City assistant manager when they won the League 1 championship in 2015. John's son Max was also on Sheffield United's books.

Leslie (Les) Strong   1984-85

Born: London 3.7.53
5'9" 10st7
Full back
FL Apps/Gls 1/0
Total Apps/Gls 1/0
Career: Crystal Palace am, Fulham 6.71 [369+3/5], Brentford 12.82 loan [5/-], Crystal Palace n/c 8.83 [7/-], (USA), Dale n/c 10.84 [1/-]. Anguilla national team coach to 1999. Petite Riviere Noire (Mauritius) advisor c.2013
Honours: Division 3 promotion 1982, Middlesex Wanderers tour to Japan 1980, Anglo-Scottish Cup final 1976

Les was a stalwart left back at Fulham for over a decade, accumulating the best part of 400 appearances and being everpresent when they were promoted in 1982. Though he missed the 1975 FA Cup Final through injury, Fulham chairman Tommy Trinder persuaded the FA to award him a special medal as he had played in all the other rounds. He did play in the Anglo-Scottish Cup Final the following term and also went on a Middlesex Wanderers tour to Japan. In 1982 Fulham played England for his testimonial. After a stint in the USA, Vic Halom, who had played with him at Craven Cottage, offered him a trial at Spotland, but the experiment lasted just 90 minutes, Dale losing 2-1 at home to Port Vale to leave them without a win at Spotland in six games. After his playing career Les returned to Craven Cottage as catering manager and matchday host. He was also involved with football in two outposts of the game, Mauritius and Anguilla, the latter featuring at the bottom of FIFA's world rankings after losing one of Les' games in charge 17-0 and another 14-1.

Michael Anthony (Mike) Fielding   1984-85
Born: Liverpool 3.12.65   5'8"
Midfield/left back
FL Apps/Gls 6/0 Total Apps/Gls 7/0
Career: Everton jnr, Barnsley app 1983, pro 8.84, Dale loan 10.84 to 14.12.84 [6/-]. Southport 9.87 to 10.87

Though a Barnsley player, Mike's only FL appearances came during a two month loan at Spotland. He initially figured in midfield in place of Shaun Reid and then at left back as one of several players tried there while Les Chapman was needed in midfield. His debut produced Dale's first home win of the season, against Peterborough, but no further victories accrued.

Anthony Peter (Tony) Moore   1984-85

Born: Wolverhampton 19.9.57
5'9" 10st12
Right back
FL Apps/Gls 1+2/0
Total Apps/Gls 1+2/0
Career: Willenhall T., Burton A., Sheffield U. 7.79 [29/-], Dale trial 4.82, Crewe A. 8.82 [17/2], York C. trial 1982-83, {Frickley Ath 1983-84 [2/- Conf]?}, Sheffield FC, Worksop T. 1983-84, Gainsborough Trinity 1983-84, Dale trial cs.84, Goole T., Dale n/c 10.84 [1+2/-], Belper T., Goole T. 1985-86
Honours: (Division 4 champions 1982)

Tony had come close to signing for Dale a couple of times before he actually did so in October 1984. He then managed just two substitute appearances and one start at right back, in successive games, becoming the 24th player used by Rochdale that term, before heading back to the non-league game. His other league experience had come a few years earlier at Sheffield United, where he played a number of games in the third division, and Crewe.

John Seasman 1984-85, 1985-88

Born: Liverpool 21.2.55
5'10" 11st7
Midfield
FL Apps/Gls 94+1/4
Total Apps/Gls 118+3/5
Career: Tranmere R. app 1971, pro 2.73 [15+2/-], Luton T. 1.75 £5000 [7+1/2], Millwall 2.76 £10,000 [157+1/35], Rotherham U. 8.80 £90,000 [93+7/25], Cardiff C. 8.84 [10+2/2], Dale loan 1.11.84 to 27.12.84 [8/-], Chesterfield 1.85 [8+2/1], Dale 7.85 £5000 [86+1/4], Northwich Victoria 7.88 [7+3/- Conf], Aylesbury U. player-coach 1988-89 [15/- Conf], Runcorn 1989-90 [28+1/4 Conf], Accrington St., Hyde U. 1991-92, Radcliffe Borough, Blackburn R. chief scout, Leeds U. academy coach
Honours: Young England XI, Division 3 promotion 1976, champions 1981, Division 4 champions 1985

John first came to notice as a youngster at Tranmere and was transferred to first division Luton when he was 19, scoring on his debut. Switching to Millwall a year later, he played over 150 games in their midfield and represented Young England in a testimonial game. A sizeable fee took him to Rotherham, where he figured in exactly 100 FL games and won promotion to the second division for the second time. He had a two month spell on loan at Rochdale during 1984-85, the first of three players from Cardiff who helped turn Dale's season around. After figuring in Chesterfield's promotion run, he returned, for a small fee, at the start of the next term, playing alongside another former Tranmere, Rotherham and Cardiff man, Ronnie Moore. He again topped 100 appearances in all games, over the next three seasons, latterly playing sometimes at right back. After several years in the non-league game he scouted for Blackburn and worked as an academy coach at Leeds. He worked for the Whizzkids charity for non-mobile youngsters, running the New York marathon to raise funds, and as the Football in the Community northern area organiser in the mid nineties. He also became a players' agent, representing David Nugent and Jon Stead amongst others.

Ian Johnson 1984-87

Born: Oldham 11.11.60
6'1" 12st
Defender
FL Apps/Gls 74+7/1
Total Apps/Gls 95+7/3
Career: Chadderton, Curzon Ashton, Dale n/c 1984, pro 7.85 [74+7/1], Altrincham cs.87 [42+4/- Conf], Droylsden 1989-90, Curzon Ashton 7.92

One of several players with links to Curzon Ashton to play for Dale over the years, Ian was a latecomer to the senior ranks, moving up from Dale's reserve side to make his FL debut just after his 24th birthday, playing alongside Joe Cooke in the absence of Bill Williams. During the following two seasons he had several long spells in the side, mainly at full-back, including the later stages of 1986-87 when Dale successfully fought off relegation, and all told topped the 100 appearance mark. An Oldham fan, while playing for Dale he joked that his favourite player when he was young was then team-mate Les Chapman! Ian subsequently played for Altrincham when they were managed by Tommy Docherty.

Stephen Jeffrey (Steve) Taylor 1984-87, 1988-90

Born: Royton 18.10.55
5'10" 10st9
Striker
FL Apps/Gls 100+1/46
Total Apps/Gls 120+1/56
Career: Bolton W. app 30.7.71, pro 25.7.74 [34+4/16], Port Vale loan 29.10.75 [4/2], Oldham A. 14.10.77 £38,000 [45+2/25], Luton T. 11.1.79 £50,000 [15+5/1], Mansfield T. 14.7.79 £75,000 [30+7/7], Burnley 24.7.80 £35,000 [80+6/37], Wigan A. 1.8.83 [29+1/7], Stockport Co. 14.3.84 [26/8], Dale 20.11.84 [84/42], Preston NE 15.10.86 £20,000 [5/2], Burnley 21.8.87 [38+7/6], Dale 3.89 [16+1/4], retired injured 1989-90, Oldham A. coach, Mossley player-manager 5.93 to 10.93, Oldham A. youth team coach 1994-95, ESP coach in USA
Honours: (Division 2 champions 1978), Division 3 champions 1982, Division 4 promotion 1987, Sherpa Van Trophy final 1988

Dale's record scorer in a post-war season, Steve won the fourth division 'golden boot' in 1985-86 when he scored 31 times, 25 of them in the league (equalling Reg Jenkins' best). Over his Dale career, he averaged virtually a goal every other game, indeed he did this with several other clubs, too, starting at Bolton in the early seventies. An excellent spell at Oldham brought a transfer to Luton where he had the misfortune to miss a first minute penalty in an FA Cup quarter-final, only being told he would be taking them in the tunnel. Despite having a five year contract he left after only a few months and worked his way around several north west clubs, winning the third division title with Burnley. Unsurprisingly Dale's player of the year in 1986 (despite his goals they still finished 18th), he became disaffected that summer when Alan Young was brought in on a much better contract than his. His move to Preston for £20,000 did not work out – though North End won promotion - due to a broken wrist soon after arriving. After a second spell at Burnley he returned to Spotland late in the 1988-89 season when Dale slid down the table after a good start under Danny Bergara. His goals helped steady the side but he was forced to retire through cartilage problems. In between stints coaching at Oldham, Steve managed Mossley, and even made a playing come-back, but lasted for just 13 games, only one of which was won. He was later an Educational Sports Programme soccer coach in the USA and ran the gym at Buckley Hall prison.

Francis (Frank) Gamble 1984-86

Born: Liverpool 21.8.61
5'9" 11st
Outside left
FL Apps/Gls 41+5/9
Total Apps/Gls 49+8/10
Career: Burscough, Derby Co. trial 3.81, signed 5.81 [5+1/2], Barrow 1982-83 [43+1/11 Conf], Dale 13.12.84 [41+5/9], Morecambe 3.86, Northwich Victoria 1987-88 [4+1/- Conf],
Southport 11.87 to 12.88
Honours: Lancashire Junior Cup (ATS Trophy) winners 1987, Northern Premier League champions 1984, Cumbrian Cup winners 1984, Northern Premier League Challenge Shield winners 1984

Frank had played a few games for Derby before a successful spell at Barrow where he scored 18 times and was their player of the year when they dominated the Northern Premier League under Vic Halom in 1984. A few months later, Halom moved to reunite him with his Barrow team-mate Barry Diamond at Rochdale and Frank became a regular on the left flank as Dale gradually edged up the table towards the end of the season. A tricky winger, he was also provider of many of Steve Taylor's goals the following term, but after losing his place moved to Morecambe where he gained a winners medal in the Lancashire Junior Cup. At Southport, he played a remarkable 24 cup ties in a year but had his contract cancelled after being sent off in one.

Donald (Don) McAllister 1984-85

Born: Radcliffe 26.5.53
5'10" 11st2
Defender
FL Apps/Gls 3/0
Total Apps/Gls 4/0
Career: Bolton W. app 1969, pro 6.70 [155+1/2], Tottenham H. 2.75 £80,000 [168+4/9], Washington Diplomats summer 1977 [25/- NASL], Charlton A. 8.81 £40,000 [55/6], Academia Setubal (Portugal) trial 1983, Tampa Bay Rowdies 4.84 [1/- NASL], Vitoria Setubal (Portugal) 1984-85, Dale trial 2.11.84, Luton T. trial 14.11.84, Dale n/c 12.84 [3/-], Barnet 3.85 [12+1/- Conf], caretaker manager 1986
Honours: Division 3 champions 1973, Division 2 promotion 1978

Don played a combined total of well over 300 games for his first two clubs, Bolton and Spurs, throughout the 1970s. Making his debut in April 1970 when he was a 16 year old apprentice, he became a regular at left back the following term - later switching to central defence - and missed only one game when Bolton won the third division title in 1973. At Spurs he missed most of the campaign when they were relegated but was the regular centre half as they gained promotion back to the top flight at the first attempt. After playing in Portugal and the USA, he had trials at both Rochdale and Luton in 1984, signing non-contract forms for Dale. He only played four games, though, one at right back, the others in central defence, Dale winning two and losing two, before heading for Barnet in the Conference and becoming their caretaker manager the following year. Don later emigrated to Sydney.

David (Dave) Redfern 1984-88

Born: Sheffield 8.11.62
6'3" 13st10
Goalkeeper
FL Apps 87
Total Apps 110
Career: Sheffield W. jnr, pro 6.81, Doncaster R. loan 1984, Dale loan 28.2.85 to 5.85, signed 7.85 £11,000 [87], Wigan A. loan 10.87 [3], Gainsborough Trinity cs.88, Manchester C. trial, Stockport Co. 7.89 £6000 [48], Buxton 1993, Emley 1993-94, Bradford PA
Honours: Division 4 promotion 1991, HFS League v Vauxhall Opel League 1988-89

Dave's progress from the junior ranks with Sheffield Wednesday was disrupted by 18 months out with a broken wrist, his senior bow not coming until he joined Dale on loan. Although making his debut in March 1984, due to earlier bad weather Dale still had 19 league games left to play and the massively proportioned 'keeper was able to help them finish in a relatively comfortable 17th place. Signed for a sizeable fee for Dale in the close season, he was everpresent until breaking a finger against Northampton eighteen months later, a run of 110 games in all competitions. However, his replacement Keith Welch then started on an even longer unbroken run in the Dale goal and Dave was never able to reclaim his place. After a season at Gainsborough Trinity when he was selected to represent the HFS League, he had a lengthy spell with Stockport, making his debut against Rochdale and winning promotion in 1991, as well as playing for several other non-league sides.

Stephen (Steve) Tapley 1984-85
Born: Camberwell 3.10.63 5'11" 11st1
Midfield
FL Apps/Gls 1/0 Total Apps/Gls 1/0
Career: Fulham app 1980, pro 10.81 [2/1], {Bournemouth loan?, Watford loan?}, Dale loan 28.2.85 to 8.3.85 [1/-], Wealdstone cs.85 [87/- Conf], Enfield cs.87 [17+1/1 Conf], Yeovil 1988 [17+4/- Conf], Wealdstone 1989, Harrow Borough, Wealdstone, Chelmsford 1993. Chelsea Football in the Community coach
Honours: Gola League Championship Shield 1985-86, FA XI v Vauxhall Opel League 1986-87, England semi-pro squad

At the opposite end of the spectrum of experience to Dale's other ex-Fulham signing in 1984-85, Les Strong, Steve had played just twice for the Cottagers and he only added one more game while at Spotland. In fact it was less than one game as he was substituted in the second half of the home defeat by Crewe in which he had stood-in for Dave Thompson on the right of midfield. He had much more success after moving down to Conference level, generally playing as a right back, winning Wealdstone's player of the year award, playing for an FA XI and being a reserve for the England semi-pro side. After retiring he worked for Football in the Community at Chelsea.

Mark Anthony (Tony) Towers 1984-85
Born: Manchester 13.4.52 5'8" 11st2
Midfield
FL Apps/Gls 1+1/0 Total Apps/Gls 1+1/0
Career: Manchester C. app 1968, pro 4.69 [117+5/10], Sunderland 3.74 £125,000 [108/18], Birmingham 7.77 to 2.81 [90+2/4], Montreal Manic 1981 to 1983 [94/10 NASL], Tampa Bay Rowdies 5.84 [9/- NASL], Vancouver Whitecaps 8.84 [8/- NASL], Dale trial 2.85 to 11.3.85 [1+1/-]
Honours: Manchester Schools, Lancashire Schools, England Schools, England Youth international 1969, 1970, England under-23s (8 caps) 1972 to 1975, England (3 caps) 1976, European Cup Winners Cup winners 1970, League Cup final 1974, Anglo-Italian Cup final 1970, Division 2 champions 1976, promotion 1980

Tony was capped at all levels by England, from schoolboys up to the senior side. Signing pro for Manchester City when he was 17 he made his league debut the same week, and a year later appeared in the City side which won the European Cup Winners Cup. He played well over a hundred games for City, making a name as a creative player in the middle of the park, and figured in the League Cup Final side immediately before moving to Sunderland in the deal which took Dennis Tuert to Maine Road. While at Roker Park he assisted their promotion to the top flight and won his three full England caps (all in May 1976), but after he moved to Birmingham, despite another promotion, his appearances were restricted by injuries and he did not play at all in 1980-81. After a lengthy spell in the USA he trained at Spotland on his return and he figured twice in the senior side, coming on as substitute for Tapley in the latter's only game and then being withdrawn himself in the next match.

David (Dave) Grant 1984-87

Born: Sheffield 2.6.60
6'0" 12st8
Left back
FL Apps/Gls 97/2
Total Apps/Gls 118/2
Career: Sheffield W. app 1977, pro 2.78 [132+1/4], Oxford U. 7.82 [24/1], Chesterfield loan 9.83 [7/-], Cardiff C. 3.84 [25/-], Dale loan 27.3.85, signed 5.85 [97/2], Macclesfield T. cs.87 [21+3/2 Conf], Mossley 1988-89, Boston U. 1988-89 to 1990 [25+9/2 Conf]
Honours: Division 3 promotion 1980, (Division 3 champions 1984)

Dave was signed on loan from Cardiff along with Phil Dwyer just before the transfer deadline in 1985 and played a large part in Dale's end of season improvement when they picked up 24 points from the 14 games that Dave played in. A no nonsense defender, he signed permanently at the end of the season and continued to play regularly at left back, though he could also double as a centre back, and missed only a handful of games in each of his two full seasons at Spotland. He had played more than 130 games for Sheffield Wednesday at the start of his career, being virtually everpresent when they were promoted to Division 2, and was put forward for an England place by his manager Jack Charlton. He left Hillsborough when he was still only 22, figuring at the start of Oxford's third division title winning campaign before his transfer to Cardiff.

Philip John (Phil) Dwyer 1984-85
Born: Cardiff 28.10.53 6'0" 13st
Central defender
FL Apps/Gls 15/1 Total Apps/Gls 15/1
Career: Mostyn School, Cardiff C. jnr 1968, pro 10.71 [468+3/41], Dale 27.3.85 [15/1], South Wales Police 5.85
Honours: Cardiff Schoolboys, Wales Schools (4 caps), Wales youth international (12 caps), Wales under-23 (5 caps) 1974 to 1976, Wales under-21 (1 cap) 1979, Wales (10 caps) 1978 to 1980, Youth Cup final 1971, Welsh Cup winners 1973, 1974, 1976, final 1975, 1977, Division 3 promotion 1976, 1983

An all time great at Ninian Park, Phil (or 'Joe' to the Cardiff fans) easily broke the Bluebirds all-time appearance record, appearing 471 times in the league and 571 in total. He was in their side beaten in the Youth Cup Final by Arsenal in 1971 and later figured in five Welsh Cup finals, winning three of them. He also gained promotion from Division Three on two occasions and was capped many times at all levels by Wales, eventually winning ten full caps and scoring against England in 1978. Originally a right back, he became a dominating centre half but also played in midfield and could do a more than useful job as a bustling centre forward. Renowned for his spirited attitude, he was once taken to hospital in an ambulance after swallowing his tongue in a match but insisted on playing the following weekend. At Spotland, the burly defender was a huge success, Dale losing only three of his 15 games at the end of a previously disappointing campaign, his new boss Vic Halom remarking that he "thought players like him were extinct". He subsequently joined South Wales Police and published an autobiography 'Mr Cardiff City' in 2011.

Peter Robinson 1984-85
Born: Newbiggin 4.9.57 6'1" 12st6
Defender
FL Apps/Gls 9+3/0 Total Apps/Gls 9+3/0
Career: Burnley jnr 1975, pro 6.76 [48+7/3], Sparta Rotterdam 7.80 £30,000, Blyth Spartans 1982, Berwick R. 1983-84, Blyth Spartans, Dale n/c 3.85 [9+3/-], Darlington 8.85 £3000 to cs.88 [110+2/5], Halifax T. loan 12.85 [3+2/-], Blyth Spartans 1988, Whitley Bay 1988-89, retired 9.91
Honours: England semi-pro international (6 caps) 1983 to 1985

Peter played a number of games for Burnley before becoming one of fairly few English players to be transferred to a top Dutch club, appearing 58 times in the Eredivisie during a couple of seasons with Sparta Rotterdam (where he was a team-mate of Louis van Gaal). Returning to his north-east roots, he was Blyth Spartans player of the year in 1983-84 and played six times for the England semi-professional side, appearing (and scoring) against Wales just a week before joining Dale as a non-contract player. He figured in most of the run-in at the end of the 1984-85 alongside Dale's other two new defenders Dave Grant and Phil Dwyer, and as Dale retained him in the summer, even though he had not had a full professional contract he still cost Darlington £3000 when he signed for them. Over the next three years he played over 100 times for the Quakers and in 1989 played against Dale for Whitley Bay in the FA Cup, having scored in the victory over Preston in the previous round. He later worked as a PE teacher.

Neil Ashworth 1984-87
Born: Southend 16.1.68
Defender
FL Apps/Gls 1/0 Total Apps/Gls 2+1/0
Career: Oulder Hill School, (Leeds U. trial 11.81), Dale as 8.83, app 8.84, pro 7.85 to 5.86, n/c 1986-87 [1/-], Castleton Gabriels 1990-91 (+ Wheatsheaf; Sunday League), (Australia), Waikato U. (New Zealand) 1992
Honours: Rochdale Schools 1982, 1983

The son of Dale hero Joe, Neil starred for Rochdale schoolboys but had a torrid time in his brief spell in the Dale's first team. An associate schoolboy and then apprentice, he made his debut in midfield in the final game of 1984-85, when Dale lost 5-0 at Aldershot. Signing on pro terms in the summer, he figured at right back against Burnley in the Lancashire Cup at the start of the new season, as Dale suffered their worst home defeat in any senior game, going down 0-7. His final appearance was as a substitute in the 4-0 League Cup defeat by Wrexham a couple of weeks later, though he was an unused substitute later in the season and remained on Dale's books for another year. He later played at various points from Castleton to Waikato.

Graham John Hurst 1984-87
Born: Oldham 23.11.67
Midfield
FL Apps/Gls +1/0 Total Apps/Gls +1/0
Career: Dale jnr 1983, n/c 1984, pro 7.85 to 5.86, n/c 1986-87 [+1/-], Mossley 3.88, Oldham T. 10.88

Graham came through the junior sides to make his senior Dale debut as substitute for fellow youngster Neil Ashworth in the final game of 1984-85, the 5-0 defeat at Aldershot. Like Ashworth he signed pro forms for the following term but did not get beyond being an unused substitute on a couple of occasions. He captained the reserves in 1986-87 but broke his arm in February and was released in the summer. He played a few NPL games for Mossley at full back.

Keith Hicks 1985-87

Born: Oldham 9.8.54
6'0" 12st
Centre half
FL Apps/Gls 32/1
Total Apps/Gls 44/1
Career: St Hugh's School (Oldham), Greenhill, Kaskenmoor School (Oldham), Middleton Juniors, Oldham A. as 27.1.70, app 7.12.70, pro 11.8.72 [240+2/10], Hereford U. 5.9.80 [201/2], Dale 3.7.85 [32/1], retired injured 12.86. (Oldham Sunday League 2.87), Hyde U. 3.87, Mossley player-manager 29.11.87, Hyde U. 9.88, {Chadderton?}, Crompton Town 1989, Castleton Gabriels 10.91, Mossley 10.91, Radcliffe Borough 2.92, Bacup Borough 1992 (+ Old Bull's Head 1.88, Dicken Green 1991, manager to 10.94; Sunday League). Dale Centre of Excellence director, Rochdale Community Football Programme director c.1994*
Honours: Oldham under-11s, Oldham Schools, SE Lancashire Boys, England youth international (2 caps) 1973, Division 3 champions 1974, Welsh Cup final 1981, Rochdale Sunday League XI 1989, North West Champion of Champions Cup 1993

Keith came through the junior sides at Oldham, making his debut alongside Dick Mulvaney and Jim Bowie (q.v.) in April 1972, before two appearances for the England youth team against Italy. Remarkably, he was an everpresent in central defence in his first season as a professional, also missing only two games in Oldham's third division championship campaign. A regular as the Latics established themselves in the second division, he eventually totalled 240 league starts before moving to Hereford. An uncompromising defender, over the next five years he passed 200 games for Hereford, too, and rejoiced in the nickname of 'Animal', being sent off against Dale. His Dale playing career was brief in comparison, as he was unlucky enough to be injured in the opening match in each of his two seasons at Spotland, the second time being forced to finish at senior level. Returning in Sunday football, he was subsequently able to play at non-league level and managed Mossley for a time. Still figuring in local football until he was 40, he was player-manager of a Dicken Green side containing other ex-Dale men such as Chris Shyne and Jason Smart who won the North West Champion of Champions Cup for Sunday League sides in 1993. In addition he headed the Dale's School of Excellence and became the long serving director of the Community Football Programme at Spotland. His son Graham joined Dale as a schoolboy in 1994 and later played one FL game.

Ronald David (Ronnie) Moore 1985-86

Born: Liverpool 29.1.53
6'0" 12st9
Centre forward
FL Apps/Gls 43/9
Total Apps/Gls 53/10
Career: Tranmere R. app, pt 5.71, pro 8.73 [248+1/72], Chicago Sting summer 1977 [22/8 NASL], Cardiff C. 2.79 £100,000 [54+2/6], Rotherham U. 8.80 £120,000 [124+1/52], Charlton A. 9.83 [60+2/13], Dale 7.85 [43/9], Tranmere R. 7.86 [75/6], player manager 2.87 to 4.87, player–coach to cs.89, assistant manager, Southport manager 2.97, Rotherham U. manager 5.97, Oldham A. manager 3.05, Tranmere R. manager 6.06 to 6.09, Rotherham U. manager 25. 9.09, Tranmere R.

manager 5.3.12 to 2.14, Hartlepool U. manager 12.14*
Honours: Liverpool & Cheshire Schools, Division 4 promotion 1976, 1989, Division 3 champions 1981. As manager; Division 3 promotion 2000, Division 2 promotion 2001, League 2 play-off final 2010

A long serving centre forward, and sometime centre half, in the lower divisions before becoming a manager, Ronnie's main contributions have been shared between Tranmere and Rotherham. Originally an apprentice defender at Prenton Park, he scored 34 goals to inspire Rovers promotion in his first season as a striker, and had already accumulated around 250 league appearances when sold to Cardiff for £100,000 when he was 26. After an uncharacteristically lean time there – Cardiff fans had ironic badges made, reading "I saw Ronnie Moore score" – he returned to his best following a move to Millmoor, his goals firing Rotherham to promotion in his first season. He spent one season at Spotland alongside Steve Taylor, Ronnie's power in the air creating many of the opportunities for his partner's record breaking campaign. Returning to Tranmere as Dale couldn't afford to keep him, he ended his career with another promotion and a total of 158 goals – with seven hat-tricks including three four goal hauls - in 510 FL games. After serving briefly as player-manager he had a stint as coach and assistant manager. He subsequently managed Rotherham, leading them to two promotions, and later returned for second spells in charge of both clubs. His time at Tranmere ended after he was found to have breached FA rules on betting but he was soon back in management at Hartlepool, rescuing them from almost certain relegation to the Conference in 2015 (at Tranmere's expense). His son Ian played for him at Tranmere, at the start of his own lengthy career as a goalscorer.

Philip (Phil) Martin-Chambers 1985-86
Born: Barnsley 10.11.53 5'7" 11st1
Left back
FL Apps/Gls 9+1/0 Total Apps/Gls 11+1/0
Career: Worsbrough HS, Barnsley jnr 1968, app 7.69, pro 10.11.71 [441+1/8], Dale n/c 8.85 [9+1/-], Hartlepool 11.85 [29/-], Rotherham U. youth coach 1986, Scarborough youth coach 3.88, assistant manager 1991, manager 3.93 to 10.93, Barrow Workingmen's Club
Cricket for Ward Green, Worsbrough Bridge, Kexbrough
Honours: Barnsley Boys, England Schools (6 caps) 1969, Division 4 promotion 1979, Division 3 promotion 1981

Phil starred for Barnsley boys when they reached the semi-finals of the ESFA Trophy and won six England schoolboy caps, being sought after by bigger clubs before becoming an apprentice with his local side. Making his debut when he was 17, he totalled a tremendous 442 FL games for the Tykes, having one run of 170 consecutive games at left back. After 17 years and two promotions with the club, captaining the 1980-81 side and having a testimonial in 1983, he would have become Barnsley's youth team coach in 1985 but manager Bobby Collins was sacked and the appointment fell through. Phil instead continued his playing career with a brief spell at Spotland – becoming Dale's first player with a hyphenated name – covering for Dave Grant and sharing in Dale's best ever start to a season, four wins and a draw in the first five games. Released for economy reasons, he spent the rest of the season at Hartlepool, before going into coaching at Rotherham and then Scarborough. He was also a useful Barnsley League cricketer, top scoring in the league in one season and topping both the batting and bowling averages in another. His elder brother David played for Rotherham and Southend, while another brother, John, was with Hereford in their non-league days.

Ronald (Ronnie) Hildersley 1985-86

Born: Kirkaldy 6.4.65
5'4" 9st2
Midfield
FL Apps/Gls 12+4/0
Total Apps/Gls 12+4/0
Career: Kirkaldy HS, Glenrothes Strollers, Manchester C. app, pro 4.83 [1/-], Chester loan 1.84 [9/-], Chester 7.84 [5+4/-], Dale n/c 8.85 [12+4/-], Preston NE 6.86 [54+4/4], Cambridge U. loan 1.88 [9/3], Blackburn R. 7.88 [25+5/4], Wigan A. 8.90 [4/-], Montreal Spirit (Canada), Halifax T. 11.91 [21+10/2], East Fife 1993-94 [47+1/4 ScL], Montrose 15.8.97 [5/- ScL], Castleton Gabriels 1998-99. Rochdalians assistant manager 2004
Honours: Lancashire Youth Cup winners 1982, Division 4 promotion 1987, Lancashire Senior Cup winners 1989-90

The diminutive Ronnie had played few senior games when he joined Dale as a non-contract player and made his debut as substitute in September 1985. He reappeared the following March and figured in midfield in most of the remaining games. He was then signed by Preston who were promoted from Division Four in his first season and later he had a number of games at Blackburn in Division 2. He played for several further clubs, including in Canada and in his native Scotland, before returning to minor football around Rochdale.

David Joseph (Dave) Tong 1985-86

Born: Blackpool 21.9.55
5'8" 10st1
Midfield
FL Apps/Gls +2/0
Total Apps/Gls +2/0
Career: Blackpool app 1972, pro 9.73 [70+8/7], Shrewsbury T. 9.78 £25,000 [156+4/8], Cardiff C. 8.82 [119+1/3], Barrow 9.85, Dale n/c 27.9.85 [+2/-], Barrow 3.10.85 [3/- Conf], Bristol C. 10.85 [19/-], Gillingham 3.86 [5/-], Cambridge U. 8.86 [4+2/-], Merthyr Tydfil 1986-87 to 1989-90 [21/- Conf]
Honours: Caligaris international tournament winners 1974, Division 3 champions 1979, promotion 1983, Welsh Cup winners 1979, 1987, final 1980, Southern League champions 1989

A highly experienced midfielder, Dave had significant spells with each of his first three clubs, totalling over 350 league games, 160 of them for Shrewsbury, and twice playing in promotion sides. His first appearances had been for Blackpool in a tournament in Italy when he scored the winner in the final against Napoli. When freed by Cardiff, he was one of several players signed by Dale on non-contract terms to make up the numbers early in 1985-86, but stayed only for a week between games for Barrow and made just two substitute appearances. He played for three further league clubs over the next year before a highly successful swansong with Merthyr. He helped them reach the Conference and win the Welsh Cup, Dave then reliving his early Italian success when the Martyrs beat Atalanta in the Cup Winners Cup.

Garry Haire 1985-86
Born: Sedgefield 24.7.63 5'6" 10st4
Outside right
FL Apps/Gls 3/0 Total Apps/Gls 3/0
Career: Oxford U. app 1980, pro 7.81, Whitley Bay 4.82, Newcastle U. trial, Bradford C. 6.83 [43+6/13], Darlington 2.85 to 1986-87 [16+9/2], Dale loan 19.10.85 to 11.85 [3/-], Scarborough loan 1985-86 [13+1/4 Conf], Scarborough trial 1986-87, Whitley Bay 1986-87, retired injured 1990
Honours: Northern League under-23s 1983, FA XI v British Universities 1983, (Division 3 champions 1985), Division 4 promotion 1985, Northumberland Senior Cup winners 1987

Garry made his FL debut after joining Bradford City and was absent only three times in his first season, netting 13 goals as City won 10 games in a row but still did not make the top four. He then had the unusual experience of being with two sides promoted in the same year when he was transferred to Darlington half way through the 1984-85 season. Dale borrowed him the following term, using him in three games on the right flank while Dave Thompson was regaining match fitness. Returning to a previous club, he netted 25 goals for Whitley Bay in 1986-87 and was substitute when they played Dale in the FA Cup, having previously knocked out two league sides. When he had to retire through injury, he had chalked up 85 goals for the Bay in total.

Anthony James (Tony) Towner 1985-86
Born: Brighton 2.5.55 5'6" 10st
Winger
FL Apps/Gls 4+1/0 Total Apps/Gls 6+2/0
Career: Brighton & HA app 1972, pro 1.73 [153+9/24], Millwall 10.78 £65,000 [68/13], Rotherham U. 8.80 £185,000 [108/12], Sheffield U. loan 3.83 [9+1/1], Wolverhampton W. 8.83 [25+6/2], Charlton A. 12.9.84 [22+5/2], Dale n/c 11.85 [4+1/-], Cambridge U. n/c 3.86 [8/-], Gravesend 1986-87, Fisher Ath. 1987-88 [56+2/5 Conf], Crawley T. 1989 to 1.92. Newhaven 1993-94, Saltdean U. 1996-97. Saltdean U. coach 2005
Honours: Division 3 promotion 1977, champions 1981, (Division 2 promotion 1979, 1986)

A first choice on the wing for his local side Brighton for five years and a great crowd favourite, he left early in the season that saw them promoted to the top flight for the first time. Tony also played regularly for Millwall and topped the 100 appearance mark at Rotherham, too, playing alongside Ronnie Moore and John Seasman following a big money transfer, and winning promotion to Division 2 for the second time. Subsequent moves proved more short lived, though he did finally play in the top division for Wolves, and Tony was yet another player recruited by Dale in 1985-86 on non-contract terms. He started only four league games, but did appear in the FA Cup match at Manchester United. He retired after playing for Crawley in another cup tie, when they met his old club Brighton. He later played and coached in the Sussex County League.

David John Mossman 1985-86
Born: Sheffield 27.7.64 5'11" 12st2
Outside left
FL Apps/Gls 8/0 Total Apps/Gls 10/0
Career: Sheffield W. jnr, pro 8.82, Bradford C. loan 3.85 [+3/1], Stockport Co. loan 10.85 [9/4], Dale £10,000 16.1.86 [8/-], Stockport Co. £7000 3.86 [28+2/1], Lincoln C. 8.87 [20+1/2 Conf], Boston U. 7.88 [28+4/4 Conf], Gainsborough Trinity 10.89, Stafford Rangers 11.89 [2+1/- Conf], Boston U. 1990-91 [6+7/1 Conf], Matlock T. cs.91
Honours: England Schools, (Division 3 champions 1985), Alliance Premier League champions 1988

A somewhat puzzling Spotland interlude saw David sign from Sheffield Wednesday for a sizeable fee by Dale standards in January 1986, but after only ten games on the left wing be sold to Stockport "for financial reasons", apparently at a loss. He only stayed at Edgeley Park for a little over a year, joining Lincoln for the season they spent out of the FL, winning the Alliance Premier League and promotion back to the league at the first attempt. However, he wasn't retained and continued to play at non-league level.

Stephen (Steve) Carney 1985-86
Born: Wallsend 22.9.57 5'10" 11st5
Central defender
FL Apps/Gls 4/0 Total Apps/Gls 5/0
Career: West Bromwich A. as, Dudley Juniors, North Shields, Blyth Spartans cs.77, Newcastle U. 10.79 £3000 [125+9/1], Carlisle U. loan 3.85 [6/-], Darlington 8.85 [10+2/-], Dale loan 24.1.86 to 2.86 [4/-], Hartlepool 3.86 [7/-], Tow Law T. 9.86, Blyth Spartans 3.87 to 5.91. RTM Newcastle assistant manager 1993-94, Newcastle Blue Star manager to 1996
Honours: Division 2 promotion 1984, Debenhams Cup winners 1978, Northern League champions 1987, 1988

The classic electrician member of a non-league giant killing side, Steve and his brother Rob figured in Blyth Spartans famous run to the fifth round of the FA Cup in 1978, Steve scoring in the victory at second division Stoke in round four. He then gained a dream transfer to Newcastle and, converting from a forward to a defender, accumulated over 130 appearances over a six year period, figuring regularly in the famous Keegan inspired side promoted to the first division in 1984. A move to Darlington proved less productive and Steve was acquired by Dale as cover during ongoing injury problems, figuring at centre half in place of Joe Cooke. Returning to Blyth for another long stint, he later managed in the Northern League, but sadly died when he was only 55.

Jason Smart 1985-89, 1992-93

Born: Rochdale 15.2.69
6'0" 12st
Central defender
FL Apps/Gls 116+1/4
Total Apps/Gls 141+2/4
Career: Oulder Hill School, Castleton Top House (Sunday League), Milton, Dale yts 1985, pro 8.86 [116+1/4], Crewe A. 7.89 £50,000 [87+2/2], Dale n/c 1992-93, Witton Albion 1992-93 [1+1/- Conf], Hyde U. loan 1992-93, Barrow 11.92, Castleton Gabriels 8.93 to at least 1998-99 (+ Dicken Green 3.93, St John's Tavern 1995-96, Industry 1996-97, Top House 1997-98, Alexander Drew 1998-99, Rochdalians 1999, Top House 1999-2000; Sunday League)
Honours: Greater Manchester Schools Cup winners, Rochdale Boys, Rochdale Sunday League XI 1995-96 and 1997-98

A local schoolboy star, Jason was a YTS trainee when drafted in at centre back to partner Joe Cooke a month after his 17th birthday. Dale had not won for 10 games but came up trumps to defeat local rivals Burnley 1-0. Winning the young player of the year award, the following term he became an automatic choice alongside John Bramhall when Keith Hicks was injured in the first match and by 1987-88 was one of the most experienced members of the young squad left to battle against relegation when most of the senior players had to be released to keep Dale from bankruptcy. When Danny Bergara left Dale for Stockport, Jason was one of the players he came back to sign, for £50,000. Released three years later, when he was still only 23, he had a brief run in Dale Reserves, subsequently playing for local side Castleton Gabriels and in Sunday football.

Carl {Thomas} Hughes 1985-86
Born: {St Helens JFM 1969}
Forward
FL Apps/Gls +0/0 Total Apps/Gls +0/0
Career: Dale yts 8.85 to 1986

Carl was a YTS lad at Spotland when called up to the first team squad for the game against Burnley in which Jason Smart made his debut. He was again non-playing substitute in two further games shortly afterwards.

Ian Measham 1985-86

Born: Barnsley 14.12.64 5'11" 11st8
Defender
FL Apps/Gls 12/0
Total Apps/Gls 12/0
Career: Huddersfield T. app 1981, pro 16.12.82 [17/-], Lincoln C. loan 8.10.85 [6/-], Dale loan 21.3.86 to 5.86 [12/-], Cambridge U. 8.8.86 [46/-], Barnet 10.88 [1/- Conf], Burnley 10.11.88 [181+1/2], Doncaster R. 16.9.93 £40,000 [29+3/-], Halifax T. trial cs.96
Honours: Division 4 champions 1992, (Division 2+ promotion 1994), Lancashire Senior Cup winners 1992-93

Despite a number of serious injuries – he twice broke his leg while an apprentice - Ian managed a 14 year professional career. He made his debut in Division Two for Huddersfield during 1984-85 and ended the following campaign with a spell on loan at Rochdale, playing in all the last 12 games, either at centre back or as a defensive midfielder. Transferred to Cambridge that summer, he was everpresnt in his first term but missed the whole of 1987-88. He then spent five years as a regular at Burnley, winning the fourth division title in 1992 and scoring one of the goals in the final game which cost Dale a play-off place. He suffered a broken neck in a match for Doncaster in February 1994 and was out of action for 14 months before fighting his way back to fitness.

Simon John Gibson 1986-87

Born: Nottingham 10.12.64
6'3" 14st
Central defender
FL Apps/Gls 3+2/0
Total Apps/Gls 9+2/0
Career: Chelsea app, pro 12.82, Swindon T. 11.83 [29+2/3], Preston NE 12.84 [42/5], Dale 8.86 £5000 [3+2/-], (Belgium cs.87), IFK Ostersund (Sweden), Herfolge (Denmark) 1988, Sandnes Ulf (Norway), Herfolge (Denmark)
Honours: Scottish youth international (8 caps)

A massively built defender, Simon won a number of Scottish youth caps while on Chelsea's books and made his debut for Swindon just before his 19th birthday, though he was sent off twice in his first season in the league. He scored on his Preston debut (also netting in a Freight Rover tie against Dale) and played about half their games over the next eighteen months as they slumped to next to bottom of the FL. At Spotland, he started as one of three centre backs but was unable to regain his place after injury and headed off to play on the continent.

John Bramhall 1986-88

Born: Warrington 20.11.56
6'2" 13st6
Centre half
FL Apps/Gls 86/13
Total Apps/Gls 107/14
Career: Stockton Heath 1974, Warrington T. 1975, Tranmere R. 7.76 [164+6/7], Bury 3.82 £10,000 [165+2/17], Chester loan 11.85 [4/-], Dale 7.86 [62/5], Halifax T. 8.88 [62/5], Scunthorpe U. 1.90 £ [32/-], Hyde U. 1991, PFA further education programme 1991, PFA staff 1997, executive 2002, assistant chief executive 2009*
Honours: Lancashire Cup winners 1982-83, final 1983-84, Division 4 promotion 1985, (1986)

John was a hugely experienced centre half, signed by Dale to replace Joe Cooke. He had played around 170 games each for Tranmere and Bury, eventually figuring in a promotion winning side in 1985. His Lancashire Cup winners medal came in 1982 when it was played as a pre-season tournament for the first time. Automatic relegation out of the league was introduced in 1986-87, and as Dale skipper, John did more than most to ensure that it wasn't Dale heading out, scoring a remarkable 10 goals from centre half, where he was everpresent, to be the side's joint top scorer. He twice scored two goals in a game, the first time a Dale centre half had managed a brace since earlier hero Davie Parkes in the 1920s. The second of them came in the remarkable game against Halifax, when, with just two more games left, Dale came from behind in the second half to win 5-3. Unsurprisingly John was voted player of the year. Again usually an automatic choice the following term, despite reputedly falling out with manager Eddie Gray after the 8-0 debacle at Orient, he broke his ankle in the last match. Dale had previously turned down a bid of £20,000 for him from Lincoln, but he was then released, just before the manager himself left the club. John spent two further seasons as a league regular, costing Scunthorpe a small fee when they signed him from Halifax, before retiring with a recurring Achilles tendon injury and concentrating on his role with the PFA. He worked on the further education programme for YTS players in the north west and eventually became PFA assistant chief executive.

Neil Mills 1983-84, 1986-87
Born: Littleborough 27.10.63
Forward
FL Apps/Gls 4+6/0 Total Apps/Gls 11+6/2
Career: Tim Bobbin c.1981, Joinery 1982-83, Tim Bobbin 1983 (Sunday League), Dale am 1983-84, Tim Bobbin, Dale 8.86 [4+6/-], Stockport Co. 8.87 [5+2/-], Castleton Gabriels, Mossley 12.87, Horwich RMI, Milton 1989, Glossop, Castleton Gabriels 1991-92, assistant manager 1993-94 to 10.94 (+ Tim Bobbin 1988, Wheatsheaf 1988 to 1991, Dicken Green 1992, (Salford 1993), St Johns Tavern 1995-96, Industry 1997-98, Top House 1998, Rochdalians 1999; Sunday League)
Honours: Lancashire Sunday Cup 1988, Rochdale Sunday League youth XI 1980, senior XI 1982 to 1985, 1995-96

A late-comer to the professional game, Neil was well known in local football around Rochdale, particularly with top Sunday League side Tim Bobbin. He had a few games in the reserves in 1983-84 but finally signed up with Dale in 1986, when chairman Tommy Cannon reputedly demanded that manager Halom sign some 'cheaper' players. Neil started all the pre-season Lancashire Cup games and was in and around the squad for the first half of the season, scoring in both the League Cup (against Burnley) and the FA Cup. He also made a few senior appearances for Stockport before stints with Castleton Gabriels and with various Rochdale Sunday League sides, winning the man of the match award when Tim Bobbin claimed the Lancashire Sunday Cup in 1988.

David Fairclough 1986-87
Born: Liverpool 5.1.57 5'9" 11st
Forward
FL Apps/Gls 0/0 Total Apps/Gls 1/1
Career: Liverpool jnr 1972, app 5.7.73, pro 14.1.74 [64+34/34], Toronto Blizzard summer 1983 [20/4 NASL], Lucerne (Switzerland) 4.7.83, Norwich C. 22.3.85 [1+1/-], Oldham A. 15.8.85 [6+11/1], Dale n/c 8.86, SK Beveran (Belgium) 18.8.86, Tranmere R. 8.89 [3+11/1], Wigan A. 8.90 [4+3/1], Knowsley
Honours: England under-21 1977, Football League champions 1976, 1977, 1979, 1980, 1983, League Cup final 1978, winners 1983, European Cup winners (1977), 1978, European Super Cup winners 1977, final 1978, UEFA Cup winners 1976, Charity Shield 1976, 1977, 1979, 1980, Division 3 play-off final 1990

Liverpool's famous 'Super Sub', David only ever started 64 FL games for the Reds but was a member of five league championship winning sides in ten seasons at Anfield. He played in two League Cup Finals (as substitute) and was a member of the famous team which won the 1978 European Cup, after being an unused substitute in the previous year's final. He had also started in the first leg and come on as substitute in the 1976 UEFA Cup Final. After unsuccessful spells elsewhere, David trained with Dale at the start of the 1986-87 season and was given a game in the Lancashire Cup, scoring in a draw at Blackburn. He was then offered a contract with Beveran in Belgium, later reappearing in the league with Tranmere, where he was still unable to shake off the substitute tag, starting only 3 games but coming off the bench 11 times. Indeed, he finished a FL career spanning 18 seasons with only 78 starts to his name.

Terence Peter Conning 1986-87

Born: Liverpool 18.10.64
5'11" 12st7
Midfield
Total Apps/Gls 40/1
Total Apps/Gls 48+3/3
Career: Liverpool app 1980, Wigan A. 1982, Liverpool University, Altrincham 1984 [58+7/13 Conf], Dale 8.86 [40/1], Weymouth cs.87 [58+3/14 Conf], Yeovil T. 3.89 £13,000 [114+8/14 Conf], Bashley 6.92, Dorchester T. 1993-94, Yeovil T. 8.94 [26+2/- Conf], Trowbridge 2.95, Bridport 1996-97, Salisbury C., Tiverton T. 1997, Weymouth reserve team coach 2002, Bridport player-manager 28.6.02, Portland U. manager 10.03, Tiverton T. player-assistant manager 1.05, Yeovil College academy manager
Honours: England schoolboy international, FA XI v NPL 1985-86, England semi-pro v Wales 1988, FA Trophy winners 1986, GMAC Cup final 1988, FA Vase winners 1998, 1999, Dr Martens League champions 1999

Peter gained a Biochemistry degree from Liverpool University and also figured with Altrincham, appearing in the side which knocked Birmingham out of the FA Cup and won the FA Trophy in 1985-86. He then signed for Dale and, in what proved to be his only campaign at league level, played a total of 51 games (possibly a record of its kind). Nominally a midfielder, he spent some of the season in the No. 9 shirt, as when netting Dale's goal in a League Cup draw with first division Watford, and also had a few games at full back. He subsequently spent a number of years back at Conference level, appearing for the England semi-pro side and costing Yeovil £13,000 when they signed him in 1989. Whilst there, he had the 'honour' of receiving the first yellow card shown in the Conference, in August 1991. He was twice a winner at Wembley in FA Vase finals with Tiverton and was still registered as a player at the age of 40, when their assistant-manager. He was also a lecturer in sport and director of football at an FE college, ran soccer schools and did some scouting before becoming a FIFA registered agent, representing Nikita Jelavic amongst others. Due to loopholes in FIFA procedures revealed by World Soccer magazine, Peter discovered that his identity had been stolen by bogus agents running internet scams, some - unwittingly appropriately - calling themselves Conning Peter!

Carl Bernard Hudson 1986-87

Born: Bradford 10.10.66
Central defender/midfield
FL Apps/Gls 13+2/1
Total Apps/Gls 18+2/2
Career: Bradford C. yts 1983, pro 1985, Dale 7.86 to cs.87 [13+2/1], Hyde U. 1987-88, Thackley 1989-90, Guiseley, Spittall Rovers. Coldstream 7.06, Eyemouth U. cs.07, Berwick T. manager cs.08, Eyemouth U. manager 1.09, Duns manager 9.13*
Honours: East of Scotland League division 1 promotion 2007

Carl had not made a senior appearance at Bradford City in the second division when he signed for Dale and all his Rochdale appearances came in a single run of 20 matches from September to December 1986. Dale generally went with three central defenders at the time, though Carl was sometimes played a little further forward as defensive midfield cover, and he was left out when Eddie Gray took over as manager. Much later, he played in the East of Scotland League when past 40 and then turned to management.

Raymond (Ray) McHale 1986-87
Born: Sheffield 12.8.50   5'6"   12st6
Midfield
FL Apps/Gls 6+1/0 Total Apps/Gls 10+2/0
Career: Hillsborough BC, Chesterfield 8.70 [123+1/27], Halifax T. 10.74 (p/e for T. Shanahan) [86/20], Swindon T. 9.76 £8000 [171+2/33], Brighton & HA 5.80 £100,000 [9+2/-], Barnsley 3.81 £60,000 [52+1/1], Sheffield U. 8.82 £20,000 [66+1/2], Bury loan 2.83 [6/-], Swansea C. 1.85 [45+2/1], Scarborough trial, Dale n/c 8.86 [6+1/1], Scarborough 1.12.86 [16/1 Conf, 25/3], Goole T. c.3.88, Guiseley manager 1988-89, Northwich Victoria 1988-89 [2/- Conf], Scarborough assistant manager 1.89, manager 11.89 to 4.93, Guiseley manager 1993-94, Scarborough manager 12.94, assistant manager 3.96, caretaker manager 1.99, Oldham A. chief scout 11.01 to 6.02
Honours: Northern Intermediate League cup winners 1969, Division 3 promotion 1981, 1984, Alliance Premier League champions 1987, Northern Premier League Cup winners 1988. As manager: NPL Division 1 champions 1994

A real veteran when arriving at Spotland - his debut was on his 36th birthday – Ray had first come to prominence as a goalscoring midfielder back in the early seventies at Chesterfield and Halifax, where he netted 16 times in 1975-76 despite their relegation. He missed very few games in four seasons at Swindon before a six figure sum took him for a short spell in the top flight at Brighton. He played in promotion sides at Barnsley and Sheffield United and while with Swansea scored a hat-trick in the Welsh Cup. Ray then spent the first half of the 1986-87 season at Spotland before joining Neil Warnock's Scarborough as they won promotion to the Football League, enabling him to take his overall tally to 599 league games. Moving into management, he won the Northern Premier League division one with Guiseley and had two stints back at Scarborough. He also worked as a tutor for the FA and was a county level squash player before moving to Spain to concentrate on golf.

Michael A. (Micky) Woods 1986-87
Born: Halifax 9.3.62
Forward
FL Apps/Gls 5+1/3 Total Apps/Gls 7+4/3
Career: Guiseley, Dale pt, n/c 8.86 [5+1/3], Colne Dynamos 23.2.87
Honours: FA Vase winners 1988, North West Counties League champions 1988

Micky had scored 16 goals at Guiseley in 1985-86 and was one of a number of players signed by Rochdale on non contract forms during the Lancashire Cup games at the start of the following term. He subsequently had to serve a long suspension left over from the previous term and made his full debut the week that Vic Halom was sacked. He scored in three of his five league starts but left for Colne Dynamos when new boss Eddie Gray paired new signings Derek Parlane and Lyndon Simmonds up front. Micky subsequently top scored in the North West Counties League with 25 goals when Dynamos won the title as well as claiming the FA Vase at Wembley in 1988.

Steven (Steve) Watson 1986-87
Born: {Bradford 1964}
Left back
FL Apps/Gls 0/0 Total Apps/Gls +0/0
Career: Rhodesway School (Bradford), Bradford C. app 1980-81, Phoenix Park 10.82, Eccleshill U., Dale n/c 8.86 to 9.86

A one time apprentice at Bradford City, Steve had been playing in minor football in Yorkshire before having a brief trial at Spotland and being an unused substitute in the Lancashire Cup tie against Bury.

Gordon T. Rayner 1986-87
Born: Bradford AMJ.56
Defender
FL Apps/Gls 0/0 Total Apps/Gls +0/0
Career: Ottley, Thackley, Whitby T., Dale n/c 8.86 to 9.86. Guiseley manager 1991, Bradford PA manager 1993 to 1997, Otley T. coach 2.04
Honours: As manager; FA Vase winners 1991, final 1992

A long serving player in Yorkshire non-league football, Gordon was another offered a trial at Spotland at the start of 1986-87, being unused substitute in two Lancashire Cup games. Coincidently, like two of Dale's other non-contract players signed at the same time, Micky Woods and Ray McHale, he was also associated with Guiseley, winning an individual merit award after taking them to successive FA Vase finals.

Peter Andrew Shearer 1986-87

Born: Birmingham 4.2.67
6'0" 11st6
Striker
FL Apps/Gls 1/0
Total Apps/Gls 2/2
Career: Cardinal Wiseman Boys School, Birmingham C. app 1983, pro 5.2.85 [2+2/-], Wimbledon loan 1985-86, Dale 4.8.86 [1/-], Nuneaton Borough 11.86 £1500 [7/- Conf], Cheltenham T. 1988-89 [19/4 Conf], Bournemouth 9.3.89 £25,000 [76+9/10], Coventry C. trial 8.93, Dundee trial, Birmingham C. 5.1.94 £75,000 [22+3/7] to 1996, Notts Co. trial 1997, Peterborough U. reserve team player-coach 1997-98, Birmingham C. junior coach 2002
Honours: England semi-pro squad 1989, Division 2 promotion 1985, Division 2+ champions 1995, Auto Windscreens Shield winners 1995

Peter had played a couple of games for Birmingham, while an apprentice, when they were promoted to the top division in 1985 and, strangely, had an even briefer FL career with Dale before eventually making his mark elsewhere. Signed as a utility man, he made a sensational debut at centre forward in place of the injured Alan Young, scoring twice in a League Cup victory over Burnley, but played only once more before Young resumed in the side and Peter was soon on the move to Nuneaton for a small fee. He resurfaced in the FL at Bournemouth in 1989, playing in various positions before making a mark as a goalscoring midfielder, and commanded a £75,000 fee when Birmingham reacquired him five years later. He helped them to victory over Dale's Northern Section Final conquerors Carlisle in the Auto Windscreens Shield and promotion back to the second tier in 1995, but after an Achilles injury made no appearances in 1995-96 before moving into coaching, reappearing at St Andrews yet again in 2002. He later worked as a PE teacher.

Alexander Forbes (Alan) Young 1986-88

Born: Kirkaldy 26.10.55 5'11" 13st4
Centre forward
FL Apps/Gls 19+9/2
Total Apps/Gls 24+9/3
Career: Kirkaldy YMCA, Oldham A. 15.7.74 [107+15/30], Leicester C. 26.7.79 £250,000 [102+2/26], Sheffield U. 31.8.82 £160,000 [23+3/7], Brighton & HA 15.8.83 £140,000 [25+1/12], Notts Co. 6.9.84 £55,000 [39+4/13], Dale 27.8.86 (exchange for D. Thompson) [19+9/2], retired 12.87, reserve team coach, Shepshed Charterhouse manager 30.3.88, Ilkeston T., Notts Co. coach, Football in the Community 1994, Chesterfield youth development c.1998, youth team coach 8.99
Honours: Scottish schools international, Division 2 champions 1980

Alan arrived in Oldham from Kirkaldy when he was 18 and made over a hundred appearances at centre forward, scoring a hat-trick against Leicester just before a quarter of a million pound move to Filbert Street. He scored twice on his debut and went on to be everpresent, scoring 14 goals when Leicester were promoted to Division One in his first season. They lasted only one season, though, and Alan had two further big money transfers in successive years, netting 12 times in only 25 second division games for Brighton. His one-time Oldham team-mate Vic Halom signed him for Dale in exchange for Dave Thompson but an accumulation of injuries meant that he was never really fit during his stint at Spotland and scored only twice in the league and managed only one game in his second season. After briefly helping with coaching the reserves, he managed Shepshed Charterhouse prior to working with Football in the Community and coaching young players. He was also assistant manager at a sports centre and reported both for Radio Leicester and the Leicester Mercury.

Robert Andrew (Robbie) Wakenshaw
1986-87

Born: Ponteland 22.12.65
5'10" 11st10
Forward
FL Apps/Gls 28+1/5
Total Apps/Gls 36+1/9
Career: Everton app, pro 12.83 [2+1/1], Carlisle U. 16.9.85 £ [6+2/2], Doncaster R. loan 3.86 [8/3], Dale 9.86 £2000 [28+1/5], Crewe A. 6.87 £2000 [18+4/1], Northwich Victoria 1988-89 [1/- Conf], Southport 2.89, Fleetwood cs.89 £5000. St George's (Douglas, Isle of Man) manager
Honours: FA Youth Cup final 1983, winners 1984, England under-19s (7 caps) 1985, Football League champions 1985, (Division 4 promotion 1989)

A star at youth level, scoring twice in Everton's Youth Cup final victory over Stoke in 1984, Robbie also scored in a 1-1 draw with Manchester United on his senior debut the same season. He made just two league appearances when Everton won the league title, but was a substitute in all the rounds of the European Cup Winners Cup except the final, coming on twice, and figured regularly for England under-19s. Just over a year later, though, he signed for Dale and figured regularly up front or on the wing for the rest of the season, scoring twice in Dale's surprise 4-2 victory at Preston that helped keep them in the league. He also scored one of Spotland's most spectacular goals, a scissor kick volley from the edge of the area in the 5-3 defeat of Halifax. Notable for his strikingly blond hair — which earned him the nickname Teddy Tint with his teammates — Robbie was sold to Crewe the following summer but missed much of the season with injury and dropped into non-league football, netting 18 goals for Fleetwood in 1990-91. He was later the manager of St George's on the Isle of Man.

Mark Rees 1986-87
Born: Smethwick 13.10.61 5'10" 11st10
Outside right
FL Apps/Gls 2+1/0 Total Apps/Gls 2+1/0
Career: Northfield T., Walsall app 1977, pro 8.79 [188+48/37], Dale loan 23.10.86 to 20.11.86 [2+1/-], Shamrock Rovers 1990, Bromsgrove Rovers 1990, Colchester U. 1990-91 [+1/- Conf], Aldershot 1991-92 [19/1 exp], Dover 1992, Sittingbourne 1992, Solihull Borough 11.92
Honours: England Schools, Division 4 promotion 1980, Division 3 promotion 1988

Mark spent twelve years in and around the first team at Walsall, but was only really an automatic choice on the right wing in 1981-82. Nevertheless, he played in two promotion campaigns and eventually figured for Walsall in Division Two. He also starred in their run to a League Cup semi-final against Liverpool, netting a famous winner against Arsenal and once scored a hat-trick in a Freight Rover tie against Derby. While out of favour in 1986, he had a brief loan spell at Rochdale, starting in two games wearing the No. 10 shirt; for some reason Dale simultaneously borrowed two right wingers, Mark and Winston White, but neither of them played at No. 7! He had a testimonial against Wolves in 1989 and eventually left Walsall the following year. After a season away, he returned to the league with Aldershot, only for them to go bankrupt and his appearances be expunged from the official record.

Eric Winston White 1986-87
Born: Leicester 26.10.58 5'10" 10st12
Winger
FL Apps/Gls 4/0 Total Apps/Gls 4/0
Career: Leicester C. app 1975, pro 11.76 [10+2/1], Hereford U. 3.79 [169+6/21], Hong Kong Rangers 1983, Chesterfield n/c 9.83 [+1/-], Port Vale n/c 10.83 [+1/-], Stockport Co. 11.83 [4/-], Bury 12.83 [125/12], Dale loan 10.86 to 12.86 [4/-], Colchester U. 2.87 [64+1/8], Burnley 10.88 £17,500 [93+11/14], West Bromwich A. 3.91 £35,000 [15+1/1], Bury 10.92 [1+1/-], Doncaster R. 1.93 [4/2], Carlisle U. 2.93 [6/-], Wigan A. 3.93 [10/2]
Honours: Division 4 promotion 1985

The cousin of earlier Dale player Everton Carr, like him Winston started out with Leicester, before a very productive spell with Hereford, playing 175 games in just over four seasons. He played for four different sides in 1983-84 before settling at Bury where he was everpresent on the right wing when they were promoted the following year. Dale borrowed him for two months at the end of 1986, but he managed only four games due to injury. He had a lengthy spell at Preston in the bottom division before a brief elevation to the second tier at West Brom, and finished his league career by again figuring for four different sides in 1992-93.

Patrick Michael (Paddy) McGeeney 1986-87
Born: Sheffield 31.10.66 5'10" 11st
Midfield/left back
FL Apps/Gls 3/0 Total Apps/Gls 3/0
Career: Sheffield U. app 1983, pro 10.84 [15+1/-], Dale loan 26.11.86 to 24.12.86 [3/-], Chesterfield 8.87 [45+4/1], Gainsborough Trinity 1989, Blackwood City (Australia), Buxton

Paddy had played a few second division games with Sheffield United in the previous two seasons when borrowed by Dale. He made his debut in midfield in the 3-3 draw with bottom club Torquay which signalled the end of Vic Halom's reign and played twice more, once at left back under caretaker Brian Taylor and once in midfield after Eddie Gray took over. His one season as a FL regular was 1987-88 when he started 35 games for Chesterfield and he later had a spell in Australia.

Brian Stanton 1986-88
Born: Liverpool 7.2.56 5'9" 10st12
Midfield/full back
FL Apps/Gls 42+7/4 Total Apps/Gls 47+10/4
Career: (Liverpool amateur league), New Brighton, Bury am 10.75, pro 3.76 [72+11/14], Huddersfield T. 9.79 £12,500 [199+10/45], Wrexham loan 3.86 [8/-], Morecambe, Dale 11.86 [42+7/4], Morecambe cs.88, Colne Dynamos 1988-89
Honours: Division 4 champions 1980, Division 3 promotion 1983

An engineering apprentice, Brian had started in the league with Bury when he was 20 but had his best spell during seven years at Huddersfield. He played over 200 times and netted an impressive 45 goals from midfield for the Terriers as they climbed from the fourth to the second division. On New Year's Day 1983 he hit a six-minute hat-trick against Bradford City, believed to be the fastest ever by a non-striker. He made his Dale debut as a non-contract player in a side selected by Brian Taylor the week that Eddie Gray was appointed manager. He played fairly regularly in midfield for the rest of the season and filled in at full back the following term as Dale successfully battled the drop.

Derek James Parlane 1986-88
Born: Helensburgh 5.5.53 6'0" 12st2
Centre forward
FL Apps/Gls 42/10
Total Apps/Gls 52/11
Career: Queens Park, Rangers 4.70 [168+34/80 ScL], Leeds U. 3.80 £190,000 [45+5/10], Bulova (Hong Kong) 9.82, Manchester C. 14.7.83 [47+1/20], Swansea C. 12.84 [21/3], Burnley trial, North Shore U. (New Zealand), South China (Hong Kong) 1985-86, Racing Jet (Belgium) cs.86, Dale 12.86 [42/10], Airdrie 12.87 [9/4 ScL], Macclesfield T. cs.88 [10+18/2 Conf], Curzon Ashton loan, Macclesfield T. player-coach 1989-90 and later director
Honours: Scotland (12 caps) 1973 to 1977, Scotland under-23s (5 caps), Scotland under-21s, Scottish League (2 caps), Scottish League champions 1975, 1976, Scottish Cup winners 1973, 1976, 1979, final 1977, Scottish League Cup winners 1978, 1979, Tennants Caledonian Cup winners 1978, final 1976, 1977, 1979, (Division 2 promotion 1985)

After scoring his first senior goal in a victory over Franz Beckenbauer's Bayern Munich in a European Cup Winners Cup semi-final, Derek won every possible honour in Scotland, appearing over 200 times for Rangers, during which time he won two Scottish League titles, three Scottish Cups and two League Cups. He also represented Scotland at under-21 and under-23 level before winning 12 full caps. Sold to Leeds for £190,000 he spent two years at Elland Road with Eddie Gray and also had a successful goalscoring stay at Manchester City, netting two hat-tricks in his first 13 games. After something of a world tour, Eddie Gray persuaded him to sign for Dale, and though not scoring prolifically himself, his partnership up front with Lyndon Simmonds brought the goals which saved Dale from the drop. Released by Dale along with other senior players the following season due to their financial crisis, Derek returned briefly to Scotland but then had a lengthy association with Macclesfield, being player, coach and eventually director of the club. Derek's father Jimmy also played for Rangers just after the war.

Keith James Welch 1986-91
Born: Bolton 3.10.68 6'0" 12st
Goalkeeper
FL Apps 205 Total Apps 252
Career: Bolton W. yts, Dale yts 8.86, pro 3.3.87 [205], Bristol C. 25.7.91 £200,000 [271], Northampton T. 7.99 [117], Tranmere R. 8.02 [2], Torquay U. 11.02 [3], Mansfield T. 2.03 [9]
Honours: Division 2+ promotion 1998, Division 3+ promotion 2000, PFA Division 4 team of the year 1991

Keith was handed his debut in a Freight Rover Trophy game against Chesterfield in January 1987, when Dave Redfern was out with a broken finger, and kept a clean sheet. He repeated that on his league debut and then performed heroics in a 0-0 draw with the third division leaders, Middlesbrough in the next round of the FRT. This proved to be just the start of a remarkable run of 226 consecutive games, playing 188 in a row in the league, until he was sent off in Dave Sutton's first game in charge – Keith's fourth manager in that time! His finest performance was probably in Dale's remarkable run to the fifth round of the FA Cup, when he performed heroically as Dale went down by a single goal to the eventual finalists Crystal Palace. After being chosen for the PFA team of the year, he was transferred to Bristol City for easily Dale's record fee of £200,000 and was again an automatic choice for most of his eight years at Ashton Gate. Promoted with City and later with Northampton, he played his 600th FL game for Torquay against Dale in December 2002.

Christopher John Hudson 1986-87

Born: Middleton 25.11.64
5'7" 10st12
Midfield
FL Apps/Gls 18+1/1
Total Apps/Gls 18+1/1
Career: Manchester C. jnr, Oldham A. n/c 10.9.82, pro 23.9.82 [16+4/-], Kramfors (Sweden) 6.86, Dale n/c 1.87 [18+1/1], Grantham 8.87 to cs.88. Football in the Community North West regional director, PFA director of community programmes c.2002, director of corporate social responsibility c.2013*

John made some league appearances with Oldham, mainly as a left back, but had been hampered by knee injuries, not figuring in the first team in his last two years at Boundary Park. After a stint in Sweden, he was yet another non-contract player at Spotland in 1986-87, generally figuring on the left of midfield. After having to retire through injury in his early twenties, he later worked as the North West regional director for Football in the Community and subsequently became PFA director of community programmes and corporate social responsibility.

Robert Lyndon Simmonds 1986-89

Born: Pontypool 11.11.66
5'5" 10st7
Striker
FL Apps/Gls 65/22
Total Apps/Gls 76/25
Career: Blackwood CS (Ebbw Vale), Cardiff C. as, Arsenal trial, Leeds U. app 1982-83, pro 7.83 [6+3/3], Swansea C. loan 10.86 [7+1/1], Dale loan 2.87, signed 5.87 £2000 [65/22], retired injured 5.89
Honours: Gwent Schools, South Wales Schools, Wales schoolboy international (11 caps), Wales youth international (5 caps)

Lyndon looked to have a big future ahead of him when he captained the Wales youth team and then scored twice, including a penalty, on his full debut for Leeds against second division leaders Portsmouth in 1985-86. The following year he scored against Dale while on loan at Swansea, but then followed his old Leeds manager Eddie Gray to Spotland just in time to help steer Dale clear of relegation with a priceless 10 goals in the last 22 games. He converted crucial penalties in three successive home wins in the last weeks of the season and the all important second in the game against Stockport that ensured survival. Signing permanently during the summer, 'Little Lyndon' missed only a couple of games and netted 15 goals, but tragically never played again, his career ended at 21 by a pelvic injury usually only seen in rugby players.

Mark Geoffrey Hunt 1986-88

Born: Farnworth 5.10.69
Forward
FL Apps/Gls 1+1/1
Total Apps/Gls 3+2/1
Career: Dale yts 7.86 to cs.88 [1+1/1]

On the YTS scheme, Mark played in Dale reserves in 1986-87 and was given the substitute berth for the final game of the season, when Dale's survival had been ensured, coming on for John Bramhall in the game at Scunthorpe. The following season he scored on his only FL start, a 1-1 draw at Exeter and also played against first division Wimbledon in the League Cup, but wasn't offered a professional contract

Geoffrey William (Geoff) Lomax 1987-89

Born: Droylsden 6.7.64
5'9" 11st8
Defender
FL Apps/Gls 70+1/0
Total Apps/Gls 85+2/0
Career: Manchester C. jnr, pro 7.81 [23+2/1], Wolverhampton W. loan 11.85 [5/-], Carlisle U. 12.85 £10,000 [27/-], Dale 7.87 [70+1/-], Chorley cs.89 [7+2/- Conf], Southport 12.89, Curzon Ashton, Dicken Green 1993-94, manager 10.94 (Sunday league), Bolton W. Football in the Community officer, FA north west regional coach
Cricket for Milnrow
Honours: Division 2 promotion 1985

Geoff played a few games for City when they were promoted back to the top division in 1985, before being sold to Carlisle. Arriving at Spotland eighteen months later, he figured first at right back but spent most of the season, during which he missed only two games, at centre back. After the mid-season loss of several experienced players for financial reason, he skippered the side and at one point was the second oldest member of the side at 23, subsequently winning the player of the year award. The following term he appeared all across the back four and in midfield, wearing eight different shirt numbers, but was not retained. He later returned to play Sunday football in Rochdale and also turned out for Milnrow 2nd XI in the summers. He worked with Football in the Community at Bolton in the mid-nineties and was a FA regional coach.

Peter John Hampton 1987-88

Born: Oldham 12.9.54
5'7" 11st2
Left back
FL Apps/Gls 19/1
Total Apps/Gls 29/1
Career: Bishop Auckland GS, Leeds U. app 1970, pro 9.71 [63+5/2], Stoke C. 8.80 £175,000 [134+4/4], Burnley 8.84 [116+2/2], Dale 7.87 [19/1], Carlisle U. 12.87 [12/-], n/c player-physio 1989-90, assistant manager to 9.97, Workington Reds manager 1998 to 2001
Honours: Durham Schools, England youth international, (European Cup final 1975), Lancashire Senior Cup final 1986

The son of the president of Crook Town, Peter joined Leeds when he left grammar school but despite a decade at Elland Road was only a regular choice in 1976-77, when Frank Gray was moved from left back to midfield. Indeed, he had been an unused substitute in the 1975 European Cup final after only four senior games. He played much more after his transfer to fellow first division side Stoke, and then in the lower divisions at Burnley (scoring against Dale in the 7-0 home Lancashire Cup defeat by the Clarets in 1985). Signed by former Leeds boss Eddie Gray in the summer of 1987, he was the Dale's regular left back until they had to let him go when the financial crisis struck in November. While at Carlisle he took on the unusual joint role of physio and non-contract player before becoming assistant to Mervyn Day and he later managed Workington.

Jamie Doyle 1987-88
Born: Glasgow 1.10.61 5'7" 11st2
Midfield
FL Apps/Gls 0/0 Total Apps/Gls 3/0
Career: Auchengill BC 1977, Partick Thistle 1978-79 [146+5/10 ScL], Motherwell 1984-85 [34+2/1 ScL], Dale trial 7.87 to 8.87, Partick Thistle 1987-88 [1+1/- ScL], Norwell Falcons, Dumbarton 1988-89 [29+6/2 ScL], Glenafton Ath. 1990 to 1993
Honours: Scotland under-21s v Denmark, Italy 1981, Scottish League XI v Irish League 1980

Jamie was an experienced Scottish League midfielder with approaching 200 games for Partick and Motherell under his belt when he was offered a trial at Spotland in the summer of 1987. He played in the Lancashire Cup games but Dale lost them all without scoring a goal and Jamie returned to Scotland. Earlier in his career, he had played for the Scottish under-21s and he also figured in the Scottish League side, made up of players from outside the top flight. His son, also Jamie, was with several Scottish lower league sides.

Mark Wilson Gavin 1987-88

Born: Bailieston 10.12.63
5'8" 10st7
Outside left
FL Apps/Gls 23/6
Total Apps/Gls 32/6
Career: High Tunstall School (Hartlepool), Leeds U. app 5.80, pro 12.81 [20+10/3], Hartlepool U. loan 29.3.85 [7/1], Carlisle U. 4.7.85 £10,000 [12+1/1], Bolton W. 27.3.86 [48+1/3], Dale 7.87 £20,000 [23/6], Heart of Midlothian 1.88 £30,000 [5+4/- ScL], Bristol C. 4.10.88 £35,000 [62+7/6], Watford 9.8.90 £250,000 [8+5/3], Bristol C. 6.12.91 £60,000 [34+7/2], Exeter C. 11.2.94 [73+4/4], Scunthorpe U. 23.8.96 [10+1/-], Hartlepool U. 25.9.97 [+3/-], Morton 1997-98 [1/- ScL]
Honours: Cleveland Boys, Durham Boys, Scottish youth trial, Freight Rover Trophy final 1986, Division 3 promotion 1990

Another ex-Leeds man, and another Scot, signed by Eddie Gray, Mark was Gray's most expensive signing when he arrived from Bolton, where he had been player of the year. An exciting winger, he was Dale's main attacking threat – and the target of uncompromising opposition defenders - in an otherwise disappointing start to the 1987-88 season, and when severe financial difficulties struck, it was no surprise that he was quickly sold, at a profit, to Hearts. Over the next few seasons he worked his way around the FL again, having most success in two spells with Bristol City after two other former Leeds men, Joe Jordan and Jimmy Lumsden – Gray's assistant at Spotland - both paid significant fees to acquire his services. After finishing playing he coached in junior football. His son Tom was a star university soccer player in the US.

Dean Anthony Walling 1987-90

Born: Leeds 17.4.69
6'0" 11st10
Forward
FL Apps/Gls 43+22/8
Total Apps/Gls 52+24/10
Career: Temple Moor School (Leeds), Leeds U. app 1985, Dale 10.7.87 [43+22/8], Kitchener Spirit (Canada) 1990, Franklin Grizzlies (Canada) 1990, Guiseley 10.90, Carlisle U. 1.7.91 [227+6/21], Lincoln C. 30.9.97 £75,000 [35/3], Doncaster R. 29.5.99 £30,000 [44+1/- Conf], Darlington trial 2.01, Northwich Victoria 2001 [8+6/- Conf], Cambridge U. 9.8.01 [20/-], Gainsborough Trinity 2002, Nuneaton Borough 2002-03 [1/1 Conf]
Honours: Leeds Schoolboys, St Kitts international 1997-98 (2 caps), Division 3+ champions 1995, promoted 1997, PFA team of the year 1995, 1998, Auto Windscreens Shield final 1995, winners, 1997, FA Vase winners 1991

Yet another former Leeds junior, Dean spent three seasons at Spotland, playing at centre forward but managed only eight goals. Remarkably, he was on the subs bench 20 times before getting a league start and was a substitute 37 times in his first season, the first in which two subs were allowed in FL games. The two goals in his first season were in the games against bottom club Newport, the second putting the final nail in County's coffin as they slipped out of the league. After a spell in Canada, 'Deano' joined Guiseley and netted 29 goals, scoring in both games in the FA Vase final. He then joined Carlisle where he was transformed into one of the best central defenders in the lower divisions, also scoring more goals than he had as a striker (and a penalty in their Auto Windscreens Shield shoot-out victory). He was their player of the year in 1995 when they were champions of the (renamed) Division 3 and was also included in the PFA divisional select XI, as he was three years later while with Lincoln, who spent £75,000 on him after he had been everpresent in Carlisle's 1997 promotion side. In 1997-98, he also had the honour of representing his father's birthplace St Kitts in international football. After retiring he started "Deano's Pro Soccer Academy" in Lincoln.

Nigel David Thompson 1987-88
Born: Leeds 1.3.67 5'7" 10st7
Midfield/left back
FL Apps/Gls 3+2/0 Total Apps/Gls 3+3/0
Career: Lawnswood School (Leeds), Leeds U. app 1983-84, pro 12.84 [6+1/-], Dale loan 8.87 to 10.87 [3+2/-], Chesterfield 3.88 to 1990 £10,000 [18+2/1], Goole T., Gainsborough Tr., Alfreton T.
Honours: Leeds City Boys, West Yorkshire Boys, England under-18 squad

A former member of the England under-18 squad, Nigel was borrowed from Leeds in August 1987 as Dale could muster only 12 outfield players for the start of the league campaign. He was injured in his first game, when he played on the right of midfield and started only twice more, on the opposite flank and at left back. He was also sparsely used in two years at Chesterfield before giving up league football due to a knee injury.

Ronald Paul (Ronnie) Coyle 1987-88

Born: Glasgow 4.8.64
5'10" 11st
Midfield FL Apps/Gls 23+1/1
Total Apps/Gls 30+1/2
Career: St Gerard's School, Celtic BC, Celtic 1981-82 [1+1/- ScL], Clyde loan 1986-87 [8/- ScL], Middlesbrough 12.86 [1+2/-], Dale 8.87 £2000 [23+1/1], Raith R. 1.88 £10,000 [248+5/9 ScL], Ayr U. 3.96 [33+1/- ScL], Albion R. cs.97 [16+3/- ScL], East Fife 1998-99 [25+1/- ScL], Queens Park 1999
Honours: Scottish Schools, Scottish youth international, Division 3 promotion 1987, Scottish Division 1 champions 1993, 1995, Scottish Division 2 champions 1997, Scottish League Cup winners 1994-95

Though winning youth international honours, Ronnie managed just a couple of games in five years with Scottish giants Celtic and had similarly few opportunities at Middlesbrough, though they were promoted at the end of his season with them. Signed by Dale for a small fee, though previously a central defender, he was a mainstay of the midfield until, like Mark Gavin, he was sold to keep Dale solvent. A tremendous servant at Raith, he figured over 250 times, twice assisting them to the championship of the Scottish first division. He was also a member of their side which played Bayern Munich in the second round of the UEFA Cup in 1995. He figured in the Ayr side promoted as champions of Division 2 and played on in the Scottish League until he was 38. Sadly he died from leukaemia at the age of only 49, just after Raith's 1994 League Cup final players met their Celtic counterparts in a benefit match for him.

Zacari David (Zac) Hughes 1987-92

Born: Bentley, Western Australia 6.6.71
Central defender
FL Apps/Gls 2/0
Total Apps/Gls 6/0
Career: St Edward's Juniors (Castleton), Matthew Moss, Balderstone School, Dale yts 7.87, pro 8.89 [2/-], retired injured 1992, Chadderton
Honours: Rochdale Schools 1985

Born near Perth in Australia but brought up locally, Zac signed on as a YTS lad when he left school and only eight league games into the season was plunged into the first team in the absence of John Bramhall. At the age of just 16 years 104 days he easily broke the record as Dale's youngest ever player. He also figured three more times in central defence soon afterwards but was injured on his only appearance in 1988-89 and had to undergo three operations. He again played just once the following term, and after another long layoff eventually made a return in the reserves in April 1991 but had to give up on a comeback the following season, meaning that his last senior game had been at the age of just 18 and a half.

Herbert Derrick Parker 1987-88

Born: Wallsend 7.2.57
5'10" 11st6
Forward
FL Apps/Gls 6+1/1
Total Apps/Gls 8+1/2
Career: Wallsend BC, Burnley app 1972, pro 2.74 [5+1/2], Southend U. 7.2.77 £10,000 [129/43], Barnsley 7.2.80 £60,000 [104+3/33], Oldham A. 19.8.83 £40,000 [54+3/11], Doncaster R. loan 19.12.84 [5/1], Burnley 11.10.85 [43/10], Haka Valkeakosken (Finland) summer 1987, Dale n/c 2.10.87 [6+1/1], Northwich Victoria 11.87 [21/9 Conf], North Ferriby U., Altrincham, Northwich Victoria 9.88 [60+18/26 Conf], Frickley Ath., Hyde U. 1991-92, Bishop Auckland, Irlam T. Ossett T.. Doncaster R. Football in the Community by 1999
Honours: Wallsend Boys, Division 4 promotion 1978, Division 3 promotion 1981

Derrick made a scoring debut for Burnley reserves when he was 15 and played a few games in the first division, but really made an impression as a goalscorer with Southend, netting 19 times when they were promoted in 1978, four of them against Torquay. He also assisted Barnsley when they were promoted to Division 2, but had spent a couple of seasons back at Burnley, by now in Division 4, and a summer in Finland prior to joining Dale. He scored on his debut against first division Wimbledon in the League Cup but only stayed for a month, mostly playing on the left flank. Remaining a regular scorer in non-league football, he netted 23 for Northwich Victoria in 1988-89. In his days with Oldham he had his cheekbone fractured in an off the ball incident with a former Barnsley teammate, which resulted in legal action, eventually settled out of court. Ironically, he later worked selling accident insurance. He also was with the Football in the Community programme at Doncaster and became a commentator on Barnsley games for Radio Sheffield.

David Christopher Mycock 1986-89, 1992-93
Born: Todmorden 18.9.69 5'10" 11st12
Left back/midfield
FL Apps/Gls 19+3/0 Total Apps/Gls 22+3/0
Career: Bolton W. as, Dale yts 7.86, pro 7.88 [19+3/-], {Chorley?}, Altrincham 1989-90 [+2/- Conf], Hyde U. 1989-90, Castleton Gabriels 2.90, (+ Dicken Green 1991-92; Sunday League), Dale am 1992-93, Walsden 1995-96 to 1997-98. Manchester FA area coach. University of Worcester Blind Football coach, England and Great Britain Blind Football coach*

David played with Dale reserves in 1986-87 and made his debut in midfield in the Freight Rover Trophy the following term while still a trainee. He then had the misfortune to make his FL debut in the infamous 8-0 defeat at Orient. After the mid-season exodus of senior players, including Peter Hampton, he had a spell at left back and played further games the following season. He was with Castleton Gabriels for a time, also figuring in Sunday football, and had some games back in the Reserves. He was area coach for the Manchester FA, but after gaining a first class honours degree became a lecturer in sports science at the University of Worcester. He coached their successful blind football team and went on to the same role with the England national team and was appointed coach to the Great Britain side for the 2012 paralympics.

73

Lee Anthony Warren 1987-89

Born: Manchester 28.2.69
6'0" 11st10
Midfield
FL Apps/Gls 31/1
Total Apps/Gls 38/1
Career: Leeds U. yts, pro 27.7.87, Dale 28.10.87 [31/1], Hull C. 25.8.88 £40,000 [141+12/1], Lincoln C. loan 20.9.90 [2+1/1], Doncaster R. 21.7.94 [115+10/3, 65+7/1 Conf], Barrow cs.00, assistant manager 5.03, Goole T. cs.05, Brigg T. 10.05, Stocksbridge Park Steels 3.07, Brigg T. cs.07, assistant manager 10.07, Bottesford T. 2009, AFC Blackburn Leisure (Hull) 2010
Honours: Durham County Schools 1985

Lee got as far as being named as the Leeds substitute, before former boss Eddie Gray added him to the former Elland Road contingent at Spotland in October 1986. A fixture in midfield for the rest of the season, when Gray moved on to second division Hull in the summer, he quickly returned to sign Lee, who was still only 19, for £40,000. After six years, during which he figured in over 150 games, he moved on to Doncaster and was one of the few players to survive their catastrophic exit from the FL, being their player of the year in their final campaign. He later served Barrow as both player and coach, appearing over 200 times. He was still playing minor football in hs 40s.

Andrew James (Andy) Duggan 1987-88, 1990-91
Born: Bradford 19.9.67 6'3" 13st
Central defender
FL Apps/Gls 4/0 Total Apps/Gls 6/0
Career: Barnsley app, pro 7.85 [1+1/-], Dale loan 11.87 to 12.87 [3/-], Huddersfield T. 9.88 [29/3], Hartlepool U. loan 8.90 [2/-], Dale 3.91 to cs.91 [1/-]
Honours: (Division 4 promotion 1991)

Andy was a powerful centre back brought in on loan in mid-season 1987-88 and was in the side which – in the midst of financial turmoil and the end of Tommy Cannon's chairmanship – recorded their first win for 20 games, 2-1 at Cambridge. After a couple of years on the fringes of Huddersfield's side and two games for Hartlepool who went on to be promoted, his second spell at Spotland was equally short and traumatic as he was injured on his debut and was released without playing again.

Stuart Mellish 1987-89, 1992-93
Born: Hyde 19.11.69 5'10" 11st3
Midfield
FL Apps/Gls 24+3/1 Total Apps/Gls 24+5/1
Career: Blackpool jnr, Dale jnr 1986, yts 7.87, pro 1988 [24+3/1], Altrincham cs.89 [3+2/- Conf], Witton Albion 11.89, Ashton U. 1990-91, Dale am 1992-93, Barrow 12.92, Southport 1.93, North Trafford 1992-93, Winsford 1993-94, Altrincham 1993-94 [1/- Conf]. Trafford 11.98. Warrington T. coach by 2014*

Stuart worked his way through the junior sides at Spotland and after several games on the bench played in 12 of the last 13 games of 1987-88 when Shaun Reid was injured, and was voted young player of the year. He played a similar number of games the following term and briefly returned from non-league football to play in the reserves, along with former youth team colleague David Mycock, during 1992-93. After a long stint in the non-league game he was assistant to Shaun Reid at Warrington when they reached the second round of the FA Cup in 2014.

John Moore 1987-88
Born: Consett 1.10.66 6'0" 11st11
Striker
FL Apps/Gls 10/2 Total Apps/Gls 10/2
Career: Sunderland app, pro 10.84 [4+12/1], St Patrick's Ath. loan 1984-85, Newport Co. loan 11.85 [2/-], Darlington loan 11.86 [2/1], Mansfield T. loan 3.87 [5/1], Dale loan 1.88 to 3.88 [10/2], Hull C. 8.88 £25,000 [11+3/1], Sheffield U. loan 3.89 [4+1/-], Utrecht (Holland) 1989-90, Shrewsbury T. 8.90 [7+1/1], Crewe A. 1.91 [+1/-], Scarborough 8.91 [3+4/1], Bishop Auckland 1992, Sing Tau (Hong Kong) 1992, Happy Valley (Hong Kong) 1997, Sun Hei (Hong Kong) 1999, Durham C. 2002-03
Honours: Division 3 champions 1988, (promotion 1989), Hong Kong XI

John spent several years at Sunderland and figured from the bench a number of times when they won the Division 3 title, but the majority of his league football was played while out on a succession of loans. One such spell saw him figure up front for Dale 10 times after Derek Parlane was released, netting twice. Eddie Gray bought him after taking over at Hull, but he remained on the fringes and eventually started just 48 games for his 10 FL clubs. He had, though, had a useful spell with Utrecht and he later starred for several years in Hong Kong, figuring for a national representative side.

Carl Stephen Harris 1987-89

Born: Neath 3.11.56
5'9" 11st
Winger
FL Apps/Gls 24+1/3
Total Apps/Gls 27+2/3
Career: Hengwrt School, Cwrtsart Secondary School, Burnley trial, Briton Ferry Ath., Leeds U. app, pro 11.73 [124+30/26], Charlton A. 7.82 £100,000 [77+3/8], Leeds U. trial 8.85, Bury 12.85 [33+5/4], Swansea C. trial 7.87, Cardiff C. trial 9.87, Airdrie trial 12.87 [1/- ScL], Dale n/c 1.88 [24+1/3], Exeter C. 12.88 £ [11+5/1], Briton Ferry Ath. cs.89, player-manager 1991, Afan Lido 1994, Maesteg Park 1994-95, Ton Pentre 1995, Afan Lido 1995-96, Caernarvon T. 1996-97, Ton Pentre 1997
Honours: Neath Schools, Wales Schools, Wales youth international (8 caps), Wales under-23s, Wales under-21s, Wales (24 caps) 1976 to 1982

Another of Eddie Gray's former Leeds colleagues to turn up at Spotland, Carl (or 'Charlie') had been a regular for Wales before he became one for Leeds, playing only a handful of first division games before his full international debut. Previously capped by Wales at all levels from schools to under-23s, injuries limited his Leeds appearances over the years, but in 1980-81 he was easily top scorer with 10 goals from the right wing. He also had three years at Charlton but figured only briefly at later clubs, for instance spending just under a year with Dale, playing on either wing, before being sold to Exeter. Later returning to Welsh League football, he played on with a variety of sides until he was 41.

Paul Anthony Hancox 1987-89
Born: Manchester 22.7.70
Forward
FL Apps/Gls +2/0 Total Apps/Gls +2/0
Career: Dale yts 1987 to 1989 [+2/-]

Paul first appeared in Dale's reserves early in 1988 and during February and March was used as substitute for the first team, twice coming on in place of Dean Walling, who was then being tried out of position on the left wing. Paul continued in the reserves the following term and was unused substitute in two of the Lancashire cup ties.

Ernest (Ernie) Moss 1987-88

Born: Chesterfield 19.10.49
6'1" 13st2
Centre forward
FL Apps/Gls 10/2
Total Apps/Gls 10/2
Career: Chesterfield Tubeworks, Chesterfield 10.68 [261/95], Peterborough U. 1.76 £16,000 [34+1/9], Mansfield T. 12.76 £18,000 [56+1/21], Chesterfield 1.79 £15,000 [105+2/33], Port Vale 6.81 £16,000 [74/23], Lincoln C. 3.83 [10+1/2], Doncaster R. 6.83 [41+3/15], Chesterfield 7.84 [90+1/34], Stockport Co. 12.86 [25/7], Scarborough 8.87 [22+1/4], Dale loan 3.88 to 5.88 [10/2], Kettering T. 8.88 [67+5/21 Conf], Matlock T. player-coach cs.90, Shepshed Charterhouse 1990, Kettering T. player-coach 1.91 [5+1/2 Conf], Boston U. assistant manager 6.92, Gainsborough Trinity manager 1995, Leek T. manager 6.98, Gainsborough Trinity manager 11.99, Kettering T. assistant manager 2000-01, Matlock T. manager 2001, Hucknall T. manager 2004-05, Belper T. manager 1.05 to 2007, Chesterfield scout, Football in the Community
Honours: Division 4 champions 1970, 1985, promotion (1983), 1984, Division 3 champions 1977

One of the great lower league goalscorers, Ernie is remembered primarily for his three spells with his home town club. Joining Chesterfield from a works team when he was 19, and netting only one league goal in his first season, he then netted 20 as the Spireites won the fourth division title in 1970, hitting four against Newport County. A powerful, old-fashioned centre forward, he hit another 20 in 1974-75 and reached 95 in his first stint before a modest fee took him to Peterborough. In a more productive spell at Mansfield, he again played in a promotion side and figured in the second tier for the only time in his career. Another 100 appearances for Chesterfield followed, already giving him a club record goals tally, and in 1983 he played in another promotion bound team, though he had left Port Vale before the end of the season. His next side Doncaster followed them up the next year and, back at Chesterfield again, he again won the fourth division title in 1985. All told he took his tally to 161 league goals for the Spireites before winding down his career, ending with a couple of months at Spotland where he scored his 245th FL goal at the age of 38. Entering management, he was still turning out in the Conference for Kettering when he was 41 and he continued to manage at non-league level for a further 15 years. He also ran sports shops with Derbyshire and England cricketer Geoff Miller, and latterly worked as a scout and as Football in the Community coach back at Chesterfield. Sadly, he was subsequently diagnosed with a rare form of dementia and Chesterfield held an 'Ernie Moss Day' early in 2015.

Danny Bruno Crerand 1987-89

Born: Manchester 5.5.69
Midfield
FL Apps/Gls 3/0
Total Apps/Gls 3/0
Career: Xaverian College, Manchester U. jnr, Chapel Villa, Dale trial 2.88 [3/-], Altrincham 1988-89 [3+1/- Conf]. Ashton on Mersey JFC coach 2005

The son of Manchester United legend, Paddy, Danny was playing in the Manchester Amateur League when given a trial by Dale, figuring in a friendly against Middlesbrough. He was then used on the right of midfield in the last three games of the season when John Seasman moved to right back. Like Paul Hancox he was also named as a substitute in the following pre-season Lancashire Cup and figured a few times in the reserves before moving on. After working as Manchester United's international sales manager, he was later a successful sports marketing consultant working with the likes of Luis Figo and Rio Ferdinand.

Simon Dean Copeland 1988-89

Born: Sheffield 10.10.68
6'1 11st8
Right back
FL Apps/Gls 27+1/0 Total Apps/Gls 37+1/0
Career: Sheffield U. yts 1986, pro 6.87, Kupio (Finland) summer 1988, Dale 7.88 [27+1/-], Gainsborough Trinity cs.89, Alfreton T.

One of several players with Sheffield United connections signed by new Dale boss Danny Bergara, Simon had suffered a broken leg while at Bramall Lane and did not play a senior game, though he did get as far as the substitutes bench. His league debut thus came in the first game of 1988-89 when Dale lost at Burnley. He figured regularly at right back, and occasionally at centre back, until Bergara left the following March.

Andrew Mark (Andy) Armitage 1988-89

Born: Leeds 17.10.68
Full back
FL Apps/Gls 33+3/0
Total Apps/Gls 42+3/0
Career: Leeds U. yts 1985, n/c 8.87, Dale 6.88 [33+3/-], Guiseley 7.89, Mt. Gravatt Hawks (Brisbane, Australia) summer 1990, Farsley Celtic, (New Zealand), Guiseley 1993-94, Farsley Celtic (+ Calverley Victoria player-manager 1993 to 1999; Bradford Sunday League). Horsforth St Margaret's Juniors coach c.2013
Honours: Northern Premier League division 1 champions 1994, NPL President's Cup winners 1994. As manager: Bradford Sunday Alliance division 2B champions 1993, division 1A champions 1998

One of two final Leeds products signed by Eddie Gray just before he left, Andy was Dale's regular left back throughout his one season at Spotland, though he played a few games in central defence. He scored twice in an FA Vase quarter final for Guiseley the following term and, after playing in Australia and New Zealand, he won the NPL division 1 title and President's Cup in a second spell with them.

David William (Dave) Sutton 1988-89

Born: Tarleton, Lancs 21.1.57
6'1" 12st7
Centre half
FL Apps/Gls 28/2
Total Apps/Gls 38/3
Career: Plymouth A. app 10.73, pro 7.74 [60+1/-], Reading loan 11.77 [9/-], Huddersfield T. 3.78 £15,000 [242/11], Bolton W. 6.85 £12,000 [98/4], Dale 7.88 [28/2], retired injured 5.89, physio, manager 1.91 to 12.94, Chorley manager to 28.10.96
Honours: Division 4 champions 1980, promotion 1988, Division 3 promotion 1975, 1983, Freight Rover Trophy final 1986

Despite his Lancastrian origin, Dave was an apprentice at Plymouth and played a couple of games when they were promoted in 1975, then establishing himself in their second division side before moving to Huddersfield. A big blond centre half, he was an everpresent when they won the fourth division title and helped them reach division two before being ruled out for a season through injury. After three seasons at Bolton, again winning promotion, he was new Dale boss Danny Bergara's only experienced signing in the summer of 1988 but lasted only until February before injuries caught up on him and he was forced into retirement. Briefly in caretaker charge when Bergara left, he trained as a physio and worked under Terry Dolan, then when Dolan and his assistant Jeff Lee left to take over at Hull, Dave was appointed manager. After signing the likes of Alan Reeves, Andy Flounders and Steve Whitehall, he came close to taking Dale into the play-offs in 1992, and the side challenged again in the following two seasons, but when Dale slipped down the league in 1994, and with his position under review by the board, he resigned. A colourful character, some of his more outlandish pronouncements had not gone down well with some supporters and he became famous for his programme notes which, for several weeks, read merely "One word of encouragement is worth ten of criticism".

Mark Cyril Smith 1988-89

Born: Sheffield 19.12.61
5'11" 11st5
Forward
FL Apps/Gls 26+1/7
Total Apps/Gls 34+2/8
Career: Sheffield U. jnr 1979, pro 14.8.80, Burton A. 1982, Buxton, Worksop T. 1983-84, Sheffield FC, Gainsborough Trinity, Shepshed Charterhouse, Kettering T. 1984-85 [25+1/13 Conf], Scunthorpe U. 9.85 [+1/-], Kettering T. 1985-86 [86+5/32 Conf], Dale 15.7.88 [26+1/7], Huddersfield T. 10.2.89 £50,000 [85+11/11], Grimsby T. 21.3.91 £55,000 [37+40/4], Kettering T. 1992-93 [1/- Conf], Scunthorpe U. 14.7.93 £20,000 [50+12/8], Boston U. 3.7.95, Gainsborough Trinity, Matlock T., Sheffield FC, Hallam, Maltby Main 1999, Buxton manager 2000, Maltby Main manager 7.9.02
Honours: FA XI 1987-88, England semi-pro squad, Division 3 promotion 1991

Another new signing with Sheffield United connections, Mark had scored 20 goals for Worksop in 1983-84 and had several successful seasons in the Conference with Kettering before moving to Spotland when he was 26. Playing up front with a variety of partners, he notched seven times in half a season and was then sold to Huddersfield for a new club record £50,000. Interestingly, after only one previous FL appearance, the timing of the move enabled him to make 47 in one season. A more or less permanent fixture in their side for two years, he also spent two seasons in the second division at Grimsby, returning to an earlier role as a winger. Appearing in non-league football until he was nearly 40, he then went into management at that level.

David Frain 1988-89

Born: Sheffield 11.10.62 5'8" 10st5
Midfield
FL Apps/Gls 42/12
Total Apps/Gls 52/13
Career: Nottingham F. as, Rowlinson YC, Norton Woodseats/Dronfield U. 1983, Sheffield U. 7.9.85 [35+9/6], Dale 18.7.88 [42/12], Stockport Co. 21.7.89 £50,000 [176+11/12], Mansfield T. loan 2.9.94 [4+2/-], (Hong Kong 3.95), Stalybridge Celtic 4.95 [41+5/4 Conf], Alfreton T., Hallam, Worksop T. 3.99. Staveley MW assistant manager 1.06
Honours: Sheffield Boys, Division 4 promotion 1991, Division 3 play-off final 1992, Division 2+ play-off final 1994, AutoGlass Trophy final 1992, PFA Division 4 team of the year 1991

Of the former Sheffield United players, the only one with league experience at Bramhall Lane (despite a late start as a professional at the age of 23 after working as a plumber), David was also the one with the biggest impact at Spotland. Playing on the left of midfield, he was Dale's main creative player and also top scored with 12 league goals. Nicknamed 'Roy of the Rovers' in the press, he unsurprisingly won the player of the year award and was even recommended for a Republic of Ireland cap by his manager. Snapped up by Danny Bergara for his new club Stockport for £50,000 he played well over 200 games for County as they came close to moving from the fourth to the new first division, David leading the side out at Wembley twice in a week in 1992. He had been selected in the PFA team of the year the previous term.

Stephen (Steve) O'Shaughnessy 1988-91

Born: Wrexham 13.10.67
6'2" 13st
Defender/midfield
FL Apps/Gls 101+8/16 Total Apps/Gls 124+11/21
Career: Leeds U. app, pro 10.85, Bradford C. 11.85 [+1/-], Dale 6.88 [101+8/16], Exeter C. £10,000 7.91 [1+2/-], Shrewsbury T. trial, Darlington 1.92 [88/2], Portmadog, Stalybridge Celtic 1994-95 to 1995-96 [48/1 Conf], Runcorn, Buler Rangers (Hong Kong), Inter Cardiff 1995, Barry T. 1995, Holywell T. 1996, Rhyl 1997, Caernarfon T. 1997, Total Network Solutions Llansantfraid 1998, Bangor C. 1998, Oswestry T. 1999, player-manager 2000, Newi Cefn Druids player-manager 6.01, Gresford Ath. 2004, Wrexham Centre of Excellence coach 8.04, Caernarfon T. manager 27.9.06, Gap Connah's Quay manager 6.08 to 6.09
Honours: Welsh youth international (6 caps). As manager: North Wales Coast Cup final 2009

A Welsh youth international, Steve was the final former Leeds junior signed by Eddie Gray immediately before his departure; coincidentally he had signed pro for Leeds the day Gray was sacked there. He had just three substitute appearance, all in different competitions, to his credit when arriving – though he had scored in a remarkable 5-0 away win at Aston Villa in the Simod Cup - but went on to play over 100 league games for Dale. The possessor of a ferocious shot – his sponsors called themselves "the Exocet boot company" - he played in midfield or central defence but was the side's top scorer in 1989-90 with 10 goals, including two in the run to the fifth round of the FA Cup. The following season "Shosh", as he was usually known, scored a legendary goal against Scarborough with a 40 yard free-kick. He later had a couple of years at Darlington, but subsequently had a much lengthier career in Welsh League football as player and then manager, also working at Wrexham's Centre of Excellence. Steve's father had also been a pro on Wrexham's books as well as a coach in Australia.

David (Dave) Allen 1987-89
Born: {Lancashire c.1971?}
Defender
FL Apps/Gls 0/0 Total Apps/Gls +0/0
Career: Dale yts 1987 to 1989. Castleton Gabriels 1992-93

A new recruit on YTS terms in 1987, Dave figured in pre-season friendlies in 1988-89 and was on the bench against Wigan in the first Lancashire Cup game, without getting on. He was later with local North West Counties League side Castleton Gabriels.

Stephen John (Steve) Wilkinson 1988-89
Born: Lincoln 1.9.68 6'0" 11st6
Striker
FL Apps/Gls 0/0 Total Apps/Gls 2+1/0
Career: Leicester C. app, pro 6.9.86 [5+4/1], Dale loan 8.88, Crewe A. loan 8.9.88 [3+2/2], Mansfield T. 2.10.89 £80,000 [214+18/83], Preston NE 15.6.95 £90,000 [44+8/13], Chesterfield 4.7.97 £70,000 [57+18/13], Kettering T. 7.00 [3+5/- Conf], Spalding loan 14.12.00. Loughborough College head of football development by 2009, Loughborough Foxes Womens FC director of football and Leicester C. academy coach
Honours: Division 4 promotion (1989), 1992, Division 3+ champions 1996

Dale took Steve on loan from Leicester in August 1988 and he played in two Lancs Cup ties, but had left before the first league game of the season. He was subsequently a huge success at Mansfield scoring over 80 goals in 200 games, an amazing five of them in a game against Birmingham in April 1990. He hit 14 when Mansfield were promoted in 1992, and 22 three seasons later. Sold to Preston, he also helped them to promotion, before three years with Chesterfield. He later worked as head of the football development centre at Loughborough College.

Stephen Paul J. (Steve) Corbett 1988-89
Born: Wolverhampton OND.69
Goalkeeper
FL Apps 0 Total Apps +0
Career: Smestow School (Wolverhampton), Derby Co. app 6.86 to 12.87, Dale trial 8.88 to 9.88, Evesham U., Worcester C., Bilston 1992, Pelsall Villa, Bilston 3.02

A former apprentice with Derby, Steve had a trial in Dale's reserves at the start of 1988-89 and was selected as substitute goalkeeper in the Rose Bowl game against Oldham. Later playing in non-league football, he also qualified as a referee.

Christopher Paul (Chris) Beaumont 1988-89
Born: Sheffield 5.12.65 5'11" 11st7
Forward
FL Apps/Gls 31+3/7 Total Apps/Gls 35+4/9
Career: Sheffield FC c.1984, Sheffield U. trial, Doncaster R. trial, Rotherham U. trial, Denaby U. 1986-87, Dale 21.7.88 [31+3/7], Stockport Co. 1.7.89 £8000 [238+20/39], Chesterfield 22.7.96 £30,000 [132+26/6], Ossett T. 2001, Sheffield FC, retired 10.02
Honours: Division 4 promotion 1991, Division 3 play-off final 1992, Division 2+ play-off final 1994, AutoGlass Trophy final 1992, 1993

Chris had first encountered his Dale manager Danny Bergara at Sheffield FC when he was 18, but it was another four years, during which he worked as an accounts clerk, before he gained a professional contract. Signed from Denaby, where he played alongside Bergara's son Simon, he made a scoring debut for Dale as substitute in the League Cup against Burnley and soon became a regular in various forward roles. However, he was one of several players to follow Bergara to Stockport and played around 300 games for them, anywhere across midfield or even at full back, missing only one game and scoring 15 goals when they were promoted in 1991. He figured in their string of Wembley appearances over the next few years, in the AutoGlass Trophy and play-off finals, scoring but being sent off in the latter in 1994 when County ended with nine men. He added another 150 games at Chesterfield, appearing in their remarkable run to the FA Cup semi-final in 1997, totalling 450 league matches despite his late start.

Neil Anthony Edmonds   1988-90
Born: Accrington 18.10.68 5'11" 11st
Forward
FL Apps/Gls 36+7/8 Total Apps/Gls 41+8/9
Career: Oldham A. app 24.4.85, pro 27.6.86 [3+2/-], Dale 9.88 [36+7/8], Karlskrona (Sweden) 1.90, Preston NE trial 1990-91, Chorley, Karlskrona (Sweden) 1991, East Bengal (India) 1991, Stalybridge Celtic 1991-92 to 1996 [81+12/5 Conf]
Honours: Hyndburn Schools, Lancashire Schools, Northern Premier League champions 1992, Indian FA Shield 1991, Calcuta League champions 1991, Durand Cup winners 1991

Neil had had few opportunities at Oldham, where he played at left back, but had a successful first campaign at Spotland, netting nine times from either a striking role or the flanks. Against Doncaster, when David Frain was sent off for disputing a contentious penalty, Neil followed him for a comment while celebrating Dale's against the odds equaliser. He hardly figured the following term, though, and left for Swedish football. He subsequently alternated spells in non-league football – winning the NPL with Stalybridge Celtic after returning to a full back role - with periods abroad, including an unusual, and highly successful, spell in Indian football.

Paul Wood 1988-89
Born: Saddleworth 20.3.70
Forward
FL Apps/Gls 2+3/0 Total Apps/Gls 2+5/0
Career: Sheffield U. yts 1987, pro 9.88 [+1/-], Dale loan 11.88 to 12.88 [2+3/-], Hyde U. 9.89

Bergara went back to Bramall Lane once more to sign Paul on loan. He stayed a month at Spotland, figuring at some point in seven matches, generally on the right wing. He had previously made just one substitute appearance for Sheffield United in a goal-less draw with West Brom. His stint at Hyde was equally brief.

Ashley Grove Fothergill 1988-89
Born: Harrogate 3.10.69
Right back/midfield
FL Apps/Gls 8+1/0 Total Apps/Gls 9+1/0
Career: Middlesbrough jnr 1984, yts 1987, Dale 10.88 [8+1/-], Wrexham trial cs.89, Whitby T. 1989, {Bishop Auckland 1990-91}, C.W. Post (USA) 1992, New York Fever (USA) 4.96 to 9.96

Ashley had been a YTS lad at Middlesbrough but was not offered a professional contract and joined Dale part way through 1988-89. He made his debut in a Sherpa Van Trophy game against Wigan in December and played a number of league games in midfield and at right back the following February and March. Indeed, he figured in three successive victories, but dropped out of the side when Malcolm Brown was signed. He later moved to New York to take a degree at Long Island, playing for the university team C.W. Post.

David Howard (Dave) Windridge 1988-89
Born: Atherstone 7.12.61 5'9" 11st
Midfield
FL Apps/Gls 5/0 Total Apps/Gls 5/0
Career: Sheffield U. jnr 1978, pro 1.79, Chesterfield 3.80 [66+12/14], Blackpool 8.83 to cs.87 [87+14/17], Ankaragucu (Turkey) 1987, Northwich Victoria 1987-88 [2/- Conf], (Finland), (Cyprus?), Cork C. 1988, Bury 11.88 [1/-], Dale loan 1.89 to 2.89 [5/-], Colne Dynamos 1989-90, Morecambe 1990-91
Honours: Division 4 promotion 1985

Originally a winger, Dave played up front, in midfield and even, at times, in defence during useful spells with both Chesterfield and Blackpool. He netted eight goals when Blackpool were promoted to Division 3 and scored after 11 seconds in a cup tie against Manchester City. Latterly struggling with injury at Bloomfield Road, after something of a world tour, he signed for Bury but played only once and was loaned to Dale for a month, figuring five times in midfield. His debut came in a victory over Burnley, but the other games produced only one point.

Carl Peter Alford 1988-90
Born: Denton 11.2.72
Forward
FL Apps/Gls +4/0 Total Apps/Gls +4/0
Career: Dale yts 11.88 [+4/-], Stockport Co. 1989-90, Morecambe loan, Burnley trial, Witton A. 11.91 [38+19/16 Conf], Macclesfield T. £1700 cs.93 [34/14 Conf], Kettering T. cs.94 £25,000 [70+2/45 Conf], Rushden & Diamonds 3.96 £85,000 [36+6/15 Conf], Dover Ath. loan 2.98 [15/7 Conf], Stevenage Borough 4.98 [78+2/50 Conf], Doncaster R. 5.00 £50,000 [12+6/- Conf], Kettering T. loan 1.01 [2+3/- Conf], Yeovil T. cs.01 [30+22/10 Conf], Nuneaton Borough loan 2002-03, Gainsborough Trinity 2003, Leigh RMI 2003-04 [1/- Conf], Woodley Sports, Nuneaton Borough, New Mills 2006-07
Honours: FA Trophy final 1992, winners 2002, Drinkwise Cup 1994, FA XI v NPL 1993-94, England semi-pro international

Carl had a very brief Dale career, just four substitute appearances as a YTS player during 1988-89, the first when he was still only 16, but went on to be one of the top strikers in the Conference. Macclesfield spent £1700 on him in 1993 and he netted 26 times for them, but after two seasons at Kettering when he netted 45 goals in only 70 starts, he commanded a massive £85,000 fee, a record between non-league clubs, when he moved to Rushden & Diamonds. He again scored prolifically at Stevenage, with 50 goals in two seasons, eventually netting 159 goals to be the Conference's fifth highest scorer up to his retirement from that level in 2004. He played in two FA Trophy finals ten years apart, scoring in Yeovil's 2002 triumph, and represented both the FA and the England semi-professional side.

William John (Billy) Roberts 1988-89
Born: Bradford 9.4.63
Forward
FL Apps/Gls 1/0 Total Apps/Gls 1/0
Career: Farsley Celtic, Dale n/c 10.88 [1/-], Farsley Celtic 3.89, Guiseley 1990, Bridlington 1992-93, Farsley Celtic, Guiseley 1993-94 to 1996-97
Honours: West Riding Senior Cup 1988, FA Vase winners 1991, final 1992, NPL division 1 champions 1994

A product of semi-pro football in Yorkshire, Billy was given a chance at league level by Dale when he was 25. Unused substitute in one game, following the sale of Mark Smith, he made his sole appearance, as one of four changes to the side, when Dale lost 3-0 at Stockport in February 1989. Scoring 22 goals back at Farsley the following year, he later figured in two FA Vase finals for Guiseley, having scored twice in the semi-final in 1991 when he played alongside Dean Walling (q.v.). In a second spell at Guiseley, he netted 31 times when they won the NPL first division and also reached the FA Trophy semi-final. His brother Allan played with him for Guiseley in their two Wembley appearances.

Malcolm Brown 1988-89, 1991-92

Born: Salford 13.12.56
6'2" 12st6
Right back
FL Apps/Gls 29/1 Total Apps/Gls 37/1
Career: Bury app 6.73, pro 12.74 [10+1/-], Huddersfield T. 5.77 [256/16], Newcastle U. 8.83 £100,000 [39/-], Huddersfield T. 6.85 £55,000 [93+3/1], Dale n/c 2.89 [11/-], Stockport Co. 6.89 [71/3], Dale 8.91 [18/1], retired 1992
Honours: Division 4 champions 1980, promotion 1974, 1991, Division 3 promotion 1983, PFA Division 4 team of the year 1990

Malcolm made his name in a long spell at Huddersfield, playing over 250 games including, remarkably, four consecutive seasons as an everpresent. During that time the Terriers twice won promotion, Malcoln netting nine goals from right back during their 1983 success, seven of them from the spot. (Oddly, Huddersfield had a whole defence made up of past and future Dale players; Malcolm plus Keith Hanvey, Dave Sutton and Peter Valentine, and also had Brian Stanton, Steve Doyle and Kevin Stonehouse in midfield). After a big move to Newcastle, he didn't figure at all for a year due to an Achilles injury, but played regularly for one season in the top flight alongside Beardsley and Waddle before returning to Huddersfield. He was one of Danny Bergara's final signings for Dale and after just 11 games followed him when he moved to Stockport. After playing in a fourth promotion campaign (he had played just once, as an apprentice, when Bury were promoted 16 years earlier), he had another short stint at Spotland before retiring.

Joseph Gerald (Joe) McIntyre 1988-89
Born: Manchester 19.6.71
Midfield
FL Apps/Gls 2+2/0 Total Apps/Gls 2+2/0
Career: Port Vale yts 1987, Dale n/c 10.88 to 5.89 [2+2/-]

A trainee at Port Vale, Joe was signed on non-contract terms by Dale and after a run in the reserves made four first team appearances, being one of three new faces for the game against Hereford in February 1989, taking over from Dave Windridge in midfield.

Paul Bernard Jones 1988-89

Born: Ellesmere Port 13.5.53
6'1" 12st9
Centre half
FL Apps/Gls 14/2
Total Apps/Gls 14/2
Career: Ellesmere Port GS, Bolton W. app 9.7.69, pro 4.6.70 [440+4/37], Huddersfield T. 18.7.83 [73/8], Oldham A. 24.12.85 £5000 [32/1], Blackpool 25.3.87 [31+6/-], (S. Africa), Wigan A. trial, Galway cs.88, {Stalybridge Celtic?}, Dale n/c 3.89 [14/2], Stockport Co. player-coach cs.89 [25/-], Capetown Spurs (South Africa), Hinckley Ath., Wilmslow Albion, Cheadle T. manager 5.92, Mossley assistant manager 11.92, Castleton Gabriels manager 1.93, Oldham A. coach 7.93, Bolton W. scout, Hull C. scout, Crystal Palace scout, Hunang Province (China) coach to 2009
Honours: Ellesmere Port Boys, Cheshire Boys, Division 3 promotion 1973, Division 2 champions 1978

A tremendous stalwart for Bolton, Paul appeared in no less than 506 games and scored 43 goals from centre half, 12 of them in 1976-77 when he came close to England selection. He was everpresent in their 1973 promotion side and was still a regular when they reached the top flight. He then figured with Huddersfield, partnering Dave Sutton in central defence and after some time away from senior football was recruited by Dale after Sutton was ruled out through injury, to help arrest an alarming slide down the league. It certainly worked, as his first three games were all won – he even scored both goals against Scarborough – and the final game of the season was his 600th in the FL. He then followed recently departed Dale boss Bergara to Edgeley Park, becoming player-coach at the start of a lengthy career coaching, managing and scouting for teams at various levels, including an unusual job in Hunang Province in China.

Christopher James (Chris) Lucketti 1988-90
Born: Littleborough 28.9.71
6'0" 13st6
Central defender
FL Apps/Gls 1/0 Total Apps/Gls 3/0
Career: St Wilfrids School, Bishop Henshaw School, Whitworth Valley, Dale am 1987-88, yts 7.88 [1/-], Stockport Co. 23.8.90, Northwich Victoria loan 9.90 [2/- Conf], Halifax T. 12.7.91 [73+5/2, 8/1 Conf], Bury 1.10.93 £50,000 [235/8], Huddersfield T. 14.6.99 £750,000 [68/1], Preston NE 23.8.01 £750,000 [184+5/10], Sheffield U. 8.3.06 £300,000 [14+3/-], Southampton loan 27.3.08 [4/-], Huddersfield T. 26.7.08 [12+1/-], Preston NE youth team coach 5.10, Fleetwood assistant manager 2013*
Honours: Rochdale Schools 1986-87, Greater Manchester Schools, Lancashire Senior Cup final 1994-95, Division 3+ play-off final 1995, promotion 1996, Division 2+ champions 1997, Championship play-off final 2005, Championship promotion 2006. As coach; League 2 play-off winners 2014

At the opposite end of an equally long career to Paul Jones, Chris made his league debut when Jones missed the game against Hartlepool just after Terry Dolan became manager. He was also selected for the first two Lancashire Cup ties the following term, but an injury in the reserves and then glandular fever meant that he did not figure in the senior side again. Illness also dogged him after he signed for Stockport, and it was at Halifax that his career took off again, despite their relegation to the Conference. At Bury he was twice player of the year and played in two promotion sides as Bury went from (the new) Division 3 to Division 1 in successive years. He accumulated over 260 appearances before an impressive fee of £750,000 took him to Huddersfield. He moved to Preston for the same amount a couple of years later and again played over 200 games, reaching the play-off final in 2005, before helping Sheffield United gain promotion to the top flight and playing at that level himself for the first time when he was 35. He finally finished his league career three years later after passing the 600 game mark. Moving into coaching, he was assistant manager at Fleetwood when they won the League 2 play-off final in 2014.

Christopher Wayne Goodison 1989-91

Born: Wakefield 23.9.64 5'8" 11st7
Full back
FL Apps/Gls 78+1/4
Total Apps/Gls 95+3/7
Career: Barnsley app 1981, pro 9.82 [31+5/-], Crewe A. 9.86 [90+4/1], Dale 6.89 [78+1/4], Seiko (Hong Kong), Hyde U. 1991, Accrington St. 1992-93, Buxton 1993-94, manager to 1.97, Chorley assistant manager, Trafford assistant manager 1999, Salford C. manager, Rossendale U. 10.04, assistant manager to 11.05. Salford C. caretaker manager 10.08. Trafford assistant manager 2010-11, Nantwich T. assistant manager 1.15*
Honours: Division 4 promotion 1989. As coach: Unibond President's Cup winners 2000, Evostick first division north play-off winners 2013

Wayne was one of new boss Terry Dolan's first signings in the summer of 1989 and missed only one game at right back as Dale managed their first top half finish since relegation 16 years earlier and reached Round 5 of the FA Cup for the first time ever. The Dale skipper for a time, he had earlier played some second division games for Barnsley and appeared around 100 times for Crewe, frequently partnering John Pemberton (q.v.) at full back and figuring during their promotion season in 1989. Released by Dale after two seasons, he moved into the non-league game and was Buxton's player of the year before taking over as their manager at the start of a string of managerial appointments.

Vincent John (Vinnie) Chapman 1989-92
Born: Newcastle 5.12.67 5'9" 11st
Full back
FL Apps/Gls 23+1/1 Total Apps/Gls 27+1/1
Career: North Tyneside College of FE, Heaton Stannington, Wallsend BC, Tow Law T. 1986, Huddersfield T. 1.88 [4+2/-], York C. loan 1988-89, Dale 7.89 [23+1/1], retired injured 6.6.92. Tingley Ath. junior coach 2001, later football development officer
Honours: Newcastle Schoolboys

One of nine debutants on the opening day of 1989-90 Vinnie must rate as one of Dale's more unfortunate players. Originally a forward, he joined Dale as a left back, but was injured in each of his first three league games for the club (and scored an own goal in the fourth) and missed almost all the remainder of the season following a cartilage operation. He eventually managed a comeback around the New Year of 1991 and shared the left back spot with Jimmy Graham. However, he did not play at all the following term due to a cruciate injury and had to give up the game. A keen Newcastle supporter, Vinnie had been signed for Huddersfield by his hero Malcolm Macdonald, but had also suffered injury problems at this stage. He was later involved with coaching juniors.

David Andrew (Dave) Cole 1989-91

Born: Barnsley 28.9.62
6'0" 11st10
Centre half
Total Apps/Gls 73+11/7
Total Apps/Gls 93+12/7
Career: Laxey (Isle of Man), Sunderland 10.83, Crewe A. loan 1983-84, St Mirren loan 1983-84, Swansea C. 9.84 [7+1/-], Swindon T. 2.85 [69/3], Torquay U. 11.86 [107+3/6], Dale 7.89 [73+11/7], Exeter C. 8.91 [+2/-], retired 1991. Merthyr Tydfil 1992-93 [12+1/- Conf], Newport AFC 1993-94, Cinderford T.
Honours: Division 4 champions 1986, Division 3/4 play-off final 1988, Gloucestershire Senior Cup winners 1994

Unusually starting out in Manx football, Dave was signed by Sunderland but went through several clubs before making his mark at Swindon, missing only two games when they were fourth division champions in 1986. However, he was injured early the following term and moved to Torquay for three years (making his debut in the 3-3 draw at Spotland which cost Vic Halom his job), before signing for Dale. A lanky centre half, he was an automatic choice in his first season, figuring in the long FA Cup run and also netting five league goals, only three fewer than the top scorer. Less of a permanent fixture the following term and sometimes figuring at right back, he signed for Exeter in 1991. He was forced to retire from league football with a neck injury after only a couple of games, but did reappear in non-league football.

Peter Ward 1989-91

Born: Durham 15.10.64
6'0" 11st10
Forward/midfield
FL Apps/Gls 83+1/10
Total Apps/Gls 104+1/11
Career: Chester-le-Street 1980-81, Watford trial, Blackburn R. trial, Newcastle U. trial, Huddersfield T. 7.1.87 [24+13/2], Dale trial 4.89, signed 20.7.89 [83+1/10], Stockport Co. 6.6.91 (£30,000 + M. Payne) [140+2/10], Wrexham £50,000 19.7.95 [117+3/14], Morecambe player/caretaker manager 1999-2000 [1/- Conf]. Stockport Co. juniors coach 2000, youth team coach 2004-05, assistant manager 1.06 (also junior coach in Xi'an, Wuhan, Beijing and Chengdu (China) summer 2002), Motherwell assistant manager 30.6.09 to 12.09, Stockport Co. coach 6.10, caretaker manager 1.11 to 3.11, coach to 7.11, scout 2012
Honours: Division 3 play-off final 1992, Division 2+ play-off final 1994, AutoGlass Trophy final 1992, 1993. As coach: League 2 play-off winners 2008

Peter worked as a roof tiler while playing for Chester-le-Street, signing for Huddersfield when he was 22. A skilful midfield player, he became an integral part of the Dale team which managed its first top half finishes for two decades and famously reached the fifth round of the FA Cup, Peter being denied a dream equaliser against Palace by a save by million pound goalkeeper Nigel Martyn. He was sold to Stockport in 1991, Mark Payne moving the other way as part of the deal, and shared in County's run of Wembley visits, scoring in the AutoGlass Northern Section final in 1993. He also played over 100 games for Wrexham before retiring with a foot injury. He was assistant to Jim Gannon back at Stockport when they beat Dale at Wembley, and then at Motherwell. He subsequently returned to County and was caretaker manager after Paul Simpson was sacked.

Colin Small 1989-90
Born: Stockport 9.11.70 5'8" 11st
Forward
FL Apps/Gls 5+2/0 Total Apps/Gls 7+2/0
Career: Manchester C. as, yts 1987, Dale 7.89 [5+2/-], Stalybridge Celtic 1990, Mossley 1991, North Reddish WMC 12.92, North Trafford/Trafford 1993-94 to at least 1997
Honours: Youth Cup final 1989, England schools international (11 caps), NWCL Trophy winners 1994, NWCL division 1 champions 1997

A schoolboy international, Colin was a promising junior at Manchester City, appearing as substitute in the 1989 Youth Cup Final, after scoring in the semi-final. He then signed for Dale and played in the first two Lancashire Cup ties but was injured in his first FL start at centre forward, subsequently having to have a cartilage operation. He had four further games late in the season but was not retained. After playing at various other levels he had a long and successful stay at North Trafford, later Trafford FC, scoring 73 goals in 182 games.

Michael Arthur (Micky) Holmes 1989-91

Born: Blackpool 9.9.65
5'8" 10st12
Midfield
FL Apps/Gls 47+7/7
Total Apps/Gls 67+8/9
Career: Yeadon Celtic, Bradford C. 7.83 [+5/-], Hamileff (Sweden) 1985, Burnley n/c 1985, Wolverhampton W. 11.85 [74+9/13], Huddersfield T. 7.88 [3+4/-], Cambridge U. 2.89 [7+4/-], Dale 6.89 [47+7/7], Torquay U. 12.90 £ [34+6/3], Carlisle U. 2.92 £15,000 [33+1/4], Northampton T. 3.93 [6/-], Telford U. 1993-94 [7+5/- Conf], Wisbech T., Moor Green, Spennymoor, South Shields, Leicester College coach, Oadby T. manager cs.08 to 5.10
Honours: Division 3 champions 1985, Division 3/4 play-off final 1987, Division 4 champions 1988, Division 4 play-off winners 1991, Sherpa Van Trophy winners 1988

Well travelled over the course of his career, Micky came to notice during a spell at Wolves when he scored in seven consecutive games in 1986-87. He assisted them to promotion and the Sherpa Van Trophy the following term, when he scored a winner at Spotland. He was a regular in midfield for a season and a half for Dale as they showed considerable improvement over previous seasons, though in October 1990 he missed a last gasp penalty against leaders Torquay that would have taken Dale top instead. Torquay, though, bought him shortly afterwards, and his new side went up via the play-offs and a penalty shoot-out at Wembley. Moving into minor football with Wisbech after suffering a back injury in a car crash, Micky subsequently lectured and coached at his local college. He was joint manager of Oadby Town with his brother-in-law and former Torquay teammate and Scottish international Matt Elliott, and his son Jordan also played for Oadby.

Robert (Robbie) Whellans 1989-90
Born: Harrogate 14.2.69 5'8" 10st9
Striker
FL Apps/Gls 5+6/1 Total Apps/Gls 7+7/1
Career: Leicester C. as, Bradford C. as, yts 1985-86, pro 6.87, Hartlepool U. loan 12.87 [8+3/1], Dale 7.89 [5+6/1], Harrogate T. cs.90, Frickley Ath., Harrogate Railway Ath., Farsley Celtic 1992-93, Guiseley 1993-94, Farsley Celtic 1994-95, Harrogate T. 2002, Radcliffe Borough loan 2003-04, Harrogate Railway Ath. 2004

A youngster at Bradford City under Terry Dolan at the same time as Steve O'Shaughnessy and Jimmy Graham, Robbie scored 21 goals in their junior sides in 1985-86 and a remarkable combined total of 54 in the Northern Intermediate League and the Central League the following year. He gained his first FL experience while on loan at Hartlepool, scoring on his debut, against Dale, but was out injured prior to his one season at Spotland. He started the first two Lancashire Cup ties at centre forward and after spending some time on the bench also started five times in the league before suffering further injury problems. He later had huge goalscoring success with Farsley Celtic, netting more than 20 goals in five out of eight seasons between 1994 and 2002, with a best of 34, and aggregating well over 150 before returning to play in his home town Harrogate again.

William (Willie) Burns 1989-91

Born: Motherwell 10.12.69
5'11" 10st10
Defender
FL App/Gls 68+4/2
Total Apps/Gls 89+4/5
Career: Forgewood BC, Motherwell as, Manchester C. yts 1986, pro 1.88, Dale 7.89 [68+4/2], East Fife 1991 to 1995 [121+4/9 ScL], Cowdenbeath 1997-98 [4/- ScL], retired injured
Honours: Scotland under-16s, Scottish Schools, Scotland youth international

The nephew of Francis Burns, of Manchester United and Scotland, Willie won youth caps for Scotland and would have made his debut for the other half of Manchester at the end of 1987-88, but broke his leg in training the day before. Originally used by Dale in a spare defender or sweeper role, he played most of his first season at left back. He missed only two games in that campaign, one of them due to suspension following his sending off in the famous game at Burnley when Dale won with nine men. In his second season, when Dale again managed to finish in the top half, he was instead used mainly as one of three central defenders, or at right back. He later played well over a hundred games in the Scottish League for East Fife before his career was ended through injury.

Kevin Stonehouse 1989-90
Born: Bishop Auckland 20.9.59 5'11" 11st1
Midfield/forward
FL Apps/Gls 13+1/2 Total Apps/Gls 20+2/4
Career: Shildon, Blackburn R. 7.79 [77+7/26], Huddersfield T. 3.83 £25,000 [20+2/4], Blackpool 3.84 £25,000 [53+2/19], Darlington 8.87 [59+13/20], Carlisle U. loan 3.89 [+3/-], Dale 8.89 [13+1/2], Bishop Auckland cs.90. Willington 1994-95, player-manager 1996-97, Murton 1997-98. Darlington Football in the Community officer 2.08, Newcastle U. scout
Honours: Division 3 promotion 1980, 1983, Division 4 promotion 1985

Kevin made his debut for Blackburn the year they were promoted to Division 2, and moved to Huddersfield just in time to help them do the same three years later. Effectively an old fashioned inside forward, he completed a promotion treble by netting 11 goals as Blackpool were promoted from Division 4 in 1985. However he was then out of action for 18 months after twice breaking his leg. Now playing on the left flank, he came back to score 13 times, including two at Spotland, for Darlington in 1987-88 and while with Dale also played mainly wide on the left, though he scored from centre forward in the FA Cup tie at Marine. He had a lengthy stint in non-league football back in the north east and worked for Football in the Community at Darlington.

Jonathan William (Jon) Hill 1989-91

Born: Wigan 20.8.70
5'10" 11st10
Full back/midfield
FL Apps/Gls 25+11/1
Total Apps/Gls 29+17/1
Career: Everton as 1984, Crewe A. yts 1986, Dale 6.89 [25+11/1], Preston NE trial cs.91, Witton Albion 9.91 [9/1 Conf], Stalybridge Celtic 1992 to 1993-94 [15+4/- Conf], retired injured. Wigan A. youth coach 1996, Manchester U. academy coach 11.99, Jordan FA youth technical director 6.09, Manchester C. academy coach 8.11, Tromso (Norway) coach 11.12, Fulham coach 12.13*
Honours: Great Britain Catholic Schools, European Catholic Schools Cup winners

Representing Great Britain in schools football, Jon scored against Italy in the European championships in Holland. He also figured in the Crewe side which reached the Youth Cup quarter finals. His only league football came with Dale, most of it in the first half of the 1989-90 season at left back, though he sometimes played in midfield, switching roles with Jimmy Graham. He was frequently on the bench in his second term, but started only three times, later playing a few games at Conference level. After retiring through injury he obtained a degree at Liverpool John Moores, becoming a PE teacher and coaching youngsters. He spent 10 years with Manchester United's academy and had a successful stint running the Jordanian international youth set-up. After a spell in Norway, Jon became first team coach at Fulham in 2013.

Jason Wiles Hasford 1989-90
Born: Chorlton-cum-Hardy 1.4.71 5'8" 10st12
Forward
FL App/Gls +1/0 Total Apps/Gls +2/0
Career: Oakwood HS, Flixton 1985, Manchester C. yts 1987, Dale 7.89 [+1/-], Witchita Wings (USA) 1990-91, Mossley 1991-92
Honours: Manchester Boys 1984, Youth Cup final 1989

Like Colin Small, Jason played in Manchester City's Youth Cup Final side in 1989, having scored four times in earlier rounds. He also scored four in an 11-1 victory over Blackpool in the Lancashire Youth Cup. After moving to Dale, he figured in a Lancashire Cup tie but his FL career was brief, coming off the bench just once, in a goalless draw against Hartlepool in September 1989 when Dale were without four regulars. He was later with Witchita Wings in Major League Soccer in the USA, scoring three times in 35 games.

Jason Dawson 1989-91

Born: Burslem 9.2.71
5'7" 11st5
Forward
FL Apps/Gls 37+18/8
Total Apps/Gls 48+21/9
Career: Stoke C. as 1985, Newcastle T., Port Vale yts 1987, Dale 7.89 [37+18/8], Macclesfield T. cs.91 [5+11/1 Conf], Leek T. 1991-92,
Stafford R. 1991-92 to 1993-4 [20+3/3 Conf]
Honours: Stoke Schools, Staffordshire County Schoolboys

A sixth former YTS lad from another club to sign on professional terms at Rochdale in 1989, Jason figured as substitute in a Lancashire Cup game but then had to wait until December to make his FL debut, coming on and scoring in a 3-0 defeat of Cambridge. His goal immediately earned him a long run in the side at centre forward in place of the injured Steve Elliott and he also scored in the defeat of third division Northampton that earned Dale their shot at Crystal Palace in the fifth round of the FA Cup. He spent much of the following campaign on the bench, though he did manage five goals, and was similarly mainly a substitute when he joined Macclesfield in the Conference.

Alan Ainscow 1989-90

Born: Bolton 15.7.63
5'8" 11st5
Midfield
FL Apps/Gls 19+1/0
Total Apps/Gls 22+4/1
Career: Blackpool app 1970, pro 7.71 [178+14/28], Birmingham C. 7.78 £40,000 [104+4/16], Everton 8.81 £250,000 [24+4/3], Barnsley loan 11.82 [2/-], Eastern U. (Hong Kong) 1983, Wolverhampton W. 8.84 [56+2/5], Blackburn R. n/c 12.85, signed 6.86 [42+23/5], Dale 7.89 [19+1/-], Horwich RMI 1990-91, Flint Town United 1990-91, Atherton Collieries 1991-92. Burscough u-17s coach 8.05
Honours: England youth international, Anglo-Italian Cup winners 1971, final 1972, Division 2 promotion 1980, Division 2 play-off final 1989, Full Members Cup winners 1987, (Lancashire Senior Cup winners 1987-88)

By far the most experienced of Terry Dolan's 1989 summer signings, Alan had made his debut in the Anglo-Italian Cup back in the summer of 1971 (when Bob Stokoe was the Blackpool boss) appearing in the final when they beat Bologna. He also appeared in the final the following year when they lost at Roma, having scored in the remarkable 10-1 defeat of Lanerossi Vicenza. He also scored on his FL debut and in 1972-73 netted double figures in the second division, including a hattrick at Preston, to be the side's top scorer. It was 1978 before he gained a move to the top division, with Birmingham, but in 1981 Everton paid £250,000 for his services. He had several further seasons in the second tier before joining Dale when he was 36, becoming skipper. He played regularly on the right flank for the first part of the campaign, but was little used thereafter until the last few weeks of the season and was then released.

Anthony John (Tony) Brown 1989-93

Born: Bradford 17.9.58
6'2" 12st7
Central defender
FL Apps/Gls 111+3/0
Total Apps/Gls 142+4/0
Career: Thackley, Leeds U. 3.83 [24/1], Doncaster R. loan 11.84 and 3.85 [14/-], Doncaster R. 7.85 [71+2/2], Scunthorpe U. 7.87 £10,000 [46+8/-], Dale n/c 8.89, signed 12.89 [111+3/-], retired injured 1993. Bradford PA, Eccleshill U. manager

Tony was 24 when he joined Leeds from Northern Counties East football and made his debut at centre back marking Leicester's Gary Lineker. He also spent a couple of years at both Doncaster and Scunthorpe, but initially joined Dale on non-contract terms as there were doubts over his fitness. In fact he made 52 appearances during the season and was one of Dale's most consistent players as they managed a top half finish. He only missed two games – both defeats - when they just missed the play-offs under Dave Sutton, but eventually had to pack up through injury during 1992-93.

Stephen Blain (Steve) Elliott 1989-91

Born: Haltwhistle 15.9.58
6'0" 11st10
Striker
FL Apps/Gls 46+6/9
Total Apps/Gls 55+8/10
Career: Nottingham F. app, pro 8.77 [4/-], Preston NE 3.79 £95,000 [202+6/70], Luton T. 7.84 £65,000 [12/3], Walsall 12.84 (exchange for D. Preece) [68+1/21], Bolton W. 7.86 £25,000 [57+3/10], Bury 29.9.88 £16,000 [31/11], Dale loan 5.10.89, signed £10,000 6.11.89 [46+6/9], Guiseley 7.91, Lostock Hall manager, Penwortham manager, Bamber Bridge manager
Honours: (Football League Cup winners 1978), Division 4 promotion 1988

Steve had a somewhat odd introduction to the senior game, Brian Clough selecting him as substitute for the League Cup Final before he actually made his first team debut. He only ever did make four appearances for Forest, but played over 200 times as a striker for Preston, netting at least 16 goals in three separate seasons. He also netted three hat-tricks for North End, one of them against Dale. He briefly figured in the top flight at Luton and later helped Bolton gain promotion from the bottom division, before Dale signed him from Bury, initially on loan and then for a £10,000 fee. He scored in his first two games but was troubled by injuries throughout his stay. Managing in non-league football, Steve also turned out for Preston in masters football.

James (Jimmy) Graham 1989-90, 1990-94

Born: Glasgow 15.11.69
6'0" 11st8
Left back/winger
FL Apps/Gls 131+6/1
Total Apps/Gls 175+7/2
Career: Avoca FC, Bradford C. yts, pro 12.9.88 [6+1/-], Dale loan 3.11.89 to 2.90 [11/-], Dale 9.7.90 £15,000 [120+6/1], Hull C. 5.8.94 [63/1], Guiseley 6.96, Lancaster C. 2.97 to 2002
Honours: Northern intermediate League champions 1988

Jimmy played under Terry Dolan at Bradford City, and Dolan signed him on loan for Dale part way through 1989-90, Jimmy figuring regularly at No. 11 for three months. He signed permanently the following summer for £15,000 and the prematurely balding figure was a fairly regularly member of the Dale side, initially in the centre of defence but mainly at left back, for the next four seasons – despite being sent off on successive Saturdays in 1992-93. Eventually totalling 183 games for Dale, he signed for Terry Dolan yet again at Hull, where he was somewhat hampered by a knee injury. Jimmy's much older brothers Arthur, David and Tommy played, respectively, for Leeds, Manchester United and Scotland, for Queens Park, and for numerous lower league sides including Scunthorpe and Scarborough. Arthur was just finishing his career at Bradford City when Jimmy signed for them. Jimmy returned to Glasgow after his playing career ended.

Andrew John (Andy) Milner 1989-94

Born: Kendall 10.2.67
6'0" 11st
Winger
FL Apps/Gls 103+24/25
Total Apps/Gls 129+31/33
Career: West London Institute, Netherfield 1986, Manchester C. 24.1.89 £7000, Dale 18.1.90 £20,000 [103+24/25], Chester 12.8.94 [106+19/24],

Hereford U. loan 10.97 [8/5], Morecambe 11.97 £10,000 [24+4/9 Conf], Northwich Victoria 1.00 [2+2/- Conf]
Rugby Union for Kendall, Cumbria Schools
Honours: Westmoreland Senior Cup 1987

Andy had actually played rugby union, at full back, to a high standard at school and only took up soccer when studying to be a PE teacher in London. He made the big step up from Netherfield to Manchester City in 1989, but didn't figure in the first team before Dale bought him for £20,000 a year later. An exciting winger, he ended his first campaign by scoring a hat-trick in a 5-2 victory over Hereford. Generally occupying the right flank, he was second top scorer in 1991-92 with 15 goals in all competitions when Dale just missed the play-offs. However he missed half the following season with an achilles problem. In 1994 he joined Chester and again played over 100 games, top scoring in 1996-97 when they made the play-offs and netting four against Doncaster. He later signed for Morecambe after scoring a 15 minute hat-trick against them while on loan at Hereford, but had to retire in 2000 due to a cruciate injury. In recent years he has worked as a counsellor for the PFA helping players suffering from depression.

Lee Edward Duxbury 1989-90

Born: Skipton 7.10.69
5'8" 11st13
Midfield
FL Apps/Gls 9+1/0
Total App/Gls 10+1/0
Career: South Craven, Bradford C. yts, pro 4.7.88 [204+5/25], Dale loan 18.1.90 to 3.90 [9+1/-], Huddersfield T. 23.12.94 £250,000 [29/2], Bradford C. 15.11.95 £135,000 [63/7], Oldham A. 7.3.97 £350,000 [222+26/32], Bury 8.03 [36+1/-], Harrogate T. 2004, Farsley Celtic 10.04 [12/1 Conf], Glenavon 1.06, Oldham A. coach 6.06 to 1.13, Eccleshill U. manager 7.13 to 7.14, Thackley manager 17.9.14 to 25.9.14
Honours: Bradford Boys 1987, Division 2+ play-off winner 1995, 1996. As manager: West Riding Cup winners 2014, Northern Counties East League Cup final

Lee was still a young hopeful at Bradford City when his former boss Terry Dolan signed him on loan for Dale and he figured in midfield in 11 successive games, including the cup tie at Crystal Palace. However, the following year he missed only one game for the Bantams – due to suspension following a match against Chester when he scored but was one of three players sent off – and he went on to play more than 200 times before a quarter of a million pound move to Huddersfield. He immediately figured in their promotion winning side, but after just a year he was back at Bradford and again secured promotion via another play-off success. An even bigger fee took him to Oldham and he went on to figure in almost 250 FL games for them, ending his career just short of 600 league games. He returned to Boundary Park a few years later as coach. After a successful year at Eccleshill, he spent just a week as Thackley boss. As a schoolboy, Lee and his mother were survivors of the tragic Valley Parade fire.

Gary Henshaw 1989-90
Born: Leeds 18.2.65 5'9" 11st8
Midfield
FL Apps/Gls 8+1/1 Total Apps/Gls 8+1/1
Career: Grimsby T. app 7.81, pro 2.83 [46+4/9], Bolton W. 6.87 [49+26/4], Dale loan 3.90 to 5.90 [8+1/1], Swansea C. trial 1991, Chorley 1991-92, Runcorn 1991-92 [7+6/- Conf], Hyde U. 1992-93, Atherton Collieries loan 9.95, Radcliffe Borough 1998-99, {Atherton LR?}, Atherton Collieries to 2001
Honours: Division 4 promotion 1988, Sherpa Van Trophy winners 1989

Gary progressed from Grimsby's junior sides to play a number of second division games in their midfield before moving to Bolton and assisting their promotion side in 1988. Danny Bergara tried to sign him for Dale the following term, but they could not afford the £25,000 asking price. Dale eventually borrowed him towards the end of 1989-90 and he appeared in midfield in eight games, four of which were won, though two of the others were heavy defeats. In a long stint with Hyde United he played almost 200 games in all.

Stephen Jonathan Francis (Steve) Milligan 1989-92
Born: Hyde 13.6.73 5'8" 9st12
Midfield
FL Apps/Gls 5/1 Total Apps/Gls 5/1
Career: Ipswich T. as, Woodley Sports, Dale yts 7.89 [5/1], Mossley trial cs.92, Castleton Gabriels cs.92, Woodley Sports 1994-95

Steve was a promising trainee at Spotland when handed his debut in April 1990 at left back, wearing No. 11, and he subsequently played in midfield while in the No. 5 shirt, scoring against Lincoln. Unfortunately he broke his leg while on holiday in Spain that summer and missed all of 1990-91. He figured in the reserves the following term, but never had another opportunity at league level.

Phillip Barry (Phil) Lockett 1989-92
Born: Stockport 6.9.72 5'9" 11st2
Midfield
FL Apps/Gls 1+2/0 Total Apps/Gls 1+2/0
Career: Dale yts 7.89, pro 7.91 [1+2/-], {Stalybridge Celtic 1992?}. Hyde U. 11.97 to 2.98. Chorley 4.02, Hyde U. loan 12.02, Leek T. 11.03, Rossendale U. 1.04, caretaker player-manager 9.04, Bamber Bridge 10.04, Congleton T. 6.05. Beechfield U. manager c.2010

Phil was a second trainee drafted into the first team squad at the end of 1989-90 and he replaced Steve Milligan during the 5-2 defeat of Hereford on the final day. Still a member of the youth team the following term, he made his sole start in the first team's midfield in Dave Sutton's first game in charge. He signed professional terms in 1991 but was restricted to the reserves, later having a lengthy non-league career, either in midfield or at right back, though making only a handful of appearances for any of his NPL clubs.

Gareth Gray 1990-92

Born: Longridge 24.2.70
6'0" 11st2
Goalkeeper
FL Apps 6
Total Apps 13
Career: Darwen 1986, Bolton W. 2.88, Dale 7.90 £5000 [6], Great Harwood cs.92, Hyde U. 9.92
Honours: Preston Schools, Lancashire Schools, Lancashire FA Youth

A time served printer, Gareth joined Bolton when he was 18 and though not appearing in their league side he did play in the Lancashire Cup against Dale when Wanderers beat them in a penalty shoot out to reach the final. He cost Dale £5000 but played only in the Leyland Daf Cup when understudying Keith Welch. When Welch was sold, Gareth had the misfortune to be injured and Dale brought in several on loan goalkeepers. Gareth did figure in a number of cup games - he is perhaps best remembered by Dale fans for somehow avoiding being sent off for a challenge outside his box against Gretna - and eventually made his league debut in October 1991. He played three games for Hyde in a week but unfortunately conceded 13 goals. A Preston fan, he played with his favourite North End player, Steve Elliott, while at Spotland.

Paul John Butler 1990-96

Born: Manchester 2.11.72
6'2" 13st
Centre back
FL Apps/Gls 151+7/10
Total Apps/Gls 183+12/10
Career: Moston Brook HS, Bradford C. as 1987, yts 1989, Dale yts 7.90, pro 5.7.91 [151+7/10], Bury 22.7.96 £125,000 [83+1/4], Sunderland 6.7.98 £900,000 [78+1/3], Wolverhampton W. loan 17.11.00, signed 31.1.01 £1,000,000 [118+1/3], Leeds U. 2.7.04 [99/4], Milton Keynes Dons 22.11.06 [17/-], Chester C. 30.7.07 to 1.09 [36/2], Sheffield U. scout, Cardiff C. scout, Stoke C. scout, Oldham A. chief scout 8.10 to 2013
Honours: Manchester Boys, Northern Intermediate League champions, Republic of Ireland v Czech Republic 2000, Republic of Ireland 'B', Division 2+ champions 1997, Division 1+ champions 1999, play-off winners 2003, Championship play-off final 2006, AutoWindscreens Shield northern final 1995

Paul switched his traineeship from Bradford City to Dale when Terry Dolan became the Dale boss and was a substitute for the first game of the 1991-92 season. His second appearance was notable, and short, as he gave away a penalty and was carried off before touching the ball. Nevertheless, he went on to establish himself in the centre of the Dale defence, partnering Alan Reeves, and after Reeves left succeeded him as player of the year in 1995 (when Dale reached the AWS northern final) and 1996. Sold to Bury for a big fee by Dale standards, two years later Sunderland bought him for £900,000, a figure upped to £1M when he joined Wolves. Already in a promotion side at Bury, he helped both Sunderland and Wolves reach the top flight, the latter via the play-offs, and almost repeated this at Leeds, where he skippered the side. He also became one of the select band of Rochdale products to become a full international when he played for the Republic of Ireland against the Czech Republic, having the unenviable task of marking the giant Jan Koller who scored twice. Winding down his career at MK Dons and Chester, where he also did some coaching, Paul ended on 597 FL appearances and 687 in all games. He was later a scout for several clubs.

Christopher (Chris) Lee 1990-91

Born: Halifax 18.6.71
5'10" 11st10
Midfield
FL Apps/Gls 24+2/2
Total Apps/Gls 36+2/4
Career: Bradford C. yts 1988, pro 7.89, Dale 14.6.90 [24+2/2], Scarborough 14.3.91 [75+3/3], Hull C. 30.7.93 [104+12/5], Guiseley 1996
Honours: Northern Intermediate League champions

The son of Jeff, the former Halifax player and Terry Dolan's assistant at several clubs, Chris started out at one of them, Bradford City, where he captained the youth team, and then signed for another when he joined Dale. He scored on his debut in the Lancashire Cup and was a regular in midfield until Dolan left, but became a target for the fans who wanted to see Micky Holmes in the side and thought that Lee snr had undue influence on team selection. Left out by Dave Sutton, he had a useful spell at Scarborough before teaming up with his father and Dolan again at Hull, where he played more than 100 times. Considering his relatively brief stay at Spotland, he figured in 12 cup ties.

Peter Costello 1990-91

Born: Halifax 31.10.69
6'0" 11st7
Forward
FL Apps/Gls 31+3/10
Total Apps/Gls 42+3/14
Career: Bradford C. yts 1987, pro 7.88 [11+9/2], Dale 7.90 £10,000 [31+3/10], Peterborough U. 3.91 £30,000 [3+5/-], Lincoln C. loan 9.91 [3/-], Lincoln C. 9.92 £15,000 [28+10/7], Halifax T. loan 10.93 [2/- Conf], Kettering T. loan 3.94 [6/4 Conf], Dover Ath. 8.94 [3+5/1 Conf], Telford U. 1994-95 [4+1/1 Conf], Instant Dict (Hong Kong) 7.95, Kettering T. 7.97 [31+6/5 Conf], Nuneaton Borough 1998-99, Instant FC (Hong Kong) 1998-99, Boston U. 12.98 [31+14/8 Conf, 13+5/-], Stevenage Borough 5.03 [8+4/1 Conf], Cambridge C. 4.04
Honours: Northern Intermediate League champions, Division 4 promotion 1991, Division 3 promotion 1992, Southern League champions 2000, Conference champions 2002

Yet another ex-Bradford City junior, Peter had played some games for them in Division 2 before joining Dale for £10,000. He was easily the leading scorer with 14 when sold to Peterborough just before the transfer deadline, but with the eccentric Barry Fry having brought in a whole set of new players Peter only made a handful of appearances as Posh gained successive promotions. He later figured with a string of clubs at Conference level, as well as playing in Hong Kong and after an eight season gap made it back to the FL – by now as a right back - when Boston gained elevation to that level in 2002 (despite Peter being sent off in the match that clinched the title).

Chris Keith Blundell 1990-91

Born: Billinge 7.12.69
5'10" 12st
Central defender
FL Apps/Gls 10+4/0
Total Apps/Gls 14+5/0
Career: Wigan A. jnr, Oldham A. yts 14.2.86, pro 17.6.87 [2+1/-], Waikato U. (New Zealand) loan 1.5.89, Dale loan 9.90, signed 11.90 [10+4/-], Northwich Victoria cs.91 [48+8/1 Conf], Winsford U. 1993. Bedians 1997-98
Honours: Warrington Boys, Cheshire Boys

Chris was borrowed from Oldham early in 1990-91 and played a number of games at centre back, but oddly enough, rarely figured after he was signed permanently, playing a couple of games in midfield. Appearing for Northwich Victoria against Yeovil, he earned the first red card shown in the Conference. Later he turned out for Bedians in the Manchester & Cheshire Amateur League.

David Wayne (Dave) Norton 1990-91
Born: Cannock 3.3.65 5'7" 11st8
Right back
FL Apps/Gls 9/0 Total Apps/Gls 11/0
Career: Aston Villa app 1982, pro 23.3.83 [42+2/2], Notts Co. 24.8.88 £30,000 [22+5/1], Dale loan 18.10.90 to 12.90 [9/-], Hull C. loan 10.1.91 [15/-], Hull C. 16.8.91 £80,000 [134/5], Northampton T. 15.8.94 £25,000 [78+4/-], Hereford U. 12.8.96 [45/1, 5+1/- Conf], Cheltenham T. cs.98 [35+1/3 Conf], Yeovil T. 7.5.99 [7+4/1 Conf], Forest Green Rovers 12.99 [43/2 Conf], joint manager 11.00, Tamworth coach 8.01, Gainsborough Trinity manager 11.01, Tamworth assistant manager 2002, Nuneaton Borough assistant manager 7.03, Grantham player-manager 2.04, Stafford R. player-assistant manager 10.04 to 8.05. Team DNF manager
Honours: England youth international, Division 2 promotion 1988, (1991), Division 3 promotion 1990, Conference champions 1999. As manager:

FA Trophy final 2001, Conference South promotion 2003, FA Trophy final 2003

Dave came through the juniors at Villa Park to play over 40 games in the top flight before moving to Notts County where he played in the side promoted to Division 2 (and, indeed in a few games at the start of the season that saw them elevated to the top flight). A solid full back, he was loaned to Dale and played regularly for two months, also spending time on loan at Hull before the latter bought him for a sizeable fee. Unfortunate to be with Hereford when they lost their league place, he could have returned when Cheltenham won the Conference title, but would have had to repay an injury insurance pay-out so continued at non-league level before going into coaching and management and working as a PE teacher. He also started his own business DNF Coaching in Nottingham and ran a side in the Midland Amateur Alliance. His brother Tracey was also in the Aston Villa youth team.

Stephen Charles (Steve) Doyle 1990-95

Born: Port Talbot 2.6.58
5'9" 11st9
Midfield
FL Apps/Gls 115+6/1 Total Apps/Gls 142+6/1
Career: Afan Lido, Preston NE as 1972, app 1974, pro 6.75 [178+19/10], Newcastle U. trial 8.82, Huddersfield T. 3.9.82 [158+3/6], Sunderland 18.9.86 £57,500 [99+1/2], Hull C. 14.8.89 £75,000 [47/2], Dale 22.11.90 £5000 [115+6/1], Chorley player-coach 4.95, manager to 4.97
Honours: Port Talbot u-15s, West Glamorgan Schools, Wales under-21 v England 1979, v Norway 1984, Division 3 promotion 1978, 1983, 1988

At Afan Lido with future Welsh international Brian Flynn as a youngster, Steve made his Preston debut at 16 years and 5 months old. A frequent performer by 1978 when they were promoted, he played for the Welsh under-21s the following year. He gained another promotion during four seasons at Huddersfield and completed a hat-trick when Sunderland bounced back from a single season in Division 3. Hull's captain, he was transferred to Dale late in 1990 and, despite lengthy injury lay-offs – he missed the last nine games of 1991-92 when Dale lost six of them to blow their promotion chance - he completed a century of appearances in their midfield to become one of only ten players to have done so with four different clubs. In all, he played 626 FL games before becoming Dave Sutton's assistant at Chorley and subsequently having a short spell as manager himself.

Ian Dominic McInerney 1990-91

Born: Liverpool 26.1.64 5'10" 11st8
Forward
FL Apps/Gls 4/1 Total Apps/Gls 4/1
Career: Newcastle Blue Star, Huddersfield T. 8.88 [5+5/1], Stockport Co. 7.89 [37+5/8], Dale loan 2.91 to 3.91 [4/1], Gateshead cs.91 [2/- Conf], Morecambe, Runcorn 1992-93 [93+19/13 Conf], Halifax T. 8.96 [11+2/1 Conf], Runcorn Halton 2.97, England FC (Qatar)
Honours: Division 4 promotion 1991, FA Trophy final 1994

Ian was Dave Sutton's first, temporary, signing for Dale when he arrived on loan from Stockport for a month, playing four games on the flanks, of which Dale won one and drew the other three. A late starter, at 24, with Huddersfield, he did not play in the league again after his loan spell, but had a long stint at Runcorn, figuring in the FA Trophy Final, and then played for England – a club side in Qatar!

Kevin Philip Rose 1990-91, 1991-93

Born: Evesham 23.11.60
6'1" 13st6
Goalkeeper
FL Apps 71
Total Apps 83
Career: Evesham U. 1976-7, Worcester C. 1977-78, Ledbury T. 3.79, Lincoln C. 8.79 £10,000, Ledbury T. cs.81 £7000, Hereford U. 3.83 [268], Bolton W. 7.7.89 £25,000 [10], Halifax T. loan 1.2.90, Carlisle U. loan 3.90 [11], Dale loan 2.91 to 3.91 [3], Dale 11.91 £10,000 [68], Kidderminster Harriers cs.93 [75+1 Conf], Redditch U. loan 1996-97, retired cs.97
Honours: FA XI 1994, England semi-pro international v Norway, Finland 1993-94

Kevin played in Hereford's 4-1 defeat at Spotland in March 1983 (when Micky French notched a hat-trick) but went on to be everpresent for five and a half seasons, accumulating 253 consecutive appearances. Understudy to Dave Felgate at Bolton, Dale borrowed him when Keith Welch was suspended following his sending-off in Dave Sutton's first game in charge. The following November, he was signed on a permanent basis and was the regular 'keeper for a season and a half as Dale twice challenged for a play-off place. Enjoying a final spell with Kidderminster Harriers, who reached the fifth round of the FA Cup, Kevin played for both an FA XI and the England semi-pro side in 1993-94.

Anthony (Tony) Colleton 1990-92
Born: Manchester 17.1.74   5'8"   10st6
Forward
FL Apps/Gls +1/0 Total Apps/Gls +1/0
Career: Dale yts 7.90 to 1991-92 [+1/-]

A member of Dale's youth team in 1990, Tony was selected as substitute for the first team for the league game against Scunthorpe when Dale had several players out injured. He came on to replace Ian McInerney on the right wing towards the end of the 2-1 win but didn't make the squad again. Indeed, though still on the books in 1991-92 he did not even figure in the reserves.

Jason Stuart Anders 1990-94

Born: Rochdale 13.3.74
5'10"   10st6
Forward
FL Apps/Gls 2+15/1
Total Apps/Gls 2+19/1
Career: Crewe A. jnr, Dale as 1989, yts 1990, pro cs.92 [2+15/1], (New Zealand summer 1992), Northwich Victoria loan 12.11.93 [3/1 Conf], Exeter C. trial 10.1.94, North Trafford 1994, Castleton Gabriels 1994-95, Whitworth Valley 4.97, Castleton Gabriels 1998-99 (+ Dicken Green 1994, Top House 1999, Tophams 2004; Sunday League)
Honours: Rochdale Schools under-14s 1988, under-15s 1989, Schools County Cup final 1989, Rochdale SL XI 1994-95

Jason starred for Rochdale Schools when they reached the County Cup Final, played at Spotland, against Wigan in 1989. "The new Ian Rush" according to his manager Dave Sutton, he figured in Dale's reserves and youth team over the next two seasons and came on as substitute for the league side on two occasions towards the end of 1990-91, the first four days before his 17th birthday. He next appeared after turning pro in 1992, being named as substitute for 13 consecutive games, and finally made two starting appearances the following March. He later played with local non-league sides Whitworth Valley and Casteton Gabriels as well as in the Rochdale Sunday League.

Stephen James (Steve) Morgan 1990-92
Born: Wrexham 28.12.70   5'9"   11st5
Forward
FL Apps/Gls 12+11/3 Total Apps/Gls 12+14/3
Career: Mold Alexandra, Oldham A. yts 13.7.87, pro 1988 [1+1/-], Wrexham loan 3.90 [7/1], Dale 3.91 £ [12+11/3], Stalybridge Celtic 1992 [13+4/2 Conf], Colwyn Bay 1993 to 1996
Honours: Deeside Schools 1982, North Wales Schools, Wales youth international 1987-88, Lancashire League division 2 champions 1988

A Welsh youth international, Steve made two substitute appearances for Oldham when he was 16, including one against Leeds in the League Cup. He was signed by Dale for a small fee in March 1991 to replace Peter Costello and made a terrific start with two goals on his debut in a victory at York, figuring in all the remaining games. However, the arrival of Andy Flounders and Steve Whitehall in the summer relegated him to the bench and he started only one further game.

Paul John Herring 1989-92
Born: Hyde 1.7.73   5'11"   11st3
Midfield
FL Apps/Gls +1/0 Total Apps/Gls +1/0
Career: Dale yts 1989, pro 7.91, Mossley cs.92, Hyde U. 1992-93, Mossley 11.93, Glossop NE 3.96

Another youngster following Lockett, Colleton and Anders into the first team squad, Paul had played in the reserves in 1989-90 and was Dale's second substitute in the game against Peterborough in April 1991 when they had eight players unavailable. He figured in the reserves after turning pro but was not called upon for the first team again, though he later played regularly for Mossley in the Northern Premier League.

Philip (Phil) Hughes 1991-92

Born: Belfast 19.11.64
Goalkeeper
FL Apps 0 Total Apps 3
Career: Burnley jnr, Manchester U. app 1981, Leeds U. 1.83 [6], Bury 6.85 [80], Wigan A. 11.87 £35,000 [99], Dale trial 8.91, Telford U. [1 Conf], Scarborough 10.91 [17], Guiseley 1992, Pontefract Colliers 1994. Leeds U. goalkeeping coach, Grimsby T. goalkeeping coach, Burnley goalkeeping coach 2004, Bolton W. goalkeeping coach 1.10, Wigan A. goalkeeping coach 7.13 to 6.14, Houston Dynamo (USA) goalkeeping coach 23.1.15*
Honours: N. Ireland youth international, N. Ireland (3 caps) 1986 to 1987, N. Ireland 1986 World Cup squad, Youth Cup final 1982, Lancashire Senior Cup winners 1986-87, NPL Division 1 champions 1994

With Gareth Gray injured, Dale were without a goalkeeper for the start of season Lancashire Cup and brought Phil in on a temporary basis. A Youth Cup finalist in 1982 with Manchester United, he had played approaching 200 games for Bury and Wigan, and won three full caps for Northern Ireland, being one of the reserve 'keepers to Pat Jennings for the 1986 World Cup and playing against England the following April. He spent most of 1991-92 at Scarborough, but suffered a dislocated shoulder. He later had a succession of appointments as a goalkeeping coach, joining his former Burnley and Bolton boss Owen Coyle in the US in 2015.

Christopher David (Chris) Thompson
1991-92
Born: Walsall 24.1.60   5'11"   12st2
Right back
FL Apps/Gls 0/0 Total Apps/Gls 2/0
Career: Bolton W. app, pro 7.77 [66+7/18], Lincoln C. loan 3.83 [5+1/-], Blackburn R. 8.83 [81+4/24], Wigan A. 7.86 [67+7/12], Blackpool 7.88 [27+12/8], Cardiff C. 3.90 to cs.90 [1+1/-], Walsall n/c 2.91 [3/-], Dale trial 8.91, Fleetwood 1991-92
Honours: England youth international 1978, Lancashire Cup winners 1983-84, final 1984-85, Isle of Man tournament final 1984-85

A teammate of Phil Hughes at Wigan, Chris was another player brought in for the 1991 Lancashire Cup ties (having played in two finals of the competition for Blackburn). He played in the No. 2 shirt, though he played most of his career up front. He was only a regular for Bolton in the second division in 1981-82 when he was top scorer with 14 goals from the left wing. However, he was a frequent performer for Blackburn as a striker, also topping their scoring charts, and for Wigan, where he appeared in a variety of roles. Sadly, he died at the age of only 52.

John Bernard Ryan 1991-94

Born: Failsworth 18.2.62
5'10"   11st7
Midfield
FL Apps/Gls 64+6/2 Total Apps/Gls 91+6/6
Career: St Peters GS, Oldham A. app 5.6.78, pro 19.2.80 [77/8], Newcastle U. 5.8.83 £235,000 [28/1], Sheffield W. 28.9.84 (£40,000 + P.Heard) [5+3/1], Oldham A. 24.8.85 £25,000 [20+3/-], Mansfield T. 28.10.87 £25,000 [53+9/1], Chesterfield 6.89 £12,500 [81+1/6], Dale 6.91 [64+6/2], Bury 1.94 [8+1/-], Stalybridge Celtic cs.94 [58+4/7 Conf], Radcliffe Borough 1996
Honours: England under-21 v Hungary 1983, Division 2 promotion 1984, Division 4 play-off final 1990

John came through the ranks at Oldham, replacing Ronnie Blair (q.v.) at left back in 1981 and missing only two games in 1982-83 when he also scored a remarkable eight goals and played for England under-21s. A big money move to Newcastle saw him team up with Keegan, Waddle and Beardsley in the side that won promotion to the top flight, but he was soon back at Oldham where he unfortunately suffered a double fracture of the leg in 1986. He arrived at Spotland at the start of Dave Sutton's first full season and though wearing his old No. 3 shirt was really employed on the right of midfield. (In Sutton's bizarre numbering scheme, actual left back Jimmy Graham was wearing No.7). 'Rhino' was a regular for over two seasons and was the subject of one of Sutton's famous pronouncements, that "every team needs a John Ryan", but nevertheless moved on to Bury after falling out of favour.

Alan Reeves 1991-95

Born: Birkenhead 19.11.67
6'0"   12st
Central defender
FL Apps/Gls 119+2/9 Total Apps/Gls 153+2/11
Career: Heswall 1984, Norwich C. 20.9.88, Gillingham loan 9.2.89 [18/-], Chester C. 18.8.89 £15,000 [31+9/2], Dale trial 1990-91, Dale 2.7.91 [119+2/9], Wimbledon 9.94 £300,000 [52+5/4], Swindon T. 23.6.98 to 2005 [190+18/12], coach, assistant manager to 2006, Brentford assistant manager to 4.07. Millwall scout, AFC Wimbledon under-21 coach 6.14*
Honours: West Cheshire League champions c.1987, PFA Division 3 team of the year 1994

Generally regarded as Rochdale's finest player of recent eras – indeed he was often referred to as "player of the year, every year", Alan had struggled to make much impression prior to joining Dale when he was 23. First used at right back, he soon switched to his best position of centre half as Dale narrowly missed out on the play-offs, and established himself as one of the best central defenders in the lower divisions. Soon after being chosen in the PFA Division 3 select XI in 1994, he was transferred to Premier League Wimbledon for a new club record of £300,000. He had a couple of seasons as a regular at the top level and then had a long spell with Swindon, playing over 200 times before a broken leg in 2005. Already on the coaching staff, he decided to retire from playing and was appointed assistant manager, later taking the same role at Brentford. His twin brother David also started out at Heswall (as did Alan's Dale teammate Steve Whitehall) and was a well-travelled striker with Bolton, Carlisle and Chesterfield amongst others (also figuring in the same 1993 PFA XI as Alan), while a cousin, Peter, played in Dale reserves in 1995. After working in sports management with his brother, Alan returned to the reincarnated AFC Wimbledon as coach.

Alexander (Alex) Jones 1991-92, 1992-94

Born: Blackburn 27.11.64
6'2" 12st8
Central defender
FL Apps/Gls 43+3/2
Total Apps/Gls 63+4/3
Career: Blackburn R. as, Oldham A. app 27.7.81, pro 2.12.82 [7+1/-], Stockport Co. loan 17.10.84 [3/-], Preston NE 3.7.86 [100+1/3], Carlisle U. 9.89 £40,000 [62+4/-], Dale 6.91 £20,000 [12+1/-], Motherwell 31.1.92 £40,000 [12/1 ScL], Dale loan 9.92, signed 11.92 £30,000 [31+2/2], Halifax T. 3.94 (exchange for J. Peake) [51/2 Conf], Stalybridge Celtic 1995-96 [27/2 Conf], Southport cs.96 [17/3 Conf], Lancaster C. 1997
Honours: Bury Boys, Division 4 promotion 1987, FA XI 1996

The son of George Jones, the well known Bury, Blackburn and Oldham centre forward of the 1960 and '70s, Alex also played for the Latics at the start of his career. He came to the fore after joining Preston, though, being everpresent in central defence (partnering Sam Allardyce) when they were promoted in 1987. Dale signed him for £20,000 in 1991 but with Reeves and Brown in central defence, he was allowed to join Motherwell half way through the season. However, in an injury crisis the following term he was re-signed and figured regularly in the second half of that season. Traded to Halifax when Jason Peake moved from the Shay, Alex continued at Conference level for several seasons, playing in an FA XI while at Stalybridge.

Mark Richard Crawford Payne 1991-93

Born: Cheltenham 3.8.60
5'9" 11st9
Midfield
FL Apps/Gls 58+4/8
Total Apps/Gls 72+7/9
Career: Bristol C. as, Bristol R. as, Bristol C. app 1977, Cheltenham T. 1978, Ledbury T., Cambuur Leeuwarden (Holland) cs.80 £7000, Stockport Co. 8.88 [77+10/16], (Holland summer 1989), Dale 5.91 (p/e for Peter Ward) [58+4/8], Chorley cs.93 [6/- Conf].
Offerton Green 1997-98
Honours: Division 4 promotion 1991

A postman while at Ledbury Town, unusually for an English player, Mark had his big chance in the Dutch Eerste Divisie, making over 200 appearances for Cambuur (where a teammate at one point was Everton star Andy King). Played initially up front and then in midfield "the postman from England" became a big favourite with the Dutch fans. He eventually returned to England in 1988 with Stockport, scoring nine times in their promotion campaign, and was then part of the deal that took Peter Ward from Spotland to Edgeley Park. A regular in midfield for a season and a half, he was sent off in his last game for Rochdale, while playing for the reserves. Also a keen golfer, he later played for Offerton in the Stockport Premier Division.

Andrew John (Andy) Flounders 1991-94

Born: Hull 13.12.63
5'11" 11.06
Striker
FL Apps/Gls 82+3/31 Total Apps/Goals 108+5/36
Career: Hull C. app, pro 24.12.81 [126+33/54], Scunthorpe U. 5.3.87 £30,000 [186+3/87], Dale 9.8.91 £80,000 [82+3/31], Rotherham U. loan 7.2.93 [6/2], Carlisle U. loan 30.10.93 [5/1], Carlisle U. loan 2.94 [1+2/-], Halifax T. 6.94 [9+8/1 Conf], Northampton T. 21.12.94 [2/-], Guandong (China) 3.95, Brigg T. 1995-96, North Ferriby U. 1996 to 1998, Goole T., County Road (Hull) c.2013
Honours: Division 4 promotion 1983, Division 3 promotion 1985, Associate Members Cup final 1984, FA Vase winners 1996, final 1997

Following the sale of Keith Welch, Dave Sutton had some money to spend and invested the largest part in Andy, who signed for £80,000, by far the largest fee ever paid by Dale. Hull's youngest ever debutant when he was 16, he played in two promotion campaigns for them, netting double figure goal tallies each time, and became one of the most prolific scorers in the fourth division at Scunthorpe. His first Dale campaign was equally successful with 19 goals in all games as Dale finished 8th. This included a famous hat-trick against Lincoln, completed by a 50 yard lob over the 'keeper. After Dale had previously turned down sizeable bids for him, he fell out of favour towards the end of his second season, but loan spells did not result in permanent transfers, even though Carlisle wanted to buy him, and his senior career faded out. He later went to play for Guandong along with another player with Dale connections, Neil Matthews. In 1996, he scored in the FA Vase semi-final to take Brigg Town to Wembley and played there again the following year for North Ferriby. He was still playing in the Hull veterans league in his fifties.

John William Halpin 1991-92

Born: Broxburn 15.11.61
5'10" 11st7
Winger
FL Apps/Gls 22+9/1
Total Apps/Gls 34+9/3
Career: Celtic BC, Armadale Thistle, Hibernian trial 1978, Celtic 9.78 [3+4/- ScL], South China (Hong Kong) loan, Sunderland loan 8.84, Carlisle U. 24.10.84 £10,000 [148+5/17], Dale 7.91 [23+9/2], Gretna cs.92, Carlisle U. Football in the Community 1992, coach 1997 to cs.99, Leeds U. scout, Carlisle U. Football in the Community 2004
Honours: Scottish youth international

John scored on his Celtic debut in a 4-0 cup victory over Queen of the South in 1982, but the majority of his senior experience came in seven seasons with Carlisle, despite breaking his leg in successive seasons and Carlisle twice suffering relegation in that time. He was a regular in the first half of his campaign at Spotland, usually playing on the left of midfield. He played for Gretna while also working for Football in the Community back at Carlisle (and playing for Carlisle Supporters Club against their Rochdale counterparts!) and later coached for the Cumbrians (at one stage assisting eccentric chairman Michael Knighton, when the latter appointed himself as manager). He returned to head the FITC programme at Brunton Park in 2004 and has also acted as the football analyst for Radio Cumbria.

Steven Christopher (Steve) Whitehall

1991-97
Born: Bromborough 8.12.66
5'9" 11st
Striker
FL Apps/Gls 212+26/75
Total Apps/Gls 262+35/95
Career: Willaston (Birkenhead Sunday League), Heswall 1986, Stork FC 1988, Southport 11.88, Tranmere R. trial, Sheffield U. trial 5.90, Dale 23.7.91 £25,000 [212+26/75], Mansfield T. 8.8.97 £25,000 [42+1/24], Oldham A. 10.7.98 £50,000 [55+21/13], Chester C. 9.00 [25+3/9 Conf], Nuneaton Borough 8.01 [10+6/6 Conf], Southport 11.01, Marine 7.03, Bamber Bridge 16.10.04, Northwich Victoria physio, Southport physio 9.06, caretaker manager 1.07
Honours: West Cheshire League champions 1988

Steve only started playing seriously in his last couple of years at school and played minor football while studying for a degree in Applied Biology at Liverpool Polytechnic. He was working as a civil servant when Dale signed him from Southport for £20,000, turning pro when he was 24. He contributed 12 goals in his first term as Dave Sutton's side challenged for promotion and in the following five seasons he was at least joint top league scorer each time. He netted 24 times in 1995-96 and notched 95 in total, easily the most since Reg Jenkins. Left out in the second half of 1996-97 by Graham Barrow, he moved to Mansfield where he had his best ever tally of 24 league goals, and then to Oldham. Back in non-league football, he gained another degree, in physiotherapy from Salford University, and then worked as a physio at Northwich and his old club Southport, temporarily managing them in 2007. His son Danny was a scholar at Spotland from 2012, scoring regularly in the junior teams before also having stints at Southport and Marine.

Kevin Charles Dearden 1991-92

Born: Luton 8.3.70
5'11" 12st8
Goalkeeper
FL Apps 2
Total Apps 2
Career: Tottenham H. yts, pro 5.8.88 [+1], Farnborough T. loan, Woking loan, Cambridge U. loan 9.3.89 [15], Hartlepool U. loan 31.8.89 [10], Oxford U. loan 14.12.89, Swindon T. loan 23.3.90 [1], Peterborough U. loan 24.8.90 [7], Hull C. loan 10.1.91 [3], Dale loan 16.8.91 to 9.91 [2], Birmingham C. loan 19.3.92 [15], Portsmouth loan 8.92, Brentford 30.9.93 [205], Barnet loan 2.99 [1], Huddersfield T. loan 11.3.99, Wrexham 6.99 [81], Torquay U. 8.01 [98+2], coach 2004-05, Boreham Wood 2.06, Brentford coach 7.06, Millwall coach 2006-07, Luton T. pt coach, Stevenage Borough pt coach, Leyton Orient pt coach 2007-08, goalkeeping coach and chief scout

6.08 (assistant caretaker-manager 1.09), Luton T. goalkeeping coach 12.14*
Honours: (Division 2 promotion 1990), (Division 4 promotion 1991), (Division 3 promotion 1992), Division 2+ play-off final 1997, Division 3+ promotion 1999, 2004, FAW Premier Cup winners 2001

Kevin was a professional at White Hart Lane for five years, during which time he made one appearance as substitute goalkeeper but had nine separate spells out on loan. One was at Spotland in 1991 when he played in the first two league games of the season, while during other loans he was with promoted clubs in three consecutive seasons. Eventually becoming a league regular when he joined Brentford, he played over 200 games including a Wembley appearance in the play-off final and promotion in 1999. His somewhat hefty build (he was over 14st by this point) earned him cult status and the nickname 'the flying pig' at Griffin Park. He also had several productive seasons at Wrexham and Torquay, winning promotion again with the latter before moving into coaching.

David Peter Williams 1991-92

Born: Liverpool 18.9.68
6'0" 12st
Goalkeeper
FL Apps 6 Total Apps 8
Career: Oldham A. yts, pro 15.8.87, Burnley 23.3.88 [24], Dale loan 2.9.91 to 10.91 [6], Crewe A. loan 1992, Cardiff C. 12.8.94 [82], Ebbw Vale cs.96, Stalybridge Celtic 1996-97 [20 Conf], Bangor C. 1997-98, Bangor C. 2000-01, Rhyl 2000-01, Caernarfon T. 2001-02, Rhyl 2002-03
Honours: Division 4 champions 1992, (Division 2+ promotion 1994), Lancashire Senior Cup winners 1992-93

David was Burnley's reserve goalkeeper when he joined Dale on loan and kept a clean sheet in a 1-0 defeat of his parent club. Indeed, Dale were unbeaten in his seven FL games, conceding only five goals, to challenge in the top six. Ironically, Dale's final match of the season, which they had to win to make the play-offs, was against newly crowned champions Burnley and David saved a penalty from Flounders in the Clarets' 3-1 win. He also saved a penalty in the Lancashire Cup Final the following term, but in 1993-94 was on the bench 46 times without making any appearances. He was, though, a regular at Cardiff for two years and then spent several seasons in the Welsh League.

Jonathan Lee (Jon) Bowden 1991-95

Born: Stockport 21.1.63
6'0" 11st7
Midfield/forward
FL Apps/Gls 73+33/17
Total Apps/Gls 92+35/19
Career: Goyt Bank Secondary, Grove U. (Hazel Grove), Oldham A. jnr, pro 22.1.80 [73+9/5], Port Vale 6.9.85 £10,000 [49+11/5], Wrexham 6.8.87 £12,500 [137+10/20], Dale 18.9.91 £10,000 [73+33/17], Oldham A. kit man and junior coach cs.95. Luton T. physio, Oldham A. assistant physio, Doncaster R. physio to 2.02
Honours: Stockport Schoolboys, Division 4 promotion 1986, Division 4 play-off final 1989, Welsh Cup final 1990

Jon was offered an apprenticeship at Spurs but decide to qualify as an electrician instead. He played a number of games for both Oldham and Port Vale, assisting the latter to promotion in 1986, but his most productive spell was four years at Wrexham. He played in the Welsh Cup final, and though Wrexham lost, winners Hereford were ineligible to represent Wales in the Cup Winners Cup and Wrexham made it through to the second round where they were defeated by Manchester United. Signed by Dale for a small fee, 'Jonny' became a huge favourite with the fans for his totally committed style. Used mainly in midfield, he was also a dangerous front man and even played central defence if needed. Oddly enough, though Dale just missed out on the play-offs in each of his first three seasons, his goal against York at the end of 1992-93 guaranteed promotion for his previous side Wrexham. Increasingly troubled by injuries, he retired in 1995 and got a job as Oldham's kit man while, like Steve Whitehall, he obtained a physiotherapy degree at Salford University. He was physio at Rochdale Hornets for a spell, as well as for several FL clubs.

Leigh Grenville Palin 1991-92

Born: Worcester 12.9.65
5'9" 10st3
Midfield
FL Apps/Gls 3/0
Total Apps/Gals 3/0
Career: Rushall Olympic, Aston Villa app 1982, pro 9.83, Shrewsbury T. loan 12.84 [2/-], Nottingham F. 11.85, Bradford C. 10.86 [65+6/10], Stoke C. 9.89 [17+2/3], Hull C. 3.90 [57/7], Dale loan 10.91 to

11.91 [3/-], Burnley 10.92 [1/-], Partick Thistle 1992-93 [5/- ScL], Halifax T. 1992-93, Tadcaster Albion, Walkington FC player-manager

Leigh was on the books of both Villa and Forest early in his career, but broke through at league level after joining Bradford City in Division 2. After losing his place in Hull's midfield following their relegation in 1991, he was loaned to Dale, but the move was not a success and only lasted 10 days. The following season he played for Partick in the Scottish Premier before dropping down to minor football. His father Grenville played for Walsall in the early sixties.

Stephen (Steve) Kinsey 1991-92
Born: Manchester 2.1.63 5'8" 10st7
Forward
FL Apps/Gls 3+3/1 Total Apps/Gls 4+4/1
Career: Manchester C. app 1.79, pro 1.80 to cs.86 [87+14/15], Chester loan 9.82 [3/1], Chesterfield loan 11.82 [3/-], Fort Lauderdale Strikers 1988 to 1990, Miami Freedom 1990, Tampa Bay Rowdies 1991, Dale n/c 10.91 to 11.91 [3+3/1], St Mirren 1991-92 [6/- ScL], Coleraine 1992, Fort Lauderdale Strikers 1992, Molde FK (Denmark) 1993, {Macclesfield T. 12.93?}. Richmond Kickers (USA) 3.96. Also Indoor Soccer for Minnesota Strikers 30.10.86, Los Angeles Lazers 10.88, Dallas Sidekicks 1989, Tacoma Stars 1990, Milwauke Wave 2.94, Detroit Neon 4.94, Tampa Bay Terror 1.96, Buffalo Blizzard 1997
Honours: England youth international 1981, 1982, Youth Cup final 1979, 1980, Division 2 promotion 1985, Full Members Cup final 1986

An England youth international and twice an FA Youth Cup finalist with City, Steve spent seven years at Maine Road and appeared in just over a hundred league games on the left flank or up front. His best season was 1984-85 when he started 33 games during City's promotion campaign, while he also scored in the remarkable 5-4 defeat by Chelsea in the Full Members Cup Final. In 1986 he went to play indoor soccer in the USA with Minnesota Strikers (scoring 63 goals in 99 games) and later played in parallel in the outdoor ASL at Fort Lauderdale. He had a brief interlude back in the UK in the winter of 1991-92, figuring with Dale, where he played mostly on the left wing, St Mirren and Coleraine, before returning to his successful US careers where he maintained a remarkable scoring rate in the various indoor leagues (e.g. 39 in only 28 games for Detroit Neon). Remaining living in Florida he ran a summer soccer camp.

Andrew William (Andy) Kilner 1991-92
Born: Bolton 11.10.66 6'0" 11st12
Winger
FL Apps/Gls 3/0 Total Apps/Gls 3/0
Career: Moorside HS, Burnley app 1983, pro 7.84 [2+3/-], IS Halmia (Sweden), Hyde U. 1986, Altrincham 1987 [18+7/3 Conf], Vanersborgs IF (Sweden)1989, Jonsereds IF (Sweden) 1990, Stockport Co. 12.90 [34+8/14], Dale loan 1.92 to 2.92 [3/-], Bury 8.92 [4+1/1], Witton Albion 1992-93 [4+1/1 Conf], Chorley 1993-94, Fredrikstaad FK (Denmark) 1994, Radcliffe Borough 1994, commercial manager 1996 to 1997. Bolton W. Football in the Community, Stockport Co. Football in the Community, Centre of Excellence director, manager 28.6.99 to 29.10.01, Sunderland scout 10.02 to 3.06. Cleveland Futbol Club (USA) coaching consultant 9.12
Cricket for Salford Schools, Lancashire under-15s, North of England Schools, Bradshaw CC
Honours: Salford Boys, England Schools (11 caps), England youth international 1984, Division 4 promotion 1991

A member of the England youth side that reached the semi-finals of the European championships, Andy was injured in an 'A' team match for Burnley on the morning before the game against West Germany. He later had a varied career, moving in and out of the FL and having numerous spells in Scandinavia. He scored 69 times in 108 Swedish league games before his only real run at league level at Stockport in 1990-91 when he scored 11 times in 21 starts on the left wing in the second half of their promotion campaign. Noted for his long throws, he was loaned briefly to Dale the following term, figuring on either flank, before resuming his travels. In 1999, he made a surprise transition from Centre of Excellence director to manager back at Stockport, later working in a variety of sports development roles and as an agent. Andy also played for the North of England Schools at cricket, as well as being a top class 200m runner, and continued to play cricket at a good level in the Bolton League.

Barry James Cowdrill 1991-92

Born: Birmingham 3.1.57 5'11" 11st4
Left back
FL Apps/Gls 15/1
Total Apps/Gls 15/1
Career: Sutton Coldfield T., West Bromwich A. 4.79 £5000 [127+4/-], Rotherham U. loan 10.85 [2/-], Bolton W. 7.88 [117+2/4], Dale loan 2.92, signed 3.92 [15/1],

Sutton Coldfield T. cs.92
Honours: Lancashire Senior Cup winners 1988-89, 1990-91, Sherpa Van Trophy winners 1989, Division 3 play-off final 1991

Barry had a long spell in the top flight with West Brom, though most of his appearances actually came after they were relegated in 1986. He was then a regular with Bolton for three years, figuring in both a play-off final and the Sherpa Van Trophy final, before joining Dale, initially on loan, for the run-in in 1991-92, when he replaced Jimmy Graham at left back. Not retained when Dale, after their excellent start, failed to make the play-offs, he returned to his original non-league club Sutton Coldfield (who coincidentally met Bolton in the Cup) and later played masters football with his old West Brom colleagues.

Carl Parker 1991-93

Born: Burnley 25.3.71
6'0" 12st
Midfield/left back
FL Apps/Gls 9+7/1
Total Apps/Gls 12+10/1
Career: Burnley yts 1987, Colne Dynamos 1989, Rossendale U. 1990, Dale 1.92 [9+7/1], Morecambe 1993, Haslingden, Padiham to 2004

Originally a YTS player at Burnley, Carl was recruited from Rossendale in 1992 and played a few games in midfield at the end of the season, scoring in the victory over Wrexham that gave Dale a chance of the play-offs with two games left, that they failed to take. He played a few games at left back the following season.

John Charles Stiles 1991-92

Born: Manchester 6.5.64
5'9" 10st12
Midfield
FL Apps/Gls 2+2/0
Total Apps/Gls 2+2/0
Career: Shamrock Rovers 1981, Vancouver Whitecaps 1983, Leeds U. 4.84 [49+16/2], Doncaster R. 8.89 £40,000 [88+1/2], Dale loan 26.3.92 to 4.92 [2+2/-], Gainsborough Trinity
Honours: Leinster Senior Cup winners 1982, Division 1 & 2 play-off final 1987

The son of World Cup winner Nobby and nephew of Leeds' Johnny Giles, John played for the latter at Shamrock Rovers, figuring for them in Europe. He was on the fringe of the Leeds team for several seasons, but did play in their FA Cup semi-final and unique 1987 play-offs, when Charlton beat Leeds in a replay to stay in Division 1, and figured regularly for two years after his former Leeds boss Billy Bremner signed him for Doncaster. With Dale suffering something of an injury crisis in March 1992, he was brought to Spotland on loan, but his debut ended in the 3-0 loss at Barnet that ultimately cost Dale a play-off place.

Mark Anthony Leonard 1991-93, 1996-99

Born: St Helens 27.9.62
5'11" 11st10
Forward
FL Apps/Gls 83+6/7
Total Apps/Gls 96+7/7
Career: Warrington T., Witton A. 1980, Everton 24.2.82, Tranmere R. loan 24.3.83 [6+1/-], Crewe A. 1.6.83 [51+3/15], Stockport Co. 13.2.85 [73/23], Bradford C. 22.9.86 £40,000 [120+37/29], Dale 27.3.92 £40,000 [9/1], Preston NE 13.8.92 £40,000 [19+3/1], Chester C. 13.8.93 [28+4/8], Wigan A. 15.9.94 [60+4/12], Dale 3.7.96 [74+6/6], retired injured 1999
Honours: England Schools, Division 3+ promotion 1994, Lancashire Senior Cup final 1995-96, 1998-99

Mark was a powerful front man who had a decent scoring rate with his other clubs but never hit it off in either of his spells with Dale. He accumulated considerable experience in the lower divisions with Crewe and Stockport, sometimes also playing in defence, and figured well over a hundred times for Bradford City in Division 2. With Dale in a strong position as transfer deadline day approached in 1992, Dave Sutton spent the hefty sum of £40,000 to bring him to Spotland to partner Andy Flounders, but sadly in the final nine games together they managed just one goal each and Dale failed to even make the play-offs. Dale recouped their money by selling him to Preston at the start of the following campaign and he subsequently played under Graham Barrow at both Chester, where they won promotion, and Wigan. In 1996 Barrow also recruited him for Rochdale and he played in various positions, including centre half, before retiring with a recurring back injury in 1999. Perhaps unexpectedly for a player of his style, his next sport was crown green bowls and he won the Merseyside Merit tournament in 2001.

Andrew John (Andy) Thackeray 1992-97

Born: Huddersfield 13.2.68
5'9" 11st
Right back
FL Apps/Gls 161+4/13
Total Apps/Gls 196+11/18
Career: Manchester C. as 1981, yts 1984, pro 15.2.86, Huddersfield T. 1.8.86 [2/-], Newport Co. 27.3.87 £5000 [53+1/4], Wrexham 20.7.88 £5000 [139+13/14], Dale 5.92 £15,000 [161+4/13], (Darlington trial 10.96), Halifax T. cs.97 [41/2 Conf, 37+1/5], Nuneaton Borough 1999 [120+6/11 Conf], Ashton United player-assistant manager 2003, Mossley 2.05, retired 11.06
Honours: Youth Cup winners 1986, Division 4 play-off final 1989, Auto Windscreens Shield Northern final 1995, Pontins Central League division 3 champions 1997, Conference champions 1998, Unibond Division 1 champions 2006

Andy was a member of the City team which beat United in the Youth Cup Final (though the FA refused to allow him to receive a winners trophy as he had been sent off in the first leg), but did not make the first team. Indeed, his first significant senior action was at Newport, where he was unable to help them avoid falling out of the league. Moving to Wrexham and gradually converting from a midfielder to right back, he was in their side which beat Arsenal in the 1992 FA Cup, thanks to Micky Thomas' famous goal. Despite him being the current player of the year, Wrexham then sold him to Dale and he became an automatic choice at right back for the next three years before suffering with a knee injury. He also weighed in with his share of goals, hitting eight in his first term including two braces against Bury, the first in bizarre circumstances when he was stuck in traffic and only arrived in time to be a second half substitute in the AutoGlass Trophy game. He is also remembered for the unfortunate decision, when skippering the side, to play against a howling gale in the first half of their AWS Northern Section final first leg at Carlisle, when Dale went in 3-0 down only for the wind to drop in the second half. When new boss Graham Barrow brought in Andy Fensome, Andy figured in some games in midfield or at left back but mainly skippered the reserves to Pontins League success. Despite the earlier problems, he was rated "probably the fittest man in football" after helping Halifax regain their league place, and he was Mossley's player of the year when they won the Unibond first division title when he was 38, eventually totalling around 750 appearances at various levels.

John (Jackie) Ashurst 1992-93
Born: Coatbridge 12.10.54 6'0" 12st4
Central defender
FL Apps/Gls 1/0 Total Apps/Gls 2/0
Career: Renton Juniors, Sunderland app 1969, pro 10.71 [129+11/4], Blackpool 10.79 £132,000 [53/3], Carlisle U. 8.81 £40,000, later player-coach [194/2], Leeds U. 7.86 £35,000 [88+1/1], Doncaster R. 10.88 £15,000 [73/1], Bridlington cs.90, Doncaster R. 11.90 to 1991-92 [66/1], Dale trial 8.92 to 9.82 [1/-], Frickley Ath., Carlisle U. Centre of Excellence coach
Honours: Division 2 champions 1976, (promotion 1980), Division 3 promotion 1982, Division 1 & 2 play-off final 1987

Jackie spent ten years at Sunderland and played regularly at centre back for three seasons during which they gained promotion to the top flight but immediately came back down again. He was everpresent when Carlisle won promotion in 1982 and accumulated around 200 games for them, latterly as player-coach, before missing only four games in two seasons at Leeds. At the end of his first term, he figured in the inaugural play-offs, when Charlton beat Leeds in a replay to remain in the top flight. Released by Doncaster in 1990, they quickly had a change of heart and he played for two further seasons. He had a brief trial at Spotland at the age of 38, playing his 616th FL game and a League Cup tie.

Andrew Paul (Andy) Howard 1992-94

Born: Southport 15.3.73
5'6" 10st2
Forward
FL Apps/Gls 4+16/3
Total Apps/Gls 7+18/3
Career: Liverpool as, yts 1989, Blackpool 9.91, Fleetwood 1991-92, Dale 7.92 [4+16/3], Fleetwood 1994

Andy made one substitute appearance in the FA Cup for Blackpool, but had the misfortune to have his one league game for them expunged when Aldershot resigned from the league. He made a string of substitute appearances for Dale early in 1992-93, making his full debut in the League Cup against Crewe in the absence of Jon Bowden. Perhaps hindered by his lack of inches, he remained on the fringe of the side for much of the season, generally playing out wide, but figured only from the bench in his second term, though he did score on his first appearance of the season.

Matthew Paul (Matt) McCormick 1992-94
Born: Rochdale 19.3.76
Winger
FL Apps/Gls +0/0 Total Apps/Gls +0/0
Career: St Cuthberts HS, Middleton NE u-16s, Dale as 1990, yts 1992 to 5.94
Honours: Rochdale Schools under-14s, under-15s

Local lad Matt joined Dale as a schoolboy, progressing to trainee status. With six of Dale's squad injured, he was named as the second substitute for the match at Shrewsbury in September 1992, but the 16 year old did not get on to the pitch in a narrow 2-1 win.

Antony M. (Tony) Beever 1991-94
Born: Huddersfield 18.9.74 6'0" 12st5
Midfield
FL Apps/Gls +1/0 Total Apps/Gls 1+1/0
Career: Colne Valley HS, Huddersfield T. jnr, Dale as 1990, yts 1991, pro 8.93 to 21.12.93 [+1/-]. {Brighouse T. 2001-02?}, (Golcar Con 2008-09; Huddersfield Sunday League)
Honours: Huddersfield Boys

Another trainee, Tony did come on when selected as substitute for the game against Doncaster in November 1992 and started the AutoGlass Trophy game at Bury when Jimmy Graham, Andy Flounders and Andy Thackeray were stuck in traffic, the latter replacing Tony when he arrived. A regular in the reserves, on one occasion deputising in goal, he was given a short professional contract in 1993 but made no further first team appearances apart from a pre-season friendly. Tony is said to have later played non-league football around his native Huddersfield, but details are lacking.

Richard Anthony Brown 1991-93
Born: Bury 2.5.75
Defender
FL Apps/Gls 0/0 Total Apps/Gls +0/0
Career: Siddal Moor HS, Dale yts 9.91 to 4.93, Bacup Borough, Mossley 1993-94, Sacred Heart 1994-95 (+ Seven Stars 1993 to at least 1996; Sunday League). {Castleton Gabriels 2003-04?} {Rochdale T. assistant manager 2011?}, FC United of Manchester youth team coach c.2012, reserve team assistant manager cs.13*
Honours: Rochdale Sunday League u-21s, Greater Manchester Inter-league Cup winners 1994

Like Tony Beever, Richard was drafted in when several Yorkshire based players were stuck in a traffic jam on the way to the Bury AutoGlass Trophy game, and was an unused substitute in what turned out to be his only first team involvement. After a spell at Mossley, where he played alongside his brother Dave, he appeared in local football, and while with Seven Stars represented the Rochdale Sunday League's under-21 side which won the Greater Manchester Cup. He was later on the coaching staff at FCUM

Steven (Steve) Mulrain 1992-94

Born: Lambeth 23.10.72
5'10" 11st7
Forward
FL Apps/Gls 3+5/2
Total Apps/Gls 4+5/2
Career: Leeds U. as 1988, yts 1989, pro 7.91, Charlton A. n/c, Dale 12.92 [3+5/2], retired 31.1.94. {Farsley Celtic?}
Honours: England Schools u-15s 1988

A member of the same England Schools side as Jamie Redknapp and Gary Flitcroft, playing against Brazil, Steve had yet to appear at senior level when signed by Dale. Scoring on his third appearance as substitute, he started in the next four games and looked to be a useful prospect when moved into midfield, but sadly suffered a badly broken foot in a freak training accident. He managed two more substitute appearances the following year plus a bizarre place on the bench as substitute goalkeeper when Dale forgot that one was required for FA Cup games. Shortly afterwards, he decided to give up football, though Dale retained his registration for 1994-95.

Timothy Joseph (Tim) Clarke 1992-93

Born: Stourbridge 19.9.68
6'3" 13st7
Goalkeeper
FL Apps 2
Total Apps 2
Career: Halesowen T., Coventry C. 22.10.90 £25,000, Huddersfield T. 28.7.91 £15,000 [70], Dale loan 12.2.93 to 3.93 [2], Altrincham loan [12 Conf], Halesowen T. 19.8.93, Shrewsbury T. 21.10.93 [30+1], Witton Albion cs.96, York C. 7.9.96 [17], Scunthorpe U. 21.2.97 [78], Kidderminster H. 10.99 [29+1 Conf, 25], Barry T. 7.01, Halesowen T. 2001, Evesham U. 2003, Weston-super-Mare, Bromsgrove R. 2005, Alvechurch 2006, Willenhall T. goalkeeping coach 2008, Halesowen T. goalkeeping coach, Evesham U. goalkeeping coach 2013, Hinkley T. goalkeeping coach 5.14*
Honours: Division 4 promotion 1999, Conference champions 2000

A very tall keeper, Tim joined Coventry from non-league Halesowen but only gained a league place at Huddersfield where he figured regularly when they finished third but lost in the play-offs. Dale borrowed him for a couple of games in 1993 when Kevin Rose, their only 'keeper, was injured, Dale picking up a win and a draw. Often the second string, he was next a regular at Scunthorpe and figured in both legs of the play-off semi-finals in 1999, but not the final at Wembley. The following year he figured in the Kidderminster side promoted to the FL. His most renowned exploits, though, were perhaps in a brief spell with Barry Town, when he helped the Welsh club reach the first round proper of the European Cup where they defeated Porto at home, though losing heavily on aggregate. He also had a long spell back in midlands non-league football before moving into coaching, and making emergency first team appearances when he was 45.

Trevor Snowden 1992-94

Born: Sunderland 4.10.73 5'8" 11st
Midfield
FL Apps/Gls 8+6/0
Total Apps/Gls 8+8/0
Career: Watford yts, Seaham Red Star, Dale 2.93 £3000 [8+6/-], (Aston Villa trial 2.93), Northwich Victoria loan 10.1.94 [7/3 Conf], Northwich Victoria cs.94 [9+1/1 Conf]

Talked up as the next Paul Gascoigne when Dave Sutton signed him from the north east – inspiring Dale fans to nickname him 'Snazza' – Trevor played a number of games in midfield in the absence of John Ryan towards the end of 1992-93. (He had had a trial at Villa after just two brief substitute appearances). He scored in a pre-season friendly against his former club Seaham, and hit a hat-trick of penalties in a reserve game, but only made it as far as the bench thereafter and soon moved on to Northwich Victoria.

Donald Richard (Don) Page 1992-93

Born: Manchester 18.1.64
5'10" 11st2
Striker
FL Apps/Gls 3+1/1
Total Apps/Gls 3+1/1
Career: (Altrincham Sunday League), Altrincham 1982 [12+14/4 Conf], Stafford R. cs.85 [14+2/4 Conf], Northwich Victoria 1985-86 [18+3/5 Conf], Runcorn 1986-87 [80+1/40 Conf], Wigan A. 23.3.89 [62+12/15], Altrincham loan 1989-90 [4/- Conf], Rotherham U. 16.8.91 [40+15/13], Dale loan 17.2.93 to 3.93 [3+1/1], Doncaster R. 17.11.93 [18+4/4], Chester 29.7.94 [22+8/5], Scarborough 4.8.95 [26+11/5], Northwich Victoria 1996-97 [+4/- Conf], Telford U. 1996-97 [10+1/1 Conf], Hyde U. 1998, Matlock T., Blyth Spartans
Honours: Division 4 promotion 1992

Don had an excellent scoring record at Runcorn, while they were in the Conference, with 40 goals in 80 games despite suffering a broken leg. He had played around 100 league games at Wigan and Rotherham, winning promotion in 1992, when he moved on loan to Dale, with Andy Flounders going the other way. He scored on his debut but Dale lost the next three games and the loanees returned to their respective clubs. Don had several shortish spells with other FL clubs before returning to the non-league game. His brother Fazial was also a non-league player with Mossley and Curzon Ashton amongst others before becoming Bolton's physio.

Noel Emmanuel Luke 1992-93
Born: Birmingham 28.12.64 5'11" 10st11
Forward
FL Apps/Gls 2+1/0 Total Apps/Gls 2+1/0
Career: West Bromwich A. app, pro 4.82 [8+1/1], Mansfield T. 7.84 [41+1/9], Peterborough U. 8.86 [270+7/27], Dale 25.3.93 to 12.4.93 [2+1/-], Boston U. 1993-94, Holbeach U. 1994-95, Corby T., King's Lynn, Raunds T.
Honours: Division 4 promotion 1986, 1991, Division 3 promotion 1992

Noel played a few first division games for West Brom and figured in Mansfield's promotion side in 1985-86, but spent most of his career at Peterborough. Originally a winger but later a midfield man, then right back, he missed only a handful of games in each of five consecutive seasons, winning successive promotions in 1991 and 1992. Though he had played a number of second division games that term, he was allowed to join Dale in March 1993, but like most of Dave Sutton's short term signings contributed relatively little to otherwise fairly successful sides. He pulled a hamstring after only half an hour of his debut and though he did figure in two more games, he was released after only a fortnight with the club. In 2013 Peterborough's fans voted him into fourth place in their list of favourite players of all time.

Martin John Hodge 1993-95

Born: Southport 4.2.59
6'2" 15st3
Goalkeeper
FL Apps 42
Total Apps 53+1
Career: Southport Trinity, Plymouth A. app 1975, pro 1.2.77 [43], Everton 1.7.79 £135,000 [25], Preston NE loan 13.12.81 [28], Oldham A. loan 22.7.82 [4], Gillingham loan 13.1.83 [4], Preston NE loan 27.2.83 [16], Sheffield W. 1.8.83 £50,000 [197], Leicester C. 31.8.88 £250,000 [75], Hartlepool U. 7.8.91 [69], Dale 12.7.93 [42], Plymouth A. 10.8.94 £10,000 [17], youth team coach 1995, Sheffield W. goalkeeping coach cs.96, reserve team coach, Dale goalkeeping coach 11.02, Leeds U. goalkeeping coach 7.04, Watford scout 10.06, Cardiff C. analyst 6.11*
Honours: Division 2 promotion 1984, PFA Division 3 team of the year 1994

A teammate of Dave Sutton at Plymouth, Martin was sold to Everton for a sizeable fee and made a number of first division appearances, before the arrival of Neville Southall resulted in Martin spending several spells out on loan. He made 214 consecutive appearances for Sheffield Wednesday, winning promotion to the top flight in his first season and being close to selection for the 1986 World Cup squad, missing out when Gary Bailey returned from injury. However he was injured in his first game for Leicester and though everpresent in his second season, later moved on to Hartlepool. Joining Dale in 1993, he was everpresent as Dale topped the table early on and again challenged for the play-off places, Martin earning a place in the PFA Select XI. When York fans called him "Sumo" (with reference to the Australian fast bowler Merv Hughes), he pulled up his shirt to show off his ample girth and was reported to the police for indecent exposure! He was transferred back to Plymouth at the start of the following campaign as he was also offered a position on the coaching side, later working as goalkeeping coach back at Hillsborough and with Lance Key at Dale. After working as a scout for Watford boss Malky Mackay, he moved with him to Cardiff as opposition analyst, also performing the same task for Wales.

Neil Peter Matthews 1993-95

Born: Manchester 2.12.67
6'0" 11st7
Defender
FL Apps/Gls 15+4/0
Total Apps/Gls 27+5/0
Career: Blackpool app 1984, pro 12.12.85 [67+9/1], Cardiff C. 8.90 £25,000 [48+4/1], Songdal (China) 5.92, Cardiff C. 4.12.92 [12+2/1], Dale 5.7.93 [15+4/-], Guandong (China) 3.95, {Macclesfield T.?}
Honours: Manchester Boys, N. Ireland youth international, N. Ireland u-23s 1989, u-21s 1990, N. Ireland 'B' 1994, Division 3+ champions 1993, Auto Windscreens Shield Northern Final 1995

Neil played at youth and under-21 level for N. Ireland while at Blackpool and then played for Cardiff, primarily at right back, either side of a short spell with Songdal in China. Back at Cardiff, he won promotion at the end of 1992-93 but then signed for Dale. Requirng a cartilage operation after just one game, he was generally reserve to Andy Thackeray at right back, though he did figure at centre half in the run to the Auto Windscreens Shield Northern Final in his second season, as Peter Valentine was cup tied. He also became the first Dale player to figure in a senior international game since World War I when he played for N. Ireland 'B' against Scotland 'B'. Signed up to play in China, again, along with Andy Flounders and Flounders' former Hull colleague Gary Swann, unfortunately both Neil and Swann were considered unfit and the English contingent were all sent home by the Chinese.

David (Dave) Lancaster 1993-94, 1995-97

Born: Preston 8.9.61
6'3" 14st
Centre forward
FL Apps/Gls 51+9/16
Total Apps/Gls 61+10/18
Career: Leyland Motors, Morecambe 1986-87, Colne Dynamos 1988, Blackpool 15.8.90 [7+1/1], Chesterfield loan 26.12.91 [12/4], Chesterfield 27.8.91 £20,000 [66+3/16], Dale 5.7.93 [37+3/14], Halifax T. 20.7.94 £7,500 [21+3/7 Conf], Bury 12.3.95 [4+6/1], Dale loan 3.96, signed 5.96

[14+6/2], Bamber Bridge loan 12.96, signed 3.97, Lancaster C. 1997-98
Honours: Lancashire ATS Trophy winners 1987, (Division 3+ promotion 1996)

Originally working as a tool maker at British Aerospace, Dave was a late comer to league football, signing for Blackpool when he was nearly 29, after scoring 66 goals in two seasons for the briefly upwardly mobile Colne Dynamos. A big old fashioned leader of the attack, he became more of a regular at Chesterfield – once netting a brace in a 4-4 draw with Liverpool in the League Cup - and then signed for Dale in 1993. He was joint top scorer with 16 in all games, including a brace against Hereford in September that put Dale top of the table and a hat-trick in the 6-2 defeat of Northampton. Sold to Halifax in the summer, but not properly replaced as Steve Whitehall's strike partner, 'Bomber' was re-signed in 1996, but did not recapture his goal scoring form. He played, appropriately, for Lancaster City with Dean Martin, Jimmy Graham and Alex Jones.

Mark Richard N. Stuart 1993-99

Born: Hammersmith 15.12.66
5'10" 11st3
Winger
FL Apps/Gls 166+36/41
Total Apps/Gls 202+42/47
Career: Queens Park R. as 1982, Hounslow, Charlton A. jnr, pro 3.7.84 [89+18/28], Plymouth A. 4.11.88 £150,000 [55+2/11], Ipswich T. loan 22.3.90 [5/2], Bradford C. 3.8.90 £90,000 [22+7/5], (Kuwait 10.92), Huddersfield T. 30.10.92 [9+6/3], Dale 5.7.93 [166+36/41], Chesterfield loan 4.8.95 to 1.9.95, Southport loan 2.99, signed 5.99 [63+5/11 Conf], Stalybridge Celtic cs.01, Guiseley 2001-02, Matlock 2005-06, Belper T. 2006-07, West Yorkshire Fire Service 2007
Honours: England schoolboys, Division 2 promotion 1986, Division 1 & 2 play-off winners 1987, Lancashire Cup final 1998-99

After playing for England Schools, Mark was offered an apprenticeship at QPR but stayed at school, studying accountancy and eventually signed pro for Charlton. He scored 12 times in their run to promotion in 1986 and managed nine in the top flight, including the winner at Old Trafford, ending the season playing in the only play-offs to allow a higher division side to maintain their status. He joined Plymouth for £150,000 and once netted four times in a reserve game for Huddersfield (which they lost 7-4!) but his career only really thrived again when he reached Spotland in 1993. Playing either on the wing, or sometimes as a striker, he was joint top scorer in his first campaign as Dave Sutton's side again challenged towards the top of the table, and after a move to Chesterfield fell through went on to net 41 league goals in just over 200 appearances over six seasons, many of them from his trade mark free kicks. In 1995 Londoner Stuart netted a brace in Dale's first ever victory in London, when they won 4-0 at Barnet. He was released to Southport by Graham Barrow on deadline day 1999, without anyone being informed. Joining the fire service, he played in non-league football until he was 40 and still continued to turn out for Charlton in masters football and for his fire brigade team, becoming a regular spectator back at Spotland.

Jamie Lee Taylor 1993-97

Born: Bury 11.1.77
5'6" 9st12
Forward
FL Apps/Gls 10+26/4
Total Apps/Gls 10+31/5
Career: Roach Dynamos, Darnhill Juniors, Manchester U. as, Oldham A. as, Blackburn R. as, Heywood St James, Dale as 1992, yts 1993, pro 1.94 [10+26/4], Altrincham cs.97, Bangor C. cs.98, Ramsbottom U. 10.01, {Heywood St James 2002 to 2004?}, Ramsbottom U. 9.07
Honours: {Manchester County Amateur Challenge Cup winners 2003}

A former associated schoolboy, Jamie became one of Dale's youngest senior players when he made his debut in a Lancashire Cup tie against Burnley aged 16 and a half. His next appearance was also against Burnley in the infamous battle of Turf Moor in the FA Cup, which ended with Jimmy Graham in hospital and three men sent off, perhaps not an ideal game for someone of Jamie's lightweight build. His first goal came in a 6-2 defeat of Northampton when he was still a week short of his 17th birthday, but his other league goals remarkably all came two seasons later in a hat-trick against Hartlepool. His single substitute appearance in 1996-97 proved to be his last senior game, despite winning the reserves' player of the year award for the second time. He was also Altrincham's player of the year the following season and while at Bangor played in Europe, in the Cup Winners Cup. {In 2003 he scored all five goals for Heywood St. James when they beat Salford Beechfield 5-4 in the Manchester Amateur Cup Final, the 'golden goal' winner coming in the 132nd minute.}

Darren Oliver 1993-95

Born: Liverpool 1.11.71
5'8" 10st5
Left back
FL Apps/Gls 22+6/0
Total Apps/Gls 25+6/0
Career: Everton as, Bolton W. yts 1988, pro 8.5.90 [3/-], Peterborough U. loan 4.10.93, Dale 8.10.93 £30,000 [22+6/-], Peterborough U. trial 23.3.95, Altrincham cs.95 [10+5/1 Conf], Barrow 1.96, Runcorn 1998-99, Winsford 1999-2000
Honours: Division 2+ promotion 1993

Darren had made a handful of appearances for Bolton when he joined Peterborough on loan and scored in the League Cup against Barnsley, before bizarrely being transferred to Dale for £30,000 after just four days. He immediately made his debut at Torquay, playing in midfield as Steve Doyle's car had broken down and he'd missed the team bus. Darren played fairly regularly for the next few months at left back but, displaced by Kevin Formby, his only run in the side the following term was ended by a suspension resulting from being sent off for handling a goalbound shot.

Paul Andrew Williams 1993-96

Born: Sheffield 8.9.63
6'3" 14st6
Striker
FL Apps/Gls 22+15/7
Total Apps/Gls 31+17/10
Career: Leeds U. jnr 1979, Distillery 1983-84, Arcadia Shepherds (South Africa) 1986, Grinaker Rovers (South Africa) 1986, Nuneaton Borough 1986-87 [4/2 Conf], Preston NE 18.12.86 [1/-], Carlisle U. trial 17.7.87, Newport Co. 12.8.87 [26/3], Sheffield U. 7.3.88 £17,000 [6+2/-], Hartlepool U. 10.10.89 £3000 [7+1/-], Stockport Co. 23.8.90 [24/15], West Bromwich A. 3.91 £250,000 [26+18/5], Coventry C. loan 10.92 [1+1/-], Stockport Co. 1.93 £25,000 [6+10/3], Dale loan 11.93 [3/2], Dale 2.94 [19+15/5], Chesterfield loan 18.1.96 to 9.2.96, Doncaster R. loan 28.3.96 [2+1/1], Altrincham cs.96 [5+2/- Conf], retired injured
Honours: N. Ireland youth international, N. Ireland v Faroe Islands 1991, Division 4 promotion 1987, (1991), Division 3 promotion 1989, Co. Antrim Shield winners 1985

Paul was with Leeds as a junior, actually playing against Dale in a friendly, but returned to Ireland to work as a coal miner and scored 22 goals in 110 games for Distillery. After a spell in South Africa he finally made his FL debut at Preston, deputising at centre back for Alex Jones, but did not figure significantly until joining Newport. Moved to play up front, he suddenly hit a purple patch while with Stockport in their promotion campaign of 1990-91. His 15 goals in 24 games induced West Brom to buy him for £250,000 and earned him a full cap for N. Ireland, albeit in a game where they could only draw with the Faroe Islands. He would have moved to first division Coventry after a loan spell, but West Brom refused to sell to their former manager Bobby Gould and Paul returned to Stockport, whose chairman was his father-in-law. He scored twice in three games on loan at Spotland in November 1993 and Dale signed him permanently the following February (apparently on much higher wages than normally offered), but he did not add to his goal tally. 'Willow' started the following season in decent form, though, with eight goals in all games by the beginning of October but did not figure significantly thereafter, being carried off unconscious on his final start in September 1995. Possibly his most memorable Dale performance came in similar circumstances when he volunteered to go in goal following Chris Clark's injury at Blackpool, on the grounds that he used to play Gaelic football! Uniquely (one would assume!) for a professional footballer, Paul's mother Betty won the Nobel peace prize as one of the organisers of the peace movement in Northern Ireland

Neil Dunford 1993-95

Born: Rochdale 18.7.67
Goalkeeper
FL Apps 2
Total Apps 3
Career: Castleton Gabriels c.8.91, (Sunday League), Dale n/c 8.93, pt 1994-95 [2], {Chorley?}. Castleton Gabriels 1998-99 (+ Milnrow 1995-96, Top House

1997-98, Alexander Drew 1998-99, Top House 1999-2000; Sunday League)
Honours: Rochdale Sunday League XI 1997-98, 1999-2000

A local brickie who was playing Sunday League football, Neil joined Dale for pre-season training in 1993, playing in two friendlies. He was Dale's first ever substitute 'keeper for a league game and the following season was a regular in the reserves and on the bench before making his league debut when Chris Clarke was out injured, immediately becoming a hero with a penalty save in a victory over Doncaster. He only played two further games though, and was next heard of playing centre forward for Milnrow back in Sunday football. He soon returned to playing in goal and represented the Rochdale Sunday League along with the likes of Top House teammates Jason Smart and Neil Mills for several seasons

Alan James Finley 1993-94
Born: Liverpool 10.12.67 6'3" 14st3
Central defender
FL Apps/Gls 1/0 Total Apps/Gls 1/0
Career: Marine, Shrewsbury T. 6.88 [60+3/2], Stockport Co. 8.90 [63+3/5], Carlisle U. loan 12.92 [1/-], Dale loan 30.12.93 to 1.94 [1/-], Runcorn 1994 to 1996 [48/2 Confl], Marine
Honours: Division 4 promotion 1991, AutoGlass Trophy final 1993

Alan had a couple of useful seasons at Shrewsbury, but was largely a reserve in four years at Stockport, though appearing a number of times when they were promoted in 1991, as stand-in for Bill Williams at centre back or Malcolm Brown at right back. He had possibly the shortest but most successful loan spell ever when he arrived at Spotland in an injury crisis among Dale defenders at the end of 1993. In his single appearance alongside Alan Reeves on New Year's Day Dale trounced Northampton 6-2. After finishing playing he was involved in youth coaching.

Gary Shelton 1993-94
Born: Nottingham 21.3.58 5'7" 11st2
Midfield
FL Apps/Gls 3/0 Total Apps/Gls 3/0
Career: Walsall app 1974, pro 1.3.76 [12+12/-], Aston Villa 18.1.78 £80,000 [24/7], Notts Co. loan 11.3.80 [8/-], Sheffield W. 25.3.82 £50k [195+3/18], Oxford U. 24.7.87 £150,000 [60+5/1], Bristol C. 24.8.89 [149+1/24], (caretaker manager 1992), Dale loan 11.2.94 to 3.94 [3/-], Chester 22.7.94, player-coach cs.95 [62+7/6], assistant manager 1998, coach 1999, West Bromwich A. coach 2000 to c.2006
Honours: England under-21 1985, Division 2 promotion 1984, Division 3 promotion 1990

Gary moved to first division Aston Villa for a sizeable fee after just a dozen starts for Walsall and scored against Spurs in his second game, later netting a hat-trick in a 5-1 defeat of Arsenal. A winger or midfield man, the bulk of his league appearances came, though, in long spells with Sheffield Wednesday and Bristol City. He missed only two games when Wednesday were promoted to the top flight in 1984 and was awarded an England under-21 cap as the permitted over-age player, also being chosen for a senior squad without getting a game. He appeared in the first division with Oxford before helping Bristol City gain promotion from the third tier. Already a highly experienced figure, he was made caretaker manager for a spell in 1992. Out of the first team picture in 1993-94 he had a month on loan at Spotland, figuring in the absence of Steve Doyle. Joining Chester, he soon became player-coach and then assistant manager. His son Andy was also at Chester, making his first league appearance two months after Gary's last, which came a month before his 40th birthday (though he remained registered as a player the following season). Gary subsequently coached at West Brom.

Jason William Peake 1993-96, 1998-00

Born: Leicester 29.9.71
5'11" 12st10
Midfield/left back
FL Apps/Gls 165+11/17
Total Apps/Gls 204+11/24
Career: Leicester C. as 1984, yts 1988, pro 9.1.90 [4+4/1], Hartlepool U. loan 13.2.92 [5+1/1], Newcastle U. trial, Halifax T. 26.8.92 [32+1/1, 27/6 Confl], Dale 23.3.94 (exchange for A. Jones) [91+4/6], Brighton & HA 7.96 £120,000 [27+3/1], Northampton T. trial cs.97, Bury 8.10.97 [3+3/-], Dale 19.6.98 [74+7/11], Plymouth A. 6.00 [7+3/2], Nuneaton Borough loan 12.00, signed 3.01 to 4.03 [57+4/4 Confl], Quorn
Honours: England Schoolboy international, Midland Youth Cup winners 1989, 1990, Lancashire Cup final 1998-99, Auto Windscreens Shield Northern final 2000

Starting out at Leicester, Jason moved to Halifax despite reported interest from Newcastle and West Brom. Though the Shaymen were relegated to the Conference, Jason did manage to score when they beat West Brom in the FA Cup, before being rescued by Dale. Soon proving himself one of their most naturally talented players, he figured regularly in midfield, or sometimes left back before asking for a transfer when Mick Docherty was sacked in the summer of 1996. Not particularly successful at Brighton, and even less so at Bury, Jason re-signed for Dale two years later and was still a regular when Dale just missed the play-offs in Steve Parkin's first season, scoring the goal of the season with a spectacular overhead kick against his old club Halifax. Again opting for a move, after a total of 215 Dale games, he joined Plymouth but was released after a change of manager, heading for Conference side Nuneaton.

Kevin Formby 1993-97

Born: Ormskirk 22.7.71
5'11" 12st
Left back/midfield
FL Apps/Gls 59+8/1 Total Apps/Gls 84+8/1
Career: Royal Marines, Exmouth T., Barrow 1.93, Burscough c.11.93, Peterborough U. trial, Burscough, Dale 24.3.94 £5000 [59+8/1], Southport cs.97 [71+14/4 Conf], Marine 2000 to 2002
Honours: Pontins League division 3 champions 1997, FA Trophy final 1998

Kevin spent five years in the Marines, playing for Exmouth Town when stationed at a nearby commando base. Originally a forward, he worked in a sports shop while playing for Barrow and was watched by several clubs when at Burscough, Dale coming in with a bid for him in March 1994. Surprisingly drafted into the side at left back he became a regular in that position until ruled out by injury in the second half of 1995-96. He rarely figured under Graham Barrow, instead winning the Pontins League division 3 title with the reserves, partnering his former first team colleague Andy Thackeray, though he did make some first team appearances in midfield. After only scoring one Dale goal, he scored on his second appearance for Southport and grabbed the winner in the FA Trophy semi-final, figuring in the final alongside Dave Thompson (q.v.). Kevin later became a competition standard darts player.

Mark Gordon Creighton 1993-95
Born: Sunderland 1976
Goalkeeper
FL Apps +0 Total Apps +0
Career: Manchester C. jnr 1987, Dale jnr 1993, n/c 1994-95

After having trials with England while with City, Mark figured in Dale's youth team and reserves for two seasons and was selected as substitute goalkeeper for half a dozen games at the end of 1993-94 as well as a couple of times the following season when usual reserve Neil Dunford was in goal. He then gave up the game to study for a degree in politics at Durham University.

Steven (Steve) Jordan 1993-94
Born: Brigg 1976
Goalkeeper
FL Apps +0 Total Apps +0
Career: Brigg GHS, Dale yts 10.93 to 5.94. Brigg T. c.2000 to 2002. {Bottesford T. 2008-09?}

Dale's YTS 'keeper, Steve was on the bench for Dale's 1-0 win at Mansfield in April 1994 but was not offered a professional contract. Earlier in the season, he had been injured during a reserve game against Manchester United 'B' which United eventually won 9-0. He played for his home town Brigg when they reached the first round of the FA Cup in 2001.

Christopher John (Chris) Clarke 1994-96

Born: Barnsley 1.5.74
6'1" 12st10
Goalkeeper
FL Apps 30
Total Apps 39+1
Career: Wolverhampton W. jnr, Bolton W. yts 1990, pro 13.7.92, Morecambe loan 1993-94, Chorley loan 1993-94, Dale 4.7.94 [30], Chorley cs.96, Barrow loan 3.98, Marine 1999 to 2002
Honours: England Youth squad 1992, Auto Windscreens Shield Northern final 1995, Unibond League v FA XI 2000

Chris played in Bolton reserves and trained with the England youth team while a YTS player and had offers of trials at Wimbledon, Motherwell and Dundee United before joining Dale in 1994. He made his debut in the Lancashire Cup victory over a Manchester United side which included the then unknown Beckham, Scholes and Neville, and after Martin Hodge opted to join Plymouth, Chris played in every game until suffering a serious head injury against Blackpool. He did return later in the season, and despite his comeback game in the reserves ending in an 8-2 defeat at Wrexham, he kept six clean sheets in the last 15 league games, also playing in the Northern Final of the Auto Windscreens Shield. However Ian Gray, who had been borrowed while Chris was out injured, was brought back permanently and Chris made only seven appearances in his second season, including the 7-0 FA Cup defeat at Liverpool. He played for Dave Sutton again at Chorley and was selected for the Unibond League representative side while with Marine.

Darren Thomas Ryan 1994-96

Born: Oswestry 3.7.72
5'10" 11st10
Forward
FL Apps/Gls 19+13/2
Total Apps/Gls 23+27/2
Career: Wolverhampton W. jnr, Shrewsbury T. yts 1988, pro 23.10.90 [3+1/-], Telford U. loan 1991-92 [1/- Conf], Chester C. 14.8.92 [5+12/2], Stockport Co. 25.1.93 [29+7/6], Dale 21.7.94 [19+13/2], Gillingham trial 20.2.96, Chester C. 3.96 [2+2/1], (Norway summer 1996), Barry T. 8.96, Total Network Solutions 1998, Merthyr Tydfil 1999, Newport Co. loan 2000, Newport Co. 2001-02, Carmarthen T. 2002-03, Haverfordwest County 2003-04, Cardiff Grange Quins, Newtown 2005, manager 10.06 to 8.10, Wolverhampton W. junior coach 2011, Airbus UK manager 3.11, Newtown manager 6.11, Northwich Victoria assistant manager 7.11, Airbus UK head coach 17.1.12, Wolverhampton W. academy coach 2013*
Honours: Shropshire Schools, Welsh Premier League champions 1997, 1998, Welsh Cup winners 1997

Darren played for a string of FL clubs but never really broke through at that level, his best spell being at Stockport. At Spotland he was the reserves' top scorer in 1994-95, with two hat-tricks to his name, and netted five against Scunthorpe Reserves the following season. He was used largely as a substitute for the first team, though he made a number of starts on the left flank at the end of his first season. He had more success with Barry Town, twice winning the Welsh Premier League and appearing in Europe when Barry became the first Welsh side to get through the two qualifying rounds of the UEFA Cup, only losing 6-4 on aggregate to Aberdeen. He also figured for numerous other Welsh clubs – playing with Steve O'Shaughnessy (q.v.) at TNS - and eventually became a manager at that level before becoming development lead coach at Wolves, where he had been a junior himself.

Alexander John (Alex) Russell 1994-98

Born: Crosby 17.3.73
5'9" 11st7
Midfield/right back
FL Apps/Gls 83+19/14
Total Apps/Gls 92+26/15
Career: Range HS (Formby), Liverpool as 1987, yts 1989, Torquay U. trial, Sheffield U. trial, Morecambe, Stockport Co., Morecambe 1992-93, Burscough 1993-94, Dale 11.7.94 £4000 [83+19/14], Glenavon loan 6.11.95 to 8.12.95, Cambridge U. 4.8.98 [72+9/9], Torquay U. 9.8.01 [152+1/21], Bristol C. 1.7.05 [42+14/6], Northampton T. loan 31.8.07 [11+2/1], Cheltenham T. loan 11.1.08 [12+1/2], Cheltenham T. 17.6.08 [19+4/2], Exeter C. loan 27.2.09 [7/-], Exeter C. 7.09 [27+2/1], Bath C. cs.10 [12/2 Conf], Yeovil T. 4.1.11 [2+12/-], Bath C. player-coach 7.11 [17+14/1 Conf], Clevedon T. cs.12 to 3.13, Bristol C. under-18s coach 3.9.12, Aylesbury U. 9.13, Tranmere R. coach 19.8.14 to 20.10.14, Oldham A. scout, Southport assistant manager 1.15*
Honours: Division 3+ promotion 1999, 2004, League 1 promotion 2007, (League 2 promotion 2009)

The son of Southport stalwart Alex snr, Alex played in Liverpool's youth team with Robbie Fowler and toured France with Sheffield United while on trial with them, but never figured at league level for either. Turning out for Burscough with Kevin Formby, he was voted player of the year after scoring 18 goals in 1993-94, four of them in a 9-3 victory over Nantwich. Following Formby to Spotland for a small fee, he only began to appear regularly in the FL in 1995-96 when replacing the injured Andy Thackeray at right back. He resumed his normal midfield role the following term and grabbed nine goals in the last three months of the season when pushed further forward. Released in 1998, he went on to win promotion with each of his next three league clubs, Cambridge, Torquay and Bristol City. Still playing in the FL at Yeovil in 2011, he finally announced his retirement in the week of his 40th birthday, in order to concentrate on his job coaching the youth sides back at Bristol City, but even then reappeared the following season. He was very briefly first team coach at Tranmere until a change of manager.

Derek Robert Hall   1994-96

Born: Ashton-under-Lyme 5.1.65 5'8" 12st3
Midfield
FL Apps/Gls 14+9/2
Total Apps/Gls 16+13/2
Career: Nova (Manchester), Coventry C. app 1981, pro 8.10.82 [1/-], Torquay U. loan 25.3.84 [10/2], Torquay U. 5.84 [45/4], Swindon T. 29.7.85 [9+1/-], Southend U. 21.8.86 [120+3/15], Halifax T. 25.7.89 [48+1/4], Hereford U. 18.7.91 [98+5/18], Dale 5.8.94 £10,000 [14+9/2], Altrincham loan 12.95 [3+1/- Conf], Hyde U. 6.96, Stalybridge Celtic, Curzon Ashton, Buxton player-manager 11.97, Milton, Woodley Sports assistant manager 10.99, Curzon Ashton player-coach 7.00, (Australia 6.02), Curzon Ashton assistant manager 10.05, Port Adelaide Lion (Australia) senior coach 2009*
Honours: Greater Manchester Schools, Division 4 champions 1986, promotion 1987

An experienced midfielder, who had first become a league regular at Torquay ten years earlier, Derek was the final one of just four summer signings by Dave Sutton in 1994. He had long spells at Southend, where he was signed by his former Torquay boss David Webb and won promotion in 1987, and then Hereford with his original Coventry manager John Sillett. In 1993 he scored the final goal against another former club, Halifax as they slipped out of the FL. He was the Bulls captain and player of the year in his last season there, but opted to join Dale. However, he was unable to make much impact in his two years and headed for non-league football, taking over as player-manager of Buxton from Wayne Goodison (q.v.) just over a year later. Derek had started out in Manchester junior football in the same Nova side as Paul Stewart (Blackpool, Spurs and England) and David Bardsley (Blackpool and QPR). He twice had stints in Australia, latterly coaching in the South Australian premier league and working as coaching director for the J & L Consulting Football (Soccer) Academy.

Owen Anthony Pickard   1994-95

Born: Barnstaple 18.11.69
5'10 11st3
Striker
FL Apps/Gls 0/0 Total Apps/Gls +1/0
Career: Plymouth A. yts, pro 7.88 [6+10/1], Hereford U. 7.92 [66+7/14], Dale trial 1.8.94, Dorchester T. 15.9.94, Yeovil T. cs.97 [63+5/27 Conf], Dorchester T. 1999, Bideford T. 2001 to 2004, Boca Seniors, Barnstaple T. manager 5.11.08 to cs.12

Owen had a couple of useful season at Hereford but when released had a trial at Spotland. He scored four times in two friendlies, against Bacup and Mossley, and came on as substitute in the Rose Bowl against Oldham, also figuring in the reserves. He scored 29 goals for Dorchester later in the season and totalled 72 for them before playing in the Conference with Yeovil. He later became manager of his local side, Barnstaple Town.

Stuart Alan Rimmer   1994-95

Born: Southport 12.10.64
5'7" 11st
Forward
FL Apps/Gls 3/0
Total Apps/Gls 3/0
Career: Everton app, pro 15.10.82 [3/-], Chester C. loan 17.1.85, signed £10,000 3.85 [110+4/67], Watford 18.3.88 £210,000 [10/1], Notts Co. 10.11.88 £200,000 [3+1/2], Walsall 2.2.89 £150,000 [85+3/31], Barnsley 5.3.91 £150,000 [10+5/1], Chester C. 15.8.91 £94,000 [213+33/67], Dale loan 29.8.94 to 15.9.94 [3/-], Preston NE loan 5.12.94 [+2/-], Marine 1998, Castleton Gabriels 2000
Cricket for Bedford Park (Southport)
Honours: England youth international 1982 (3 caps), FA Youth Cup final 1982, Division 4 promotion 1986, Division 3+ promotion 1994

An England youth international and Youth Cup finalist with Everton, after joining Chester Stuart scored a debut hat-trick and hit 21 goals in 23 games at the start of their promotion run in 1985-86, including four against Preston on his 21st birthday, before being injured. Rather small for a front man, two seasons later he scored 27 times, with a hat-trick just before expensive but unsuccessful moves to Watford and then Notts County. Regaining his scoring touch at Walsall, with a hat-trick in his second game, he returned to

Chester in 1991, taking his tally for the club to 134 goals in 360 FL games and playing in a second promotion campaign. In 1994 Dave Sutton had hoped to buy him, and took him on loan briefly, but in the end he continued at Chester until 1998. He did play in Rochdale again, with Castleton Gabriels and was also a club cricketer.

Matthew James (Matt) Dickins 1994-95
Born: Sheffield 3.9.70 6'4" 14st
Goalkeeper
FL Apps 4 Total Apps 5
Career: All Saints RC School (Sheffield), Sheffield U. yts, pro 1.7.89, Leyton O. loan 1989, Lincoln C. 27.2.91 [27], Blackburn R. 27.3.92 £250,000 [1], Blackpool loan 22.1.93 [19], Lincoln C. loan 19.11.93, Grimsby T. loan, Dale loan 14.10.94 to 7.11.94 [4], Stockport Co. 13.2.95 [12+1], Altrincham cs.96 [42 Conf], Boston U. loan 9.9.98 [3 Conf], Sheffield FC 1999-2000
Honours: Division 2 promotion 1992

Matt made a promising start to his career at Lincoln and after only a year was bought by Kenny Dalglish for Blackburn for £250,000. He played one game for Rovers when they were promoted in 1992, but in October 1994 arrived for an ill-fated loan spell at Spotland. He conceded four times in the first half of his debut and a total of 15 in four league games, sadly earning himself legendary status at Spotland for all the wrong reasons. He did resume his league career at Stockport and was everpresent for Altrincham in 1996-97 despite their relegation from the Conference.

Richard Sharpe 1994-95

Born: Wokingham 14.1.67
5'11" 11st7
Forward
FL Apps/Gls 9+7/2
Total Apps/Gls 15+8/3
Career: West Ham U. jnr, Leyton Orient jnr, Southend U. c.1984, (Sunday football), Florida Tech 1990 to 1993, Cocoa Expos (Orlando, USA) 1994, Dale 5.10.94 [9+7/2], Cocoa Expos (USA) 3.95, Colorado Rapids 3.96, Carolina Dynamos 2.97, retired injured. Indoor soccer for Cocoa Expos 1994.
Honours: NCAA Division II champions 1991. All American XI 1991, 1992. 1993.

Having been a junior at West Ham, Richard won a degree scholarship to Florida Institute of Technology in 1989 and became the record goalscorer in NCAA history with 49 goals in a season and 137 in his four year career, as well as being record 'points' scorer, including 'assists', and being selected for the All American XI three seasons in a row. (He has since been inducted into the Florida Tech Sports Hall of Fame). He netted 33 goals in just 15 games for Cocoa Expos in the US Indoor Soccer League, plus a hat-trick in the All Star game, before spending the winter with Dale. He made his debut in the AWS against Wigan in November and despite being sent off in Dave Sutton's last match in charge, was in the squad regularly, at least as substitute, until returning to the States the following March. He subsequently played Major League Soccer with Colorado Rapids and was a Camp America soccer coach.

David Anthony (Dave) Bayliss

1993-2002, 2005-06
Born: Liverpool 8.6.76
5'8" 11st
Defender
FL Apps/Gls 173+17/9 Total Apps/Gls 202+23/9
Career: Halewood CS, Speke T., Liverpool as, Chester C. as, Marine jnr, Dale yts 1993, pro 10.6.95 [169+17/9], Luton T. 7.12.01 [28+9/-], Chester C. loan 16.12.04 [9/-], Wrexham 11.7.05 [21+1/-], Dale loan 24.2.06 to 3.06 [4/-], Lancaster C. cs.06, Barrow 11.06, joint-manager 12.07, manager 2.12 to 5.11.13
Honours: Knowsley schoolboys, (Lancashire Cup final 1998-99), Auto Windscreens Shield Northern final 2000. Division 3+ promotion 2002. As manager; Conference North play-off winners 2008, FA Trophy winners 2010

Dave wrote to youth team boss Jimmy Robson for a trial at Spotland in 1992 and joined the staff as a YTS lad the following year, appearing in a pre-season friendly against Guiseley. He made his league debut in April 1995 against Barnet when Paul Butler was missing. Over the next five seasons he played in about half Dale's games, either in central defence, where he was remarkably successful considering his lack of height, or at full back. He finally become a fixture in the side at centre back under Steve Parkin in 2000-01 when Dale missed out on the play-offs on the final day. However, a falling out after Parkin's departure saw Dave also leave, joining promotion rivals Luton and being sent off when the two sides met. He did return to Spotland on loan in 2006, during Parkin's second spell in charge, before embarking on a stint at Barrow which saw him become joint manager and lead the side to promotion to the Conference in 2008 and victory in the FA Trophy Final two years later. He left after the club investigated 'an incident' between the manager and irate fans with Barrow struggling back in the Conference North in 2013.

Philip Andrew Shore 1994-96
Born: Rochdale 1978
Goalkeeper
FL Apps +0   Total Apps +0
Career: Oulder Hill School, Dale jnr 1993, Hull C. trial c.8.94, Dale yts 11.94 to 3.96

Initially with Dale in 1993-94, Philip also had a trial at Hull prior to his involvement in the first team at Spotland, when he was still 16, being named as substitute goalkeeper for the cup tie against Walsall the following November. He was subsequently used regularly in this role, and would have been allowed to appear for part of the final game of the season at Fulham only for Dale to be blitzed 5-0 and Mick Docherty thought better of throwing him in. He was still a member of the youth team in 1995-96 but by then Dale had two professional 'keepers in Gray and Clark. Philip would have been very familiar with Willbutts Lane, even before signing, as his father ran the Church Inn by the corner of the ground.

Ian James Gray 1994-95, 1995-97

Born: Manchester 25.2.75
6'2" 12st
Goalkeeper
FL Apps 78
Total Apps 97
Career: Oldham A. yts 1991, pro 16.7.93, Dale loan 18.11.94 to 2.95 [12], Dale 17.7.95 £20,000 [66], Stockport Co. 8.97 £200,000 [14+2], Rotherham U. cs.00 [38+2], Huddersfield T. cs.02 [29], retired injured 12.04
Honours: Division 2+ promotion 2001, Division 3+ promotion 2004

Brought in after Matt Dickins' spell, Ian kept a clean sheet on his debut and later conceded just one goal in a run of five league games, also helping Dale reach the Northern Final of the Auto Windscreens Shield, though his loan had ended before the games against Carlisle. In the summer, Mick Docherty persuaded Oldham to sell him for £20,000 and he was Dale's regular No. 1 for two seasons before a fee ten times that size took him to Stockport. However, by the time a tribunal had set the fee at £200,000, County's new boss had also bought Eric Nixon from Manchester City and Ian managed only a few games over the next three years. He had more chances at Rotherham and Huddersfield, winning promotion with both of them, but his career was ended by a broken hand during Huddersfield's run to the 2004 play-offs. While with Dale, he had been chosen for the Football League's under-21 side to face their Italian counterparts, but had to withdraw as Dale had a match the same night.

Peter Valentine 1994-96
Huddersfield 16.4.63 5'10"
12st
Centre half
FL Apps/Gls 49+1/2 Total Apps/Gls 58+1/2
Career: Huddersfield T. jnr, app 1979, pro 16.4.81 [19/1], Bolton W. 18.7.83 [66+2/1], Bury 23.7.85 [314+5/16], Carlisle U. 18.8.93 £10,000 [27+2/2], Dale 18.11.94 £15,000 [49+1/2], retired injured 4.96
Honours: Lancashire Senior Cup winners 1986-87, final 1992-93

Peter first joined Huddersfield as a member of their under-11 side and worked his way up to figure in their league side when he was 18. He became a regular after a move to Bolton in 1983 and then spent eight years at Gigg Lane, accumulating over 350 league and cup appearances. Brought to Spotland as a somewhat delayed replacement for Alan Reeves just before Dave Sutton – with whom he had played at Huddersfield – lost his job, Peter was first choice centre half until a succession of injuries forced him to retire. Mick Docherty wanted to add him to the coaching staff, but this fell through due to financial constraints.

Craig Whitington 1994-95
Born: Brighton 3.9.70 5'11" 12st4
Forward
FL Apps/Gls 1/0 Total Apps/Gls 1/0
Career: Worthing T., Crawley T. 1990, Scarborough 19.11.93 £50,000 [26+1/10], Huddersfield T. 12.8.94 £20,000 [1/-] contract cancelled 2.96, Dale loan 25.11.94 to 12.94 [1/-]. Crawley T. 1996-97, Rottingdean U. 1999. Whitehawk 2005, Brighton NE player and secretary 2007, Three Bridges 2008
Honours: Division 2+ promotion 1995, Brighton League division 2 champions 2008, JW Whittington Cup winners 2008, Brighton & Hove Cup winners 2008

After a possible move from non-league Crawley to Omonia Nicosia did not materialise, Craig had a useful first FL season playing up front for Scarborough to earn a move to Huddersfield in 1994. Soon afterwards he had the misfortune to arrive at Spotland on loan the week Dave Sutton was sacked, figuring in the home defeat by Hartlepool that sealed Sutton's fate. Reappearing with former club Crawley, with whom he had scored 72 goals in 173 games, he was out of the game through injury for a while before continuing in Sussex minor football, even helping create a new club. His father Eric played for Brighton and Crawley.

Dean Stacey Martin 1994-97

Born: Halifax 9.9.67
5'11" 11st10
Midfield
FL Apps/Gls 45+8/0
Total Apps/Gls 55+10/2
Career: (Huddersfield Sunday League), Halifax T. app 1984, pro 10.9.85 [149+4/7], Scunthorpe U. 8.7.91 [100+6/7], Halifax T. loan 17.10.94 [5+1/- Conf], Dale loan 13.1.95 to 17.2.95 [2+2/-], Dale 16.3.95 [43+6/-], Halifax T. loan 8.1.97 to 29.1.97 and 20.2.97 to 4.97 [17/2 Conf], Lancaster C. cs.97, Stalybridge Celtic 2.98 [11+1/- Conf], Bohemians 1998-99, Lancaster C. 2000-01, Bradford PA 4.02

Playing Sunday League football with the son of a Halifax scout, Dean joined the Shaymen as an apprentice and went on to appear over 150 times in the first team. He also made a century of appearances for Scunthorpe before being loaned to Dale in January 1995 when Mick Docherty was finally confirmed as Dave Sutton's successor. When Shaun Reid was ruled out for the rest of the season, Dean was signed permanently and was a regular in midfield the following term, famously scoring with a flying header against Darlington to earn the FA Cup visit to Liverpool. Only appearing in the Lancashire Cup ties in 1996-97, he returned to original club Halifax, now down in the Conference, and continued in the non-league game for several seasons

John Steele Deary 1994-97

Born: Ormskirk 18.10.62
5'10" 12st4
Midfield
FL Apps/Gls 90+1/10
Total Apps/Gls 107+1/15
Career: Everton as, Blackpool as, app 1978, pro 13.3.80 [285+18/43], Burnley 18.7.89 £30,000 [209+6/23], Dale 30.1.95 £25,000 [90+1/10], Southport 8.97 [13/4 Conf], retired 10.97

Honours: Division 4 promotion 1985, champions 1992, Division 2+ play-off winners 1994, Lancashire Senior Cup winners 1992-93

John worked his way through the junior sides at Blackpool, making his FL debut under Alan Ball. A midfielder with a good goalscoring record, he played well over 300 games, top scoring with 13 goals when Blackpool were promoted in 1985 and netting 53 in all. He then made 200 appearances for Burnley, helping them win the fourth division title in 1992 – playing in the final game win which denied Dale a play-off place – and then move up to the renamed Division 1 two years later. A colleague of Mick Docherty at both Blackpool and Burnley, he was Docherty's first permanent signing for Dale and scored the winner on his debut in February 1995. He was a regular in the Dale midfield for two and a half seasons, taking his overall tally to 609 FL games – and unusually trained to be a referee while still a FL player. After moving to Southport he suffered a suspected heart attack after a game and was forced to retire.

Graham Paul Shaw 1994-96

Born: Stoke 7.6.67
5'9" 11st5
Forward
FL Apps/Gls 13+9/0 Total Apps/Gls 17+13/1
Career: Newcastle T., Stoke C. app 1983, pro 10.6.85 [83+16/18], Preston NE 24.7.89 £70,000 [113+8/29], Stoke C. 12.8.92 £70,000 [23+13/5], Plymouth A. loan 8.94 [6/-], Dale 23.3.95 to 3.96 [13+9/-], Leek T. 1996. Stockport Co. chief executive 4.11 to 10.11
Honours: Youth Cup final 1984, Division 2+ promotion 1993

Graham played quite regularly for Stoke in the second division for four seasons as a slightly built but speedy forward. After three years at Preston, netting 17 goals in all in 1991-92, he returned to his home town (Tony Ellis (q.v.) moving the other way) to help the Potters regain their place in the second tier. He moved to Rochdale in March 1995 but, already suffering from back injuries, made little impact and disappeared from the scene the following January. He subsequently studied criminal law at Staffordshire University. He wrote a column in online magazine Total Football, reflecting the legal side of the game and was briefly the chief executive at Stockport.

Ian Philip Thompstone 1995-96

Born: Bury 17.1.71
6'0" 13st
Utility player
FL Apps/Gls
11+14/1
Total Apps/Gls
16+17/2
Career: Manchester C. yts 1987, pro 1.9.89 [+1/1], Oldham A. 25.5.90, Exeter C. 23.1.92 [15/3], Halifax T. 14.7.92 [31/9], Scunthorpe U. 25.3.93 £15,000 [47+13/8], Dale 28.7.95 [11+14/1], Bury trial cs.96, Scarborough 8.96 [12+7/2], Bury c.3.97, Atherton LR 4.97, Flixton 1997-98, Tottington U. 1997-98, Walshaw Sports am c.2001

Ian scored in his only City appearance, as substitute against Middlesbrough in April 1988, making him their youngest ever FL goal scorer. Though with both City and Oldham when they won promotion to the top flight, he did not play during either campaign. He did figure regularly at Halifax in 1992-93, netting a hat-trick from centre half against Northampton and then switching to centre forward. Transferred before their demotion to the Conference, he was still easily top scorer with nine goals, but at Scunthorpe he usually figured in midfield or at full back. Dale's only outfield signing in the summer of 1995, despite starting only 11 league games he played in all four roles, making him also a useful substitute. He was released by the board after Docherty was sacked.

Paul Anthony Joseph Moulden 1995-96

Born: Farnworth 6.9.67
5'8" 11st3
Striker
FL Apps/Gls 6+10/1
Total Apps/Gls 11+10/6
Career: Bolton Lads Club 1981-82, Manchester C. app 1983, pro 7.9.84 [48+16/18], Bournemouth 2.8.89 £160,000 [32/13], Oldham A. 23.3.90 £225,000 [17+21/4], Brighton & HA loan 14.8.92 [11/5], Birmingham C. 12.3.93 £150,000 [18+2/5], Huddersfield T. 23.3.95 [+2/-], Dale trial 23.8.95, signed 28.9.95 [6+10/1], Accrington St. 6.96, Bacup Borough 12.97, Castleton Gabriels 1999-00. Bolton Lads Club coach, Manchester C. academy coach 4.06 to 2009

Honours: England Schools (3 caps), England youth international, Youth Cup winners 1986, Division 2 promotion 1989, champions 1991, Division 2+ promotion 1995

The son of former Dale player Tony, Paul earned a place in the record books when he scored a phenomenal 340 goals in a season with Bolton Lads Club, 289 of them in 40 league games. Snapped up by Manchester City, he represented England at youth level, scored against Manchester United in the Youth Cup Final and was leading scorer for the reserves three times. Coming back from the first of three broken legs during his career, he top scored with 13 goals when City were promoted in 1989 but was then sold to Bournemouth as part of the deal taking Ian Bishop (q.v.) to Maine Road. Netting 13 times by March, he moved on to Oldham (while Bournemouth, 12th when he left, were relegated) and helped the Latics earn promotion to the top flight in 1991. Despite one further expensive move, his career rather petered out due to further injuries and a lack of games under Birmingham boss Barry Fry. He signed for Dale just after the start of the 1995-96 season and scored a hat-trick on his full debut in the Auto Windscreens Shield. A brace in the first round of the FA Cup gave him six goals in four games, but despite a few further starts, mainly in cup ties, he didn't add to his tally. Working his way around local minor football, he later coached his original Bolton junior team and then Manchester City's academy sides.

Jason Paul Hardy 1995-96

Born: Manchester 14.12.69 5'10" 11st4
Left back
FL Apps/Gls 5+2/0
Total Apps/Gls 5+2/0
Career: Burnley yts cs.86, pro 20.7.88 [38+5/1], Halifax T. loan 1.92 [+4/-], Halifax T. 1.7.92 [20+2/2, 8/- Conf], Prestwich Heys 1994-95, Bamber Bridge 1994-95, Dale trial 20.7.95, signed 24.8.95 [5+2/-], Salford C. 1996-97, Hyde U. 1998-99. Mossley cs.02
Honours: Division 4 champions 1992

Jason made one substitute appearance for Burnley while a YTS player and figured fairly frequently at left back, or sometimes left midfield, in his first two seasons after turning pro. Little used thereafter by the Clarets, he was in the same Halifax side as Ian Thompstone and after their relegation spent two seasons outside the league before being offered a trial at Spotland. Signed up as defensive cover, he played a handful of games at left back in the absence of Kevin Formby. He was one of ten members of Burnley's 1992 fourth division championship squad to turn out for Dale at some point.

Neil Nicholas Mitchell 1995-96

Born: Lytham 7.11.74
5'6" 10st
Midfield
FL Apps/Gls 3+1/0
Total Apps/Gls 3+1/0
Career: Blackpool yts 1991, pro 28.11.92 [39+28/8], Dale loan 8.12.95 to 1.96 [3+1/-], Southport loan 3.96 [8/4 Conf], Macclesfield T. 8.96 [19+7/4 Conf, 2+4/-], Hull C. trial 1.98, Morecambe 9.2.98 [2+4/- Conf], Chorley 8.99. (Bloomfield Veterans 7.04; Sunday League). Lytham St. Annes YMCA coach 2013*
Honours: Blackpool Schools, Lancashire Schools, England Schools under-15s 1989, England under-18s, Division 4 promotion 1992, Conference champions 1997, (Division 3+ promotion 1998)

An England schoolboy and under-18 international (figuring in the same side as Nicky Butt and Paul Scholes), Neil made his league debut as substitute a week before his 17th birthday and scored for Blackpool against Dale in the FA Cup a week after his 18th. He figured fairly frequently, albeit often from the subs bench, for a couple of seasons before being loaned to Dale. He played three times as a stand-in for Dale's more regular midfielders, his debut coming in Dale's only victory in 15 league games. He figured in the Macclesfield side which won promotion to the FL in 1997 but soon returned to non-league football, later turning out for a team of former Blackpool players in Sunday football while coaching junior sides.

James Richard Price 1994-97

Born: Preston 1.2.78
5'9" 11st
Left back
FL Apps/Gls 3/0
Total Apps/Gls 3/0
Career: Dale yts 1994-95, pro 3.96 [3/-], Chorley 1997-98, {Altrincham 1997-98?}, Radcliffe Borough 1999-2000 to at least 2003-04. Charnock Richard c.2009
Honours: NPL division 1 play-off winners 2003

James played in Dale's youth team in 1994-95 before breaking his leg. He reappeared in the reserves the following season and made three first team appearances at left back when Kevin Formby was injured in January 1996. Unfortunately suffering another fracture that March, he was given a professional contract but was only ever an unused substitute in 1996-97. He figured for Radcliffe Borough when they reached the first round proper of the FA Cup for the first time in 2000.

James Anthony Proctor 1995-96
Born: Doncaster 25.10.76 5'8" 10st5
Midfield
FL Apps/Gls 1+2/0 Total Apps/Gls 1+2/0
Career: Bradford C. yts 1993-94, Dale trial 9.95, signed 2.10.95 [1+2/-], Chorley cs.96, Guiseley 1997-98, Worcester Wildfire (USA) 1998, Boston Bulldogs (USA) 1999, Connecticutt Wolves (USA) 2000, Boston Bulldogs 2001, Weston Mass Pioneers (USA) 2002 to 2003, New Hampshire Phantoms (USA) 2004 to 2005; BB-N (Cambridge, USA) assistant coach 1999, New England Eagles (USA) coach 1999, Worcester Academy (USA) coach 2000*

James had been at Bradford City as a junior, but signed for Dale when they released him and he was unused substitute for the game in January 1996 in which fellow youngster James Price made his debut. His own chance came in three games in April all of which ended in defeat with Dale missing a whole string of senior players. He later emigrated to the USA where he had a much more successful career. As well as playing professionally, he simultaneously worked for the Soccer 101 Academy before becoming head soccer coach at Worcester Academy in Massachusetts while still in his mid twenties. He was also manager of his own soccer camps business.

Kevin William Pilkington 1995-96

Born: Hitchin 8.3.74
6'2" 13st
Goalkeeper
FL Apps 6 Total Apps 6
Career: Harrowby U., Manchester U. yts 1990, pro 6.7.92 [4+2], Dale loan 2.2.96 to 3.96 [6], Rotherham U. loan 22.1.97 [17], Celtic loan 1997-98, Port Vale 1.7.98 [23], Aberystwyth T. cs.00, Wigan A. trial 2.9.00, Mansfield T. 8.9.00 [167], Notts Co. 4.7.05 [141], Luton T. loan 12.11.09 [7 Conf], Luton T. 20.5.10 [15 Conf], Mansfield T.

loan 26.10.10 [10 Conf], (also Ilkeston T. goalkeeping coach 16.9.11), Notts Co. player/goalkeeping coach 20.2.12 [2+1]*
Honours: England Schools, Youth Cup winners 1992, Premier League champions 1996, Division 3+ promotion 2002, Division 3+ play-off final 2004

A member of the 1992 Youth Cup winning side with Beckham and Giggs, Kevin made a handful of appearances for Manchester United as understudy to Peter Schmeichel. He played six games on loan at Spotland when Ian Gray was injured, but Dale didn't win any of them. The following term he played three times as United won the Premier League title, but on the downside was in goal when they lost to York in the League Cup (after York had beaten Dale in the previous round). Most of his league games came in the lower divisions in lengthy spells with both Mansfield and Notts County during which he accumulated over 300 appearances, winning promotion with Mansfield in 2002. He kept a clean sheet in the play-off final two years later, only for the Stags to lose on penalties after a goalless draw. In 2009-10 he was limited to Notts' reserves, remarkably having to understudy Peter Schmeichel's son Kasper, and joined Luton in the Conference. After returning as County's goalkeeping coach he had to make occasional emergency appearances, appearing aginst Scunthorpe in 2015 just after his 41st birthday.

Lance William Key 1995-96, 1997-99

Born: Kettering 13.5.68
6'2" 14st6
Goalkeeper
FL Apps 33 Total Apps 37
Career: Histon 1984, Sheffield W. 14.4.90 £10,000, York C. loan 1991-92, Oldham A. loan 12.10.93 [2], Portadown loan 1994-95, Oxford U. loan 26.1.95 [6], Lincoln C. loan 11.8.95 [5], Hartlepool U. loan 15.12.95 [1], Dale loan 1.3.96 to 5.96 [14], Dundee U. 7.96 [4 ScL], Tranmere R. loan 1996-97, Sheffield U. 3.97, Blackburn R. trial cs.97, Dale 8.97 [19], Rushden & Diamonds trial 7.12.98, Northwich Victoria loan 18.12.98, signed 2.99 [69 Conf], Altrincham loan 1999-2000 [15 Conf], Kingstonian 6.01, Histon 9.04 player-coach, Wivenhoe T. 9.08, Rushden & Diamonds goalkeeping coach 7.10 to 5.11, Cambridge U. goalkeeping coach cs.12 to 6.13, Histon assistant manager 7.14*
Honours: England semi-pro international 2002-03, Southern League champions 2005, Conference South champions 2007

Lance was on the books of ten FL clubs, yet totalled only 51 league appearances, the majority of them for Dale. Although with Wednesday for six years, he was behind Woods, Turner and Pressman in the goalkeeping hierarchy and his league bow came for Oldham in the Premier League when they won 1-0 at Chelsea, Lance being voted man of the match. He did appear once for Wednesday, as substitute in an FA Cup tie when Pressman was sent off, but his first run of senior games came when on loan at Rochdale in 1996, his debut coinciding with a 2-1 win at Preston, Dale's first for 13 games. After a stint with Dundee, he went on a pre-season tour with Blackburn, but when Ian Gray was sold on the eve of the 1997-98 season, Lance was brought back to Spotland and played every game until the signing of Dale legend Neil Edwards. His only appearances in 1998-99 were in the Lancashire Cup and in an FA Cup tie against Rotherham, when Edwards arrived late for the kick-off, Lance keeping clean sheets each time. After spells in the Conference, Lance appeared well over 100 times for both Kingstonian – with whom he earned a call up to the England semi-professional side – and his original club Histon, who worked their way through the 'pyramid' to reach the Conference themselves in 2007. Lance later became goalkeeping coach at Rushden & Diamonds, but was reregistered as a player and turned out in a local cup tie when he was 42. Lance's brother Richard was also a goalkeeper with Exeter and Cambridge.

Francis Michael (Franny) Powell 1995-96
Born: Burnley 17.6.77 6'2" 12st
Forward
FL Apps/Gls +2/0 Total Apps/Gls +2/0
Career: {Dale jnr 1993?}, Burnley yts 1993-94, Dale n/c 9.95 [+2/-], Southport cs.96 to 1998 [+2/- Conf]. Kelbrook U. c.2007, Rossendale U. 2009-10, Colne U. 2010-11, {Kelbrook player-manager 2011?*}

Franny had been a YTS player (and unused substitute for the first team) at Burnley before signing for Dale when he was 18. Unfortunately injured playing for the reserves soon after arriving, he hit a hat-trick for them the following April, when he also made two substitute appearances for the first team in successive defeats at Colchester and Cambridge. He was then on Southport's books, playing in a friendly against Dale, but broke his leg in his first competitive game for them and was out of the game for 18 months. He was later a prolific scorer in minor football.

Paul Lyons 1995-97

Born: Leigh 24.6.77
5'8" 10st2
Left back
FL Apps/Gls 1+2/0
Total Apps/Gls 1+2/0
Career: Manchester U. yts 5.7.93, pro 1.8.94, Dale trial 2.7.95, n/c 9.95, pro 7.96 [1+2/-], Radcliffe Borough 12.96, Bacup Borugh 1998 to 2000. {Unsworth 2002-03?}

A former Manchester United YTS player, Paul joined Dale in September 1995 and made his debut at left back in a dire 4-0 defeat by Barnet when Dale were shorn of eleven potential first team players the following April. He was also substitute in the remaining five games of the season and signed a short term professional contract in the summer but was not included in the first team squad again.

Neil Keith Barlow 1994-97

Born: Bury 24.3.78
6'0" 12st
Defender
FL Apps/Gls 1+1/0
Total Apps/Gls 1+1/0
Career: Dale yts 1994-95, pro. 3.96 to 5.97 [1+1/-]. Baildon Trinity Athletic c.2001, player-manager 2002-03, committee 4.10*

Neil played in Dale's youth team in 1994-95 and figured in the reserves the following season, being drafted into the first team by Mick Docherty in April 1996, just after being offered a professional contract. After a useful substitute appearance against Cambridge, he started the next match against Barnet in the absence of all Dale's senior central defenders (he was partnered by midfielder Dean Martin) but gave away a goal after just 16 seconds and was carried off after a mistimed challenge five minutes later, the game ending in a 4-0 defeat. He reappeared in the reserves the following December but did not make the senior squad again. He later worked as a sports development officer for Bradford Council and had a long involvement with Baildon Trinity Athletic.

Andrew Brian (Andy) Fensome 1996-98

Born: Northampton 18.2.69
5'8" 11st2
Right back
FL Apps/Gls 80+2/0
Total Apps/Gls 92+2/0
Career: Rushton School, Norwich C. app 1985, pro 16.2.87, Newcastle U. loan 11.88, Bury T. 1989, Cambridge U. 21.11.89 [122+4/1], Preston NE 8.10.93 £7500 [93/1], Dale 3.7.96 [80+2/-], Barrow cs.98 [26+2/- Conf], Morecambe 1998-99 [114+5/- Conf], Lancaster C. 7.02. Preston NE junior coach, Barnsley coach, Hereford U. assistant manager 22.6.10 to 4.10.10, Accrington & Rossendale College girls coach, Preston NE academy coach 2012, youth team coach 2.13*
Honours: Division 4 play-off winners 1990, Division 3 champions 1991, Division 3+ play-off final 1994, champions 1996. As coach: Herefordshire Senior Cup winners 2010

Andy finished his first season as a league player with a successful appearance in the first play-off final to be played at Wembley and Cambridge followed this up by winning the third division title the following year. Following manager John Beck to Preston, he was everpresent and player of the year in 1994-95 but was released after North End won the (new) third division title. One of new Dale boss Graham Barrow's first signings in the summer of 1996, he was the regular right back for two seasons before a lengthy stint in the Conference. He later returned to Preston as a coach at their centre of excellence and worked as a summariser for radio Lancashire before a short lived spell as assistant manager at Hereford. He also worked for Disney Soccer Academy and Premier League Academies in the USA and ran the Preston North End football camp in Australia. He also played for North End veterans at both football and cricket.

Wayne Anthony Dowell 1996-97

Born: Durham 28.12.73
5'10" 12st6
Left back
FL Apps/Gls 6+1/0
Total Apps/Gls 8+1/0
Career: Burnley yts 1991, pro 27.3.93 [6/-], Witton Alb. loan 1993-94 [6/- Conf], Carlisle U. loan 29.3.96 [2+5/-], Dale 25.7.96 [6+1/-], Scunthorpe U. trial 1997, Doncaster R.

4.8.97 [1/-], Northwich Victoria 8.97 [+1/- Conf], Accrington St. 10.97, Barrow 3.99 [5+1/- Conf]. Colne FC 8.02
Honours: Durham County Schools

Wayne had played just a handful of league games before joining Dale, and though selected at left back in the Lancashire Cup ties he was then ruled out with a stress fracture of the shin. When he did make the league side, Dale did not concede a single goal in the four games that he completed, but he suffered concussion in the game at Brighton and a pulled hamstring against Orient and did not play subsequently. His Doncaster career was even shorter, Wayne being substituted after 30 minutes of the first game of the season and released the following week.

Andrew James (Andy) Farrell 1996-99

Born: Colchester 7.10.65
5'11" 12st
Midfield/defender
FL Apps/Gls 113+5/6
Total Apps/Gls 133+6/6
Career: Stanway Rovers, Colchester U. app 1982, pro 21.9.83 [98+7/5], Burnley 7.8.87 £13,000 [237+20/19], Wigan A. 22.9.94 £20,000 [51+3/1], Dale 3.7.96 [113+5/6], Morecambe 1.8.99 [30+1/- Conf], Leigh RMI 3.7.00 to 5.04 [61+4/- Conf]. Burnley junior coach, youth team coach 2011 (joint caretaker manager 2012)*
Honours: Division 4 champions 1992, Division 2+ play-off winners 1994, Sherpa Van Trophy final 1988, Lancashire Senior Cup winners 1992-93, final 1995-96, 1998-99

Andy first came into the Colchester defence just before turning pro and had just four league appearances to his credit when facing Manchester United in the League Cup. After around 100 games he joined Burnley and was a stalwart of their side alongside later Dale teammate John Deary in midfield. He figured over 330 times in seven seasons, including two Wembley finals, and helped the Clarets to the fourth division title in 1992. He played in every shirt number from 1 to 11, once deputising in goal for Chris Pearce (q.v.) when he was sent-off. His next stop was Wigan, where he played under Graham Barrow and Barrow quickly obtained his signature when he took over at Spotland. Initially used in midfield, he also figured at centre back, at left back and even wore the number 9 shirt for a spell. He spent three seasons as a regular for Dale but left when Barrow was sacked. Including the Conference, he played well over 600 senior games and was still at Leigh RMI when he was 38, subsequently working for Burnley's centre of excellence, briefly acting as joint caretaker-manager. Andy's daughter Emily won a football scholarship in the USA.

Keith John Hill 1996-2001

Born: Bolton 17.5.69
6'0" 12st6
Central defender
FL Apps/Gls 171+5/6
Total Apps/Gls 197+5/7
Career: Blackburn R. app 1985, pro 9.5.87 [89+7/4], Plymouth A. 23.9.92 [117+6/2], Dale 3.7.96 [171+5/6], Cheltenham T. 06.01 [2+3/-], Wrexham loan 10.01 [12/1], Morecambe 2002 [19+1/- Conf], Dale youth team coach 2004, manager 12.06, Barnsley manager 6.11 to 12.13, Dale manager 1.13*
Honours: Lancashire Cup winners (1987-88), 1989-90, Division 2 promotion 1992, Division 3+ promotion 1996, (2002). Auto Windscreens Shield Northern final 2000. As manager; League 2 promotion 2010, 2014

When Keith first arrived at Spotland in 1996, noone could have guessed the impact he would have over a decade later. He had captained Blackburn Rovers when only 19 and was a regular at centre back in the side promoted to the top flight under Kenny Dalglish in 1992, but figured just once as a substitute in the first Premier League season. After four seasons at Plymouth, appearing in the side that won promotion in 1996, he joined Dale and was virtually everpresent at centre half alongside Alan Johnson in his first season, missing games only through suspension following two red cards. A third dismissal came in controversial circumstances after just 20 seconds at Orient the following term, but Keith remained a regular throughout Graham Barrow's reign, often as one of three centre backs. He retained his place under Steve Parkin, but after 200 senior games was released along with defensive partner Mark Monington when Dale agonisingly missed out on the play-off places in 2001. After short playing stints elsewhere he returned to Spotland as youth team coach during Parkin's second spell in charge, also turning out for the reserves. In December 2006, Parkin and assistant Tony Ford were dismissed with Dale perilously close to the foot of the table after seven defeats in eight games and Keith was handed the job of caretaker-manager. After an unlucky defeat in his first game, his new charges amazingly won successive games 4-0, against Boston and away at Grimsby, and the chairman had no need to look further for the new boss! By the season's end, Dale had remarkably risen to 9th in the table and the following year, in their centenary season, Keith and former teammate Dave Flitcroft led them all the way to Wembley in the play-off final. Disappointment there, and again the following term when they lost in the play-off semi-final, failed to derail the "Hillcroft" revolution and in 2010, Keith became only the second Dale manager to win promotion. They followed this up by matching their previous best in the third tier, finishing ninth and claiming some notable scalps along the way including doing the double over promoted Southampton. The following summer, though, an on again off again saga ended with the managerial team following in the footsteps of their mentor Steve Parkin by taking over at Championship side Barnsley. However, when he was dismissed eighteen months later, with the Tykes in relegation trouble, Keith returned to Spotland and set about repairing the damage done in his absence. Putting together a new team, he remarkably fired them to promotion again, following up with an even better 8th place finish in League 1 in 2015.

Andrew Scott (Andy) Gouck 1996-98

Born: Blackpool 8.6.72
5'10" 12st12
Midfield
FL Apps/Goals 58+8/8
Total Apps/Gls 65+9/8
Career: Blackpool yts 1988, pro 4.7.90 [121+27/12], Dale 25.7.96 [58+8/8], Southport cs.98 [90+1/4 Conf], Morecambe cs.01 [28+14/4 Conf], Accrington St. 2.03 [20+6/5 Conf], Fleetwood 2004 (+ Bloomfield Veterans 7.06; Sunday League)
Honours: Lancashire Senior Cup winners 1993-94, 1994-95, 1995-96, Division 4 promotion 1992

Andy came through the ranks at Blackpool, having his first lengthy run in midfield during their promotion success in 1992, though he did not play in the play-off final itself. After four more seasons when he played about half their games – including three successive Lancashire Senior Cup Final victories - he moved to Dale. He figured regularly in their midfield for a couple of seasons, despite a hernia operation, and hit the winner when a nine-man Dale remarkably came back from a goal down to beat Doncaster. He then spent a number of seasons playing Conference football, scoring a tremendous goal for Accrington in a televised cup tie, before turning out for the Bloomfield Veterans side run by his father.

Michele Joseph (Mike) Cecere 1996-97

Born: Chester 4.1.68
6'0" 11st4
Striker
FL Apps/Gls 2+2/1
Total Apps/Gls 5+3/1
Career: Oldham A. app 28.11.84, pro 17.1.86 [35+17/8], Huddersfield T. 11.11.88 £100,000 [50+4/8], Stockport Co. loan 3.90 [+1/-], Walsall 23.8.90 £25,000 [92+20/32], Exeter C. 13.1.94 [34+9/11], Dale 8.96 to 12.96 [2+2/1]
Honours: Division 4 promotion 1989

With attention on the growing number of overseas players, in 1996 Dale managed to sign an Italian, even if he was born in Chester! A lanky central striker, Mike had started out at Oldham in Division 2, netting all the goals, as substitute, in a 3-0 defeat of Blackburn in May 1987. The following week, his late goal took the Latics' play-off against Leeds to extra time before they went down on away goals. He cost Huddersfield a six figure fee but, though never a fixture in the side, had better fortune in front of goal at Walsall, netting 16 times in 1992-93. His stay with Rochdale was brief, despite netting when coming on at Swansea on the opening day, his only starts coming in December before he gave up due to injury.

Kevin Gray 1996-97
Born: Manchester 5.4.78
Goalkeeper
FL Apps 0 Total Apps 1
Career: Stockport Co. yts 1994, Dale trial 1995-96, Dale 7.96, Caernarfon T. 1997-98

The brother of Dale's first choice 'keeper Ian, Kevin had a trial at Spotland towards the end of 1995-96 and was briefly signed up as his brother's understudy at the start of the following term. His one appearance came in a Lancashire Cup defeat at Morecambe.

Alan Keith Johnson 1996-2000

Born: Wigan 19.2.71
6'0" 14st
Central defender
FL Apps/Gls 59+3/4
Total Apps/Gls 69+3/5
Career: Wigan A. yts 1987, pro 1.4.89 [163+17/13], Lincoln C. 15.2.94 £60,000 [57+6/-], Preston NE loan 1.9.95 [2/-], Sing Tau Sports Club (Hong Kong) summer 1996, Dale 15.8.96 [59+3/4], retired injured 1999-2000. St Helens T.
Honours: Lancashire Cup final 1998-99

A hard man of a central defender, noted for his intimidating crewcut image, Alan was a cult figure at Spotland before injury terminated his career. After approaching 200 games in five years at Wigan, he had a shorter stint at Lincoln before heading off to play in Hong Kong. When he returned he phoned former Wigan colleague Joe Hinnegan at Spotland, and with the departure of trialist centre half Trevor Matthewson, Alan went straight into the side five days later. He went on to be everpresent and won the player of the year award but an injury in pre-season 1997 limited him to one appearance in the 'A' team until making a comeback during 1998-99. Injured again, he was retained for the following year, and after being on the bench, nearly got one last game but suffered a calf strain in training. Retiring with cruciate damage, he attempted a return with St Helens Town, but the knee gave way again.

Michael Anthony (Mickey) Brown 1996-97

Born: Birmingham 8.2.68 5'9" 11st12
Winger
FL Apps/Gls 5/0
Total Apps/Gls 5/0
Career: Shrewsbury T. app 1984, pro 11.2.86 [174+16/9], Bolton W. 15.8.91 £100,000 [27+6/3], Shrewsbury T. 23.12.92 £25,000 [66+1/11], Preston NE 30.11.94 £75,000 [11+5/1], Dale loan 13.9.96 to 10.96 [5/-], Shrewsbury T. loan 12.12.96, signed 10.1.97 £20,000 [111+50/16], Boston U. 7.01 [21+5/3 Confl], Chester C. cs.02 [6+17/- Conf], Nuneaton Borough 3.03 [10/2 Conf], Newtown 2003-04, Shawbury U. 9.07, Shrewsbury T. fitness coach 2009
Honours: (Division 2+ promotion 1993), Division 3+ champions 1994, 1996, Conference champions 2002

Mickey became a legend at Shrewsbury with three separate spells during which he figured in a club record 418 league games, and later returned to the New Meadow in the appropriate role - for a man who played until he was 40 - of fitness coach. A speedy winger, he assisted the Shrews to the (renamed) third division title in 1994, and after the second of his expensive moves away, repeated that at Preston, though he spent most of his spell at Deepdale sidelined with cartilage trouble. He figured briefly on loan at Spotland, replacing the veteran Dave Thompson on the right wing for five games, before Shrewsbury re-signed him. He later won the Conference title with Boston but did not appear in the league with them. Unsurprisngly, Mickey has been voted into Shrewsbury's Hall of Fame.

Peter Robert (Robbie) Painter 1996-99
Born: Wigan 26.1.71

5'11" 12st2
Striker
FL Apps/Gls 101+11/30
Total Apps/Gls 116+14/31
Career: Chester C. yts 1987, pro 1.7.88 [58+26/8], Maidstone U. 16.8.91 £30,000 [27+3/5], Burnley 27.3.92 £25,000 [16+10/2], Darlington 16.9.93 £25,000 [104+11/28], Dale loan 10.10.96, signed 1.11.96 £15,000 [101+11/30], Halifax T. 7.99 [46+12/8], Gateshead cs.01, Bradford PA cs.02, Ossett T. 2003, Emley 2004, Guiseley 8.05, Glasshoughton Welfare 2005
Honours: Lancashire Senior Cup winners 1992-93, final 1998-99, Division 4 champions 1992, Division 3+ play-off final 1996

Robbie (or Peter as he was then referred to) made his debut at 16 in November 1987. By 1989-90 he was figuring regularly in midfield for Chester, subsequently moving on to Maidstone during their brief tenure in the FL. Next joining Burnley, he helped them win Division 4, scoring the last ever goal in the division, before it was rebranded as the new Division 3, in the match that cost Dale their play-off place. Going up front regularly while at Darlington, he appeared at Wembley in a play-off final and was involved in the fastest ever red card, when an opposition goalkeeper brought him down after just 19 seconds. With Dale struggling for goals – just seven in the first 10 league games – he was brought in on loan in October 1996 and after netting four times in his first five games was unsurprisingly signed permanently a month later. The following term was his best and he was voted player of the year after missing just one game and scoring 17 league goals. He was not offered the new contract he wanted during 1998-99, though, and left at the end of the season. After a couple of seasons at Halifax, he had a lengthy stint in non-league football.

Mark Bailey 1996-99

Born: Stoke 12.8.76
5'9" 10st12
Midfield
FL Apps/Gls 49+18/1
Total Apps/Gls 57+20/1
Career: Stoke C. yts 1991, pro 12.7.94, Dale trial 8.96, signed 10.10.96 [49+18/1], Northwich Victoria trial cs.99, Winsford U. 8.99, Lancaster C. 11.99, Northwich Victoria 1.00 [50+11/4 Conf], Lincoln C. 10.01 [97+1/1], Macclesfield T. 7.04 [25+1/-], Peterborough U. trial 8.06, Stafford R. 9.06 to 5.07 [2/- Conf]
Honours: Clayton Schools, Staffordshire Boys, Midland Youth Cup winners, (Lancashire Cup final 1998-99), Division 3+ play-off final 2003

The son of 1970s Port Vale midfielder Terry, Mark was a member of the Stoke side that won the Midland Youth Cup and reached the quarter final of the FA Youth Cup, and played one pre-season game for them after turning pro. Following a couple of months' trial in the reserves, Mark signed for Dale and made his senior bow in December 1996 when he was preferred to Alex Russell in midfield for a number of games. A regular choice the following term until losing the right midfield slot to new signing Gary Jones, he figured in a variety of roles before his release in 1999. Returning to the league with Lincoln, by now as a right back, Mark scored in the play-off final for the Imps in 2003 and again in the semi-final the following term – remarkably matching the tally for the whole of his FL career. He again reached the play-offs with Macclesfield, coincidentally losing to Lincoln.

Glenn Alan Robson 1996-99

Born: Sunderland 25.9.77
5'11" 11st7
Forward
FL Apps/Gls +10/0 Total Apps/Gls +10/0
Career: Murton CW, Dale trial 9.96, signed 13.11.96 [+10/-], Harrogate T. 9.98, Spennymoor, Blyth Spartans cs.99, Durham C. 2002-03, Oldham A. trial 7.7.03, Darlington 30.7.03 [3+3/-], Durham C. 11.03, Morpeth T., Consett, Brandon U., Shildon, Stokesley loan 11.10, Newton Aycliffe, RCA Sunderland 12.11, Bedlington Terriers 7.12, Durham C. 8.8.14*
Honours: Pontins League division 3 champions 1997

Glenn was a trialist striker from the north east who eventually spent just over two years at Spotland. Figuring in the reserve side which won division 3 of the Pontins (Central) League, he made his FL bow in February 1997 (the only debutant in the second half of the season), but was restricted to a number of appearances from the bench. Top scorer (and player of the year) for the reserves the following term, albeit with just seven goals, he then moved to Harrogate where he netted 23 times in his first season. He scored 86 goals in 125 games with Blyth Spartans before linking up briefly with Darlington where he finally started three FL games in 2003, subsequently returning to a long spell with various clubs in the Northern League.

Lee Brendan Martin 1996-97
Born: Huddersfield 9.9.68 6'0" 13st
Goalkeeper
FL Apps +0 Total Apps +0
Career: Huddersfield T. yts 1985, pro 7.87 [54], Blackpool 7.92 [98], Bradford C. loan 1996, Dale n/c 11.96, Halifax T. 8.97 [32 Conf, 37], Macclesfield T. 7.99 [52+1], goalkeeping coach, Huddersfield T. 11.03, goalkeeping coach and physio 5.04 to 2008, Tranmere R. physio 2.10 to 6.10
Honours: England Schools, Lancashire Senior Cup winners 1993-94, 1994-95, 1995-96, Pontins League division 3 champions 1997, Conference champions 1998,

Lee was an experienced 'keeper, brought in as reserve to Ian Gray during 1996-97, but spent his time at Spotland entirely on the bench, though he did help the reserves win their league. He had made his league debut with Huddersfield in the second division in 1987 and appeared quite regularly with Blackpool (winning the Lancs Cup three times). After the Dale, he helped Halifax return to the FL before completing the circle back to Huddersfield. Having by this point obtained a physiotherapy degree from Salford University, he worked as the Terriers' goalkeeping coach and physio before assisting Tranmere's physio turned manager Les Parry and also running his own physiotherapy practice.

Andrew John (Andy) Barlow 1997-99

Born: Oldham 24.11.65
5'9" 11st1
Left back
FL Apps/Gls 60+7/1
Total Apps/Gls 64+8/1
Career: Hulme GS, Oldham A. as 3.11.82, pro 31.7.84 [245+16/5], Bradford C. loan 1.11.93 [2/-], Blackpool 13.7.95 [77+3/2], Dale 7.7.97 [60+7/1], Ramsbottom U. cs.99 (also Huddersfield T. academy coach 8.99), PFA regional coach 2.00
Honours: Division 2 champions 1991, Lancashire Senior Cup winners 1995-96, final 1996-97, (1998-99)

Andy was on Oldham's books while at grammar school and made his debut in midfield immediately after turning pro at 18, subsequently gaining a regular place at full back. In 1987 he figured at left back in the play-offs against Leeds and four years later he was everpresent when the Latics were promoted to the first division for the first time for 70 years. Less used in the top flight, he nevertheless had well over 250 league games to his credit, over 11 seasons, when he moved to Blackpool. After playing every game in 1996-97, he was signed by Dale and was the usual left back for much of the next two years. For the final game of 1998-99, after Graham Barrow was sacked, he helped select the team, playing on the left wing and scoring his only Dale goal in a draw at Brighton. Released by the board during the summer, he became a regional coach educator for the PFA and was also a PFA committee member.

Mark Colin Carter 1997-98

Born: Liverpool 17.12.60
5'9" 12st6
Striker
FL Apps/Gls 7+4/2
Total Apps/Gls 8+5/2
Career: Liverpool jnr, South Liverpool 1979, Bangor C. 7.81 [70+4/27 Conf], Runcorn 7.84 [249+6/145 Conf], Barnet 20.2.91 £40k [7+4/1 Conf, 62+20/30], Bury 10.9.93 £6000 [113+21/62], Dale 17.7.97 [7+4/2], Gateshead loan 13.11.97 to 9.2.98 [9/1 Conf], Ashton U. 6.98, Runcorn player-coach 1.99, player-manager 1999-2000, Radcliffe Borough 2.01, Glossop NE 9.01, Accrington St. scout (+Aintree Valentine over-40s; veterans league) Cricket for Bootle
Honours: FA Trophy final 1984, 1986, Gola League Championship Shield winners 1985, Conference champions 1991, Division 3+ promotion 1993, 1996, Division 3+ play-off final 1995, Division 2+ champions 1997, Lancashire Senior Cup final 1994-95, England semi-pro international (11 caps)

Mark, or Spike as he was nicknamed, was a legendary goalscorer at Conference level, netting 145 times in six and a half seasons for Runcorn, during which he played in his second FA Trophy Final and scored 41 goals in all games in 1986-87. Signed by Barry Fry as Barnet moved up to the FL he scored 19 times in his first season at that level and helped Barnet win promotion in his second. In January 1993, he was involved in a possibly unique occurrence when he and the other three substitutes all scored. Moving on to Bury he hit 50 goals in three seasons as Bury first reached the play-offs and then won promotion from the bottom division and Mark top scored as they immediately won the (new) second division title. Perhaps surprisingly allowed to leave at that point, he signed for Dale, but the move never worked out. Mark drifted back to the non-league game netting a total of 34 goals for Ashton United and his old club Runcorn in 1998-99. He played until he was 41, subsequently working as a press officer at both Liverpool and Everton and turning out for Aintree Valentine over-40s. He remains the England semi-pro international record goalscorer with 13 in 11 games.

Andrew Michael (Andy) Scott 1997-98

Born: Manchester 27.6.75
6'0" 12st11
Left back
FL Apps/Gls 1+2/0
Total Apps/Gls 1+2/0
Career: Blackburn R. jnr 1990, yts 1991, pro 4.1.93, Cardiff C. 9.8.94 [14+2/1], Pontypridd T. loan 1.12.95, Bath C. loan 29.3.96 [10/2 Conf], Merthyr Tydfil loan 21.9.96, Bath C. loan 30.12.96 [12/0 Conf], Dale trial 4.97, signed 8.8.97 [1+2/-], Leigh RMI 1998-99, Stalybridge Celtic 22.8.98 [17+3/- Conf], Southport 25.1.02 [19+15/- Conf], Lancaster C. 6.03, Kidsgrove Ath. cs.06, Altrincham 1.07 [6+1/- Conf], Hyde U. cs.07, Radcliffe Borough 26.8.07

Dale were low on numbers at the start of the 1997-98 season and signed Andy on the eve of the first league game, in which he made his debut as a late substitute. His only start, at left back in the absence of Andy Barlow, came in a home defeat by Orient the following January. His earlier FL experience at Cardiff had almost all come in the first three months of 1994-95, when he replaced another left back later with Dale, Damon Searle. Andy subsequently spent a decade in senior non-league football, generally playing in midfield.

Stephen Michael Bywater 1997-98

Born: Manchester 7.6.81
6'3" 12st10
Goalkeeper
FL Apps 0
Total Apps 1
Career: Collyhurst & Moston, Moston Juniors, Fletcher Moss, Dale jnr 1994, as 7.95, yts 5.97, West Ham U. loan 18.2.98, signed 7.6.98 £300,000 [57+2], Wycombe W. loan 23.9.99 [2], Hull C. loan 23.11.99 [4], Wolverhampton W. loan, Cardiff C. loan, Coventry C. loan 3.8.05 [14], Derby Co. 12.8.06 £225,000 [149+1], Ipswich T. loan 31.1.08 [17], Cardiff C. loan 4.3.11 [8], Sheffield W. loan 20.9.11, signed 1.1.12 [32], Millwall 24.6.13 [6+1], Gillingham loan 14.8.14 [13], Doncaster R. 16.1.15 to cs.15 [21]
Honours: England youth team in Norway summer 1996, England u-16s 1996-97 (5 caps), England u-17s, England u-21s (6 caps), FA Youth Cup winners 1999, Division 1+ play-off final 2004, Championship play-off winners 2005, 2007, League 1 promotion 2012

Stephen's great grandfather had been with Aston Villa and Stoke pre-war and grandfather Les was Dale's goalie in the late 1940s, while his father Dave was also a goalkeeper, playing for Halifax and Dale reserves before working as a coach at Spotland. Unsurprisingly, given that pedigree, Stephen was the 'keeper in the first ever Dale under-14s squad and figured in the 'A' team when still 14, but already 6'1" tall. He made his first team debut in the pre-season friendlies in August 1997 and after being substitute in several early season games, played his one senior game for Dale in a 6-1 Auto Windscreeens Shield defeat by Carlisle the following January, aged just 16 and a half. Already an England international in his age group, a first for a Dale player, he signed a pre-contract with West Ham, joining them officially, for £300,000 on his 17th birthday. He won a Youth Cup winners medal in his first season and continued to earn Dale further monies as he made his Premier League debut – for the last two minutes of a remarkable 5-4 victory over Bradford City when Hislop went off injured – and appeared for England under-21s. In 2005, he came on as sub when West Ham won their PL place back via the play-off final and after over 50 games for the Hammers – and several loan spells - he was again a Championship play-off winner with Derby two years later. He figured 150 times in the league for the Rams before winning promotion for a third time with Sheffield Wednesday. In 2015 Stephen played for his 13th FL club, Doncaster Rovers.

Craig Smith 1997-98

Born: Mansfield 2.8.76
6'1" 13st7
Forward
FL Apps/Gls 1+2/0
Total Apps/Gls 1+3/0
Career: Derby Co. yts 1993, pro 9.8.95, Dale loan 25.8.97 to 25.9.97 [1+2/-], Rushden & Diamonds loan 2.98 [1+1/- Conf], Burton A. 1998-99, Hinckley T. 2001-02

Craig was a professional with Derby for three seasons, but his only league appearances came in a short loan spell at Spotland at the start of the 1997-98 season. His debut as substitute was brief as he was then substituted himself. He started the following week, at home to Peterborough, but all three of his league appearances ended in defeats. After joining Burton he scored against his former club Derby in a friendly.

Nicholas John (Nick) Irwin 1995-98
Born: Salford 25.12.78
Defender
FL Apps/Gls +0/0 Total Apps/Gls +0/0
Career: Dale yts 6.95, n/c 28.4.97, pro 8.97, Loughborough University 1998, {Daisy Hill 8.09?}

Nick joined Dale when he was 16 and figured in the 'A' team and youth team from 1995-96. The youth team player of the year, he was an unused sub in a couple of pre-season games after turning pro in 1997 and was in the squad for three FL games, also without getting on. Though a regular in the reserves, his only first team appearance was as substitute in the friendly against Bolton for the opening of the new stand. He subsequently attended Loughborough University, where he played in a friendly against Aston Villa, marking Stan Collymore.

James Ian Cook Bryson 1997-99
Born: Kilmarnock 26.11.62
5'11" 12st12
Midfield
FL Apps/Gls 43+11/1 Total Apps/Gls 51+11/3
Career: Ayr U. BC, Hurlford U. 8.81, Kilmarnock pt 22.10.81 [194+21/40], Sheffield U. 24.8.88 £40,000 [138+17/36], Barnsley 12.8.93 £20,000 [16/3], Preston NE 29.11.93 £42,500 [141+10/19], Dale 21.7.97 [43+11/1], Bamber Bridge cs.99. Preston NE academy coach (+ AC Sporting (Preston); veterans league)
Honours: Division 3 promotion 1989, Division 2 promotion 1990, Division 3+ play-off final 1994, Division 3+ champions 1996, Lancashire Senior Cup winners 1996-97

Graham Barrow's third experienced signing in the summer of 1997, Ian actually missed the first couple of months of the season through injury. He had originally spent seven years at Kilmarnock, scoring a penalty on his debut as an 18 year old and appearing well over 200 times before heading for Sheffield United in 1988. Proving a bargain at £40,000, he was a regular member of the side which won successive promotions, missing only a handful of games and chipping in with his share of goals from the left wing. He played in the top flight for three seasons, indeed he scored twice in a 6-0 thrashing of Spurs, and later had a long run in the side at Preston where he appeared in over 150 games. He scored a spectacular overhead kick in the 1994 play-off final defeat at Wembley and was in their third division championship winning side two years later. His second term with Dale was more productive than his first and he figured regularly in midfield, taking his overall tally to 591 FL and Scottish League appearances and 99 goals. As senior pro he helped David Hamilton organise the side for the final game of the season after Graham Barrow's departure, but left in the summer. Ian later became an academy coach back at Deepdale and played in veterans' football, as well as commentating for Radio Lancashire and working for Sky's Football First.

Graham Lancashire 1997-2001

Born: Blackpool 19.10.72
5'10" 11st12
Striker
FL Apps/Gls 54+29/23
Total Apps/Gls 62+34/28
Career: Accrington & Rossendale College, St. George's HS, Burnley yts 1989, pro 1.7.91 [11+20/8], Halifax T. loan 20.11.92 [2/-], Chester C. loan 21.1.94 [10+1/7], Preston NE 23.12.94 £55,000 [11+12/2], Wigan A. loan 12.1.96 [4/3], Wigan A. 8.3.96 £35,000 [16+10/9], Dale 2.10.97 £40,000 [54+29/23], Hednesford T. cs.01 to 2003. Burnley junior coach c.2009, academy operations manager 1.12*
Honours: Blackpool & District Schools, Lancashire Schools, Division 4 champions 1992, Division 2+ promotion 1994, (Division 3+ promotion 1994), Division 3+ champions (1996), 1997, Lancashire Cup final 1998-99, Auto Windscreens Shield Northern final 2000.

Graham was a noted lower league goalscorer who unfortunately spent more time injured than playing, not least at Spotland where he started only 54 league games in four seasons yet netted 23 goals. He scored eight goals in seven games for Burnley early in their 1991-92 promotion winning season, including a hat-trick against Wrexham on only his third start. Two years later he was promoted twice, seven goals during a loan spell at Chester significantly aiding their cause before he returned to Turf Moor in time to be unused substitute in their play-off final. He was in a championship winning side again in both 1996 and 1997, though making only a handful of appearances each time. Dale risked £40,000 to acquire him a few months later, and he maintained his excellent strike rate while starting as many games as he had for all his previous clubs, though when he retired he had still only managed 180 games (with 52 goals) spread over ten years. He worked organising football events as well as coaching juniors at Burnley before becoming operations manager at their academy.

Neil Ryan Edwards 1997-2005

Born: Aberdare 5.12.70
5'9" 11st10
Goalkeeper
FL Apps 239
Total Apps 280+1
Career: Leeds U. as 1983, yts 1987, pro 10.3.89, Huddersfield T. loan 17.8.90 and 3.1.91, Shelbourne loan, Stockport Co. 3.9.91 £5000 [163+1], Dale 3.11.97 £25,000 [239], Bury 5.7.05 [24], retired injured 2006. Carlisle U. goalkeeping coach 2006, Bolton W. goalkeeping coach 2007, Wales under-19s goalkeeping coach, Liverpool under-18s goalkeeping coach 2012*
Honours: Mid-Glamorgan Schools, Wales under-15, under-16, under-18, Division 3 play-off final 1992, (Division 2+ promotion 1997), AutoGlass Trophy final 1992, 1993, Lancashire Cup final 1998-99, Auto Windscreens Shield Northern final 2000.

Widely regarded as one of Dale's finest ever goalkeepers, Neil trained with Leeds from the age of 12 and represented Wales at several age groups, eventually making one senior appearance for Leeds in the Zenith Data Systems Cup. Missing playing for Wales under-21s because of a broken ankle in training, he joined Stockport for a small fee in 1991 and, taking over from Dave Redfern (q.v.), ended his first season with Wembley appearances in both the play-off and AutoGlass Trophy finals, repeating the latter the following year. He lost his place to fellow Welshman Paul

Jones in 1996 and a year later joined Dale for £25,000. Immediately becoming a huge favourite with the fans, 'Taffy' made light of his oft-reported lack of inches and remained Dale's regular stopper until injuries cost him most of the 2001-02 season, though he returned in time to figure in Dale's first ever play-off campaign. Continuing for three further seasons he was eventually overtaken as first choice by his protégé Matt Gilks and had one last, injury interrupted season at Bury before turning to coaching. Well known for his varying hair styles, Neil was also Dale's club captain for some time and ended with a record tally for a Dale goalkeeper of 281 appearances, surpassing Mike Poole and Keith Welch. The substitute appearance came when he missed the start of a cup tie and took over from Lance Key when he finally arrived at the ground.

John Patrick Pender 1997-99

Born: Luton 19.11.63
6'0" 13st12
Central defender
FL Apps/Gls 14/0
Total Apps/Gls 16+1/0
Career: Wolverhampton W. app 1980, pro 8.11.81 [115+2/3], Charlton A. 23.7.85 £35,000 [41/-], Bristol C. 30.10.87 £50,000 [83/3], Burnley 18.10.90 £70,000 [171/8], Wigan A. 22.8.95 £30,000 [67+3/1], Dale 22.7.97 £11,500 [14/-], retired injured 10.98
Honours: Irish youth international, Republic of Ireland under-21s (5 caps), Division 2 promotion 1983, 1986, Division 2/3 play-off final 1988, Division 3 promotion 1990, Division 4 champions 1992, Division 2+ play-off winners 1994, Division 3+ champions 1997, Lancashire Senior Cup winners 1992-93

A well built central defender, John gave good service to a number of league clubs over a 17 year career. He played over 100 times for Wolves as they bounced up and down between the first and second divisions in the early '80s, also helped Charlton gain a place in the top flight and though playing only in the first 10 games, was involved in another promotion at Bristol City. The most expensive move of his career took him to Burnley in 1990. He was an automatic choice for four years, gaining further promotions as skipper of the Clarets as they moved up from Division 4 to the renamed Division 1. Arriving at Spotland for a sizeable fee by Dale standards in 1997, after yet another promotion (the sixth of his career) with Wigan, he was injured pre-season and only made his debut in November. Injured again the following February, he was forced to retire with a damaged knee, like his intended central defensive partner Alan Johnson.

Adam Maurice Reed 1997-98

Born: Bishop Auckland 18.2.75
6'0" 12st
Central defender
FL Apps/Gls 10/0
Total Apps/Gls 12/1
Career: Darlington yts 1991, pro 16.7.93 [45+7/1], Blackburn R. 9.8.95 £200,000, Darlington loan 21.2.97 [14/-], Dale loan 5.12.97 to 4.2.98 [10/-], Darlington 7.98 [80+14/2], York C. trial cs.03, Harrogate T. trial cs.03, Whitby T. 15.8.03. Middlesbrough academy physio*

Adam made his mark as a promising teenager at Darlington, inducing Blackburn to splash £200,000 on him. However, he never made their first division side and with Dale missing three of their regular defenders, they took him on loan midway through 1997-98. He played regularly, partnering John Pender in central defence before Keith Hill returned to the side. He subsequently re-signed for Darlington but in five years was never an automatic choice, though he had two or three lengthy spells in the side. He then obtained a degree in physiotherapy and subsequently worked at Middlesbrough.

Graeme Atkinson 1997-98, 1999-2002

Born: Hull 11.11.71
5'8" 11st3
Outside left/left back
FL Apps/Gls 45+12/5
Total Apps/Gls 54+14/6
Career: Hull C. yts 1988, pro 6.5.90 [129+20/23], Porirua Viard U. (NZ) loan summer 1990, Preston NE 7.10.94 £80,000 [63+16/6], Dale loan 12.12.98 to 12.1.98 [5+1/-], Brighton & HA 5.3.98 [16/-], Scunthorpe U. 2.11.98 [+1/-], Scarborough 18.2.99 [15/1], Dale 1.7.99 [40+11/5], Lancaster C. cs.02, Tamworth 2.03, Spennymoor, Southport 8.03 to 10.03, Preston NE academy coach, Myerscough College coach 9.05, Barrow chief scout 7.08, ECFA under-17/19 performance analyst 2013*
Honours: Division 3+ champions 1996, (promoted 1999), Lancashire Senior Cup winners 1996-97, Auto Windscreens Shield Northern final 2000.

Graeme played almost 150 league games for Hull, figuring in every match in 1992-93, mostly in central midfield but also on the left flank or at left back. He only missed two games in 1995-96 when Preston won the new Division 3 title, partnering Ian Bryson in midfield, but suffered with injuries while at Deepdale and teamed up again with Bryson during a month's loan at Rochdale, playing on the left wing. After several unproductive moves, Graeme reappeared at Spotland in 1999 and played in the majority of games as Steve Parkins's side just missed out on the play-offs, doubling on the left wing or left wing back and scoring a memorable last minute winner at Rotherham. He missed all of 2000-01 with a cruciate ligament injury, and although playing a few games when Dale did make it to the play-offs the following year, he was released by the board after John Hollins left the club. After playing non-league football, he coached at Preston's academy and lectured on football at Myerscough College. He also acted as a performance analyst for England Colleges and for Opta.

Gary Roy Jones 1997-2002, 2003-12

Born: Birkenhead 3.6.77
5'10" 12st
Midfield
FL Apps/Gls
449+21/74
Total Apps/Gls
508+27/80
Career: Birkenhead Inst., Liverpool jnr, Tranmere R. jnr 1991, Ashville 1992, St. Joseph's (Wallasey Sunday League), Caernarfon T. c.1995, Swansea C. 11.7.97 [3+5/-], Dale loan 15.1.98, signed 19.2.98 [123+17/22], Barnsley 30.11.01 £175,000 [56/2], Dale loan 13.11.03, signed 19.2.03 [326+4/52], Bradford C. 22.6.12 [81+1/8], Notts Co. 8.14 [39+4/3]
Honours: Cheshire County schools, Cheshire junior cup final, Lancashire Cup final 1998-99, Auto Windscreens Shield Northern final 2000, League 2 play-off final 2008, winners 2013, League 2 promotion 2010, League Cup final 2013

By far Dale's all-time appearance record holder, Gary spent at least part of 14 seasons at Spotland. His professional career had actually got off to a rather slow start as, though offered a contract by Watford while at Caernarfon, he was 20 before he signed for Swansea and had played only a handful of games before a loan to Dale early in 1998. Soon signed permanently by Graham Barrow, he helped revive Dale's season as they won half of their last 16 games though still finishing only 18th. Relatively little used the following term, he might well have been released, but his career was revived under Steve Parkin, partnering Dave Flitcroft in midfield as Dale twice just missed the play-offs. He followed Parkin to Barnsley in 2001, but with Dale struggling in 2003-04, Alan Buckley brought him back to Spotland just before Buckley himself was replaced by the returning Parkin. A fixture in the side thereafter, when former teammate Keith Hill became manager Gary led Dale's drive for the play-offs, missing only three games and chipping in with sevn goals, and had the ultimate honour of leading the side out at Wembley in 2008. Despite spells out injured, he was still skipper as Dale finally won promotion two years later and had an amazing first season up in League 1. He played in every match and notched easily his best ever goals tally, top scoring with 17 in the league and 19 in total. The first Dale player to pass 400 FL games and 500 games in total, he left after Dale's disastrous 2011-12 season under Steve Eyre and John Coleman (his eighth Dale boss), having accumulated 470 FL, 23 FA Cup, 16 FL Cup, 17 Associate Members Cup (under its various guises) and five play-off games, totalling 45,495 minutes of action! Moving to Bradford City at the age of 35, he had another remarkable season as the Bantams incredibly became the first fourth tier side since Rochdale in 1962 to reach the League Cup Final - beating Aston Villa and Arsenal along the way – and then returned to Wembley to win the play-off final. He finally ended his FL career in 2015 after 659 games.

Paul Carden 1997-2000

Born: Liverpool 29.3.79
5'8" 11st10
Midfield
FL Apps/Gls 30+15/0
Total Apps/Gls
36+20/0
Career: Blackpool yts 1996, pro 7.7.97 [+1/-], Dale trial 2.98, pro 3.3.98 [30+15/-], Hull C. trial 13.1.00, Chester C. loan 13.3.00 [9+2/-], Chester C. cs.00 [49+2/1 Conf], Doncaster R. cs.01 £10,000 [10+6/1 Conf], Chester C. 11.02 £4000 [77+4/3 Conf, 36+4/-], Peterborough U. 4.7.05 [43+1/-], Burscough 20.10.06, Burton A. 10.06 [27+1/1 Conf], Accrington St. 5.7.07 [4/-], Cambridge U. loan 11.07 [2/- Conf], Cambridge U. loan 3.1.08 [15/- Conf], Wrexham 24.5.08, Cambridge U. 23.6.08 player-assistant manager [102/3 Conf] (caretaker manager 7.09 to 8.09), Luton T. loan 18.2.11 [8+2/- Conf], Luton T. player-coach 27.8.11 to 1.13 [1/- Conf], Blackburn R. junior coach 7.13, Southport assistant manager 10.14, manager 1.15*

Honours: Lancashire Cup final 1998-99, Conference champions 2004, Conference play-off final 2008, 2009, England semi-professional international 2006-07

Paul made his only Blackpool appearance in a local derby with Preston screened on Sky and a few months later joined Dale, initially on trial. He played seven games before the end of the season and figured regularly on the right of midfield or at right back in the second half of 1998-99. Almost entirely restricted to the bench following the arrival of Tony Ford and Dave Flitcroft, Paul joined Chester. He played for them when they lost their league place but returned to captain them to the Conference title in 2004, also being voted their player of the year the following term. Moving on to Peterborough he became involved in the bizarre 'Big Ron, football manager' reality tv show before having his contract cancelled and heading for Burton Albion via a convenient move to his brother Adam's club Burscough, outside the transfer window, and captaining the England non-league side. He returned briefly to the FL with new boys Accrington but then had several spells with Cambridge, playing in two play-off finals and becoming assistant manager. Later boss of Southport, he brought in his one-time Dale midfield partner Alex Russell as his assistant.

David Gray 1996-99

Born: Rossendale 18.1.80
6'2" 13st7
Forward
FL Apps/Gls +3/0
Total Apps/Gls +4/0
Career: Dale yts cs.96, pro 7.98 [+3/-], Chorley loan 4.1.99, {Clitheroe loan 1999?}, Atherton Collieries cs.99, Rossendale U. 1999-2000, Northwich Victoria 1999-2000 [9+9/2 Conf], Rossendale U. cs.00, Accrington St. 7.02, Bacup Borough 2002-03, Salford C. 6.11.03, Chorley 7.04, Bacup Borough 1.05, Curzon Ashton 2005-06, Barnoldswick T. 8.09, Silsden 8.10, Rossendale U. 9.10, Padiham, Barnoldswick T. 10.11, Bacup Borough 30.11.12
Honours: North West Counties League champions 2001, Lancashire FA Trophy final 2013

A member of Dale's youth team in 1996-97, David was an unused substitute in the next to last game of 1997-98. He netted five of a Dale side's seven goals in a pre-season friendly against Accrington at the start of the following term and made four substitute appearances but was released at the end of the season. Making a few appearances at Conference level, he subsequently played North West Counties League football for a variety of teams.

Paul Sparrow 1998-99

Born: Wandsworth 24.3.75
6'1" 11st4
Full back
FL Apps/Gls 21+4/2
Total Apps/Gls 29+5/2
Career: Crystal Palace as 1988, yts 1991, pro 13.7.93 [1/-], Preston NE loan 8.3.96, signed 15.3.96 [20/-], Dale 2.7.98 [21+4/2], Lancaster C. 9.99, Kendall T. 8.05, Chorley 3.08
Honours: Wimbledon Schoolboys, Division 3+ champions 1996, Lancashire Senior Cup winners 1996-97, final 1998-99

Paul had spent two years at Preston, prior to joining Dale, playing a number of games when they won the (new) third division title (replacing the injured Andy Fensome, q.v.) and captaining their reserves in 1997-98. He played fairly frequently, in either full back berth, for much of his season at Spotland, but Graham Barrow used a variety of full back pairings and Paul was not retained, moving on to a long spell in the non-league game, coincidentally figuring alongside Fensome at Lancaster City. He also worked at Myerscough College, with another former Preston and Dale player, Graeme Atkinson and obtained a degree in physiotherapy.

Dean Anthony Stokes 1998-2000

Born: Birmingham 23.5.70
5'9" 11st12
Left back
FL Apps/Gls 28+2/0
Total Apps/Gls 40+2/0
Career: Dale jnr, Castleton Gabriels, (Rochdale Sunday League), Milton, Armitage 90 c.1990, Redditch U., Halesowen T. 1992, Port Vale 15.1.93 £5000 [53+7/-], Dale 15.7.98 [28+2/-], Leek T. cs.00, Newcastle T., Stafford Rangers 8.02, Newcastle T., Alsager T. 2005-06, player-manager 1.07, Eccleshall coach 3.08, Rochdale T. player-manager 6.09
Honours: Rochdale Sunday League under-21s, Division 2+ promotion 1994, Anglo-Italian Cup final 1996, Lancashire Cup final 1998-99, (Auto Windscreens Shield Northern final 2000).

Dean was brought up in Rochdale and was a junior at Spotland as well as playing in local amateur football before moving back to the midlands. Signing for Port Vale when he was 22, he made just over 50 appearances, playing fairly regularly in their 1994 promotion campaign and figuring in the final of the Anglo-Italian cup against Genoa at

Wembley, before Graham Barrow recruited him in 1998. He played in the first nine league games but was then injured and only regained his place for the final game of the season, when caretaker boss David Hamilton brought him back. Used reasonably frequently in Steve Parkin's first season, though he was often a substitute, he then returned to the non-league game, reappearing in Rochdale as manager of Rochdale Town (the former Castleton Gabriels). Dean was also a PE teacher in Manchester and was featured in an article in the 'Times Ed' in 2002. His brother Danny played as a striker in the Rochdale Alliance League for a number of sides including the Ratcliffe Arms, and for Spotland Meths who won the Lancashire Amateur League Division 2 in 2006.

Mark David Monington 1998-2001

Born: Bilsthorpe 21.10.70 6'1" 14st
Central defender
FL Apps/Gls 90+5/12
Total Apps/Gls 107+5/16
Career: Burnley jnr 1987, pro 23.3.89 [65+19/5], Rotherham U. 28.11.94 £50,000 [75+4/3], Dale 6.7.98 [90+5/12], Boston U. cs.01 [25/- Conf, 1/-], Halifax T. loan 23.11.02, signed 27.12.02 [47+6/7 Conf], retired injured 2005-06
Honours: Division 4 champions 1992, Division 2+ promotion 1994, Lancashire Senior Cup winners 1992-93, final 1998-99, Auto Windscreens Shield Northern final 2000, Conference champions 2002

A solidly built centre half, Mark spent six seasons on the fringe of the Burnley side as they progressed from the old fourth to the new first division. He was also one of the three men sent off in the infamous cup tie against Dale in 1994. He had four seasons with Rotherham without becoming a regular, but at Spotland he was first choice for two of his three seasons, winning the player of the year in 1998-99. A major threat at set pieces, 'Mono' netted twice on three occasions, and scored six goals in eight games during 2000-01. On the other hand, he was sent off three times, two of them against his previous club Rotherham. Released after Dale just missed the play-offs in 2001, he joined Boston, and despite being sent off on his debut, helped them gain a league place.

Isidro (Izzy) Diaz Bernabé 1998-99

Born: Valencia, Spain 15.5.72 5'7" 9st6
Winger
FL Apps/Gls 12+2/2
Total Apps/Gls 14+4/2
Career: Valencia (Spain) jnr, Torrente (Spain) jnr, CD Teruel (Spain) 1991-92, Real Zaragoza 'B' (Spain) 1992-93, CF Balaguer (Spain) 1994-95, Wigan A. 25.7.95 [57+19/16], Wolverhampton W. 8.8.97 [1/-], West Bromwich A. trial 11.97, Wigan A. 18.12.97 [1+1/-], Tranmere R. trial, Dale 14.8.98 [12+2/2], FC Cartagonova (Spain) c.12.98, Leca FC (Portugal) 1999, GD Chaves (Portugal) 1999-2000, Leca FC (Portugal) 2005-06, Barakaldo CF (Spain) 2006-07, CD Laredo (Spain) 2009, retired 2010
Honours: Division 3+ champions 1997, Lancashire Senior Cup final 1995-96

One of Wigan's 'Three Amigos', with Roberto Martinez and Jesus Seba, Izzy was a former Zaragoza reserve (playing over 60 times for their 'B' team in the Spanish League) recruited from Spanish third division side Balaguer by the then English third division side at the start of their rise up the leagues. Signed for Dale by ex-Wigan boss Graham Barrow, his goal at Carlisle earned their first victory of the 1998-99 season, but after a dozen games on the right wing he returned to Spain. He spent most of the following decade in Portugal, most notably 165 appearances with Chaves in the Liga da Honra (second tier), finally retiring from the Spanish lower leagues when he was 38.

Mark Thomas Williams 1998-99

Born: Liverpool 10.11.78
6'0" 11st2
Right back
FL Apps/Gls 11+3/1
Total Apps/Gls 15+3/1
Career: Salesian HS, Tranmere R. yts 1996, Barrow 1.98, Dale trial 19.8.98, signed 18.9.98 [11+3/1], Rotherham U. 5.3.99 [10+1/-], retired injured 2000. Hereford U. 8.01 [12+1/1 Conf], Chester C. 3.02 [6+5/- Conf], BAFA (Brunei) cs.02 to 2006.
Honours: Unibond League champions 1998

Though he almost joined Oldham from Tranmere, Mark's only senior experience before signing for Dale was five games in the Northern Premier League for Barrow. He played a number of games at right back in the middle part of 1998-99 and scored the winning goal against Halifax in only his third game. Against Swansea, he was mistakenly booked for a foul actually committed by Paul Carden and later sent off when he received a second yellow card. The red was subsequently rescinded and Carden had to serve the suspension instead! Mark ended the season at Rotherham, but suffered a serious injury in the following pre-season which ended his FL career. He did make a come-back in the Conference and later played in Brunei under the management of Mick Lyons, the former Everton defender, in the Malaysian Premier League. While there, Mark and another player just escaped the Bali terrorist bombing when they went outside to check on an England game and were among the rescuers dragging people from the building.

Miguel Juan de Souza 1998-99

Born; Newham 11.2.70
5'11" 13st8
Striker
FL Apps/Gls 5/0
Total Apps/Gls 5/0
Career: {Brighton & HA 1987, East Ham 1988?} Clapton 1988-89, Charlton A. 4.7.89, Bristol C. 1.8.90, {Cheltenham T. 1990?}, Yeovil T. 1991 [22/- Conf], Dorchester T. 1991, Bashley 1992, Dagenham & Redbridge 1992-93 [21/8 Conf], Birmingham C. 1.2.94 £25,000 [5+10/-], Bury loan 25.11.94 [2+1/-], Wycombe W. 27.1.95 £80,000 [73+10/29], Peterborough U. 26.3.97 £50,000 [20+16/5], Southend U. loan 8.9.97 [2/-], Dale loan 28.10.98 to 28.11.98 [5/-], Rushden & Diamonds 1999 [38+14/14 Conf], Boston U. 6.00 [7+2/1 Conf], Farnborough loan 20.10.00, signed 26.1.01 [8+4/1 Conf], St Albans C. 12.8.02, player-coach 5.04, Boreham Wood 2004-05, Dulwich Hamlet 2004-05, Chesham U. 2005, Wealdstone 2006, Chesham U. Ladies coach 7.06, Leyton O. youth coach 2009, Clapton 9.12, Leyton O. head of youth recruitment 2013*
Honours: Ryman League champions 2001, (Division 3 champions 1995)

Miguel was a well travelled striker inside and outside the FL whose best spell came with Wycombe, not least when he hit hat-tricks in both games against Bradford City in 1995-96 and totalled 18 league goals for the season. Dale borrowed him from Peterborough three years later, but after a promising debut he made little impact. He later had a long spell with St Albans City figuring over 100 times (and simultaneously gaining a degree in sports science), and after playing for Chesham managed their ladies team. He returned to play for Clapton when he was 42 before heading Orient's youth development.

Michael Andrew Holt 1998-2000
Born: Burnley 28.7.77

5'10" 11st12
Forward
FL Apps/Gls 25+13/7
Total Apps/Gls 30+17/9
Career: Blackburn R. jnr, Preston NE 16.8.96 [12+24/5], Macclesfield T. loan 25.9.98 [3+1/1], Dale loan 16.11.98, signed 15.1.99 [25+13/7], Northwich Victoria loan 20.1.00 [5/- Conf], Accrington St. cs.2000, St Patrick's Ath. 2000, Derry C. 2003, St Patrick's Ath. 2004, Dublin C. 2005, Nelson cs.05, Barnoldswick T. 8.06, Padiham to 2009, Lancashire Police player-coach
Honours: Auto Windscreens Shield Northern final 2000. North West Counties League division 2 promotion 2006

A promising junior at Blackburn, where he netted 28 times in 33 games for the youth team, he turned pro with Preston instead, scoring 34 times in 39 games for their reserves and netting against Spurs in the League Cup in only his third senior outing. Unfortunate to be injured the day new boss David Moyes took over, he had few first team opportunities and was allowed to move on to Dale. His best moment was probably the televised game against Hull, when he scored twice and Moyes was the match summariser! Joint top scorer, albeit with seven goals, in his first (half) season, he was rarely used after Steve Parkin arrived, indeed neither he nor the other joint leading scorer in 1998-99, Andy Morris, scored a single league goal the following term. After a stint in Ireland, Michael scored 36 goals in a season at Nelson and joined the Lancashire Police, playing for and coaching their team.

Andrew Dean (Andy, 'Bruno') Morris 1998-2000

Born: Sheffield 17.11.67
6'4" 15st12
Centre forward
FL Apps/Gls 26+6/7
Total Apps/Gls 30+7/8
Career: Rotherham U. jnr, pro 29.7.85 [+7/-], Chesterfield 12.1.88 [225+40/56], Exeter C. loan 4.3.92 [4+3/2], Dale

23.12.98 [26+6/7], Scarborough loan 16.9.99 to 12.99 [6+3/2 Conf], Hucknall T. cs.2000, Chesterfield Football in the Community 2000 to 5.13
Honours: Division 4 play-off final 1990, Division 3+ play-off winners 1995

A cult hero at Chesterfield, Andy was a massively proportioned striker who took his nickname from heavyweight boxer Frank Bruno. He spent a decade at Saltergate, netting just over 50 goals, figuring at Wembley in the first play-off final to be held there, and playing his part in the amazing FA Cup run of 1997. Chesterfield came within a refereeing decision of reaching the Final, the officials not noticing another effort cross the line after Bruno had given the Spireites the lead, the game with Middlesbrough eventually ending 3-3. He had a testimonial against Notts Forest the following season and wrote a column in the local Chesterfield newspaper, but temporarily left the club to sign for Dale late in 1998, finishing as joint top scorer thanks to a hat-trick against Chester. He almost certainly also became their weightiest ever outfield player. Only starting one league game after Steve Parkin signed Clive Platt, Andy soon returned to Chesterfield to work in their Football in the Community programme, eventually totting up 25 years service for the club.

Philip Alan (Phil) Priestley 1998-2001

Born: Wigan 30.3.76
6'0" 12st9
Goalkeeper
FL Apps 2+1
Total Apps 3+1
Career: Abraham Guest HS, Wigan A. jnr, Atherton Laburnum Rovers, Leyland Motors, Wigan A., Atherton LR, Dale 23.9.98 [2+1], Scarborough loan 24.11.00 [6 Conf], Chester C. loan 27.2.01 [5+1 Conf], Bangor C. cs.01, Prescot Cables cs.04, Stalybridge Celtic 1.11.04, Bangor C. 1.05, FC United of Manchester 8.05, Radcliffe Borough 9.05, Chorley 10.05 (joint caretaker manager 2006-7), FC United of Manchester coach 10.07, Radcliffe Borough 1.08, FC United of Manchester 3.08, Bangor C. academy coach, Radcliffe Borough 4.08, Skelmersdale 2009, Runcorn Linnets 16.10.09, Charnock Richard 2010, Prescot Cables 11.10, Leigh Genesis player-coach 12.10, Runcorn manager 2011, Atherton LR player-manager 2012 to 6.13, AFC Blackpool, Atherton Collieries 1.14, Southport goalkeeping coach*
Honours: (Auto Windscreens Shield Northern final 2000), Welsh Cup final 2002, Lancashire FA Trophy final 2009

Signed as goalkeeping cover from the exotically named Atherton Laburnum Rovers, Phil was with Dale for three seasons but made only two and a half FL appearances. His first was in a 1-1 draw with Plymouth in January 1999, the others the following term, each time when Neil Edwards was injured. Remarkably, apart from his one league and one cup start, he was on the bench for every one of Dale's other 54 matches in 1999-2000. He was also on the bench a number of times in the next season before being replaced as Edward's understudy by the up and coming Matt Gilks. In his first year at Bangor he was chosen in the League of Wales team of the season. A big favourite with the Bangor fans, who nicknamed him Elvis, he played in the UEFA Cup and the InterToto Cup (against Transylvanian opposition) as well as scoring a league goal and totalling well over 100 games. He later spent several years alternating between the newly formed FC United of Manchester and Radcliffe Borough, playing against Dale in friendlies on several occasions. He also worked for coaching firm Just4Keepers. Phil's father Alan was a goalkeeper with Southport and Phil later became their goalkeeping coach.

Jason Lee Lydiate 1998-99

Born: Manchester 29.10.71
5'11" 12st3
Central defender/midfield
FL Apps/Gls 14/1
Total Apps/Gls 14/1
Career: Manchester U. as 1985, yts 1987, pro 1.7.90, Bolton W. 19.3.92 [29+1/-], Blackpool 3.3.95 £75,000 [81+5/2], Scarborough 6.8.98 [26+1/1], Dale loan 12.2.99 to 5.99 [14/1], Bamber Bridge cs.99, Winsford U. 1999, Finn Harps 8.99, Hyde U. 2.03 to cs.03. Dale junior coach c.2011*
Honours: Salford Boys, Division 2+ promotion 1993, (Division 1+ promotion 1995), Lancashire Senior Cup winners 1995-96

Jason captained the Manchester United side -also containing another Salford Boys product then going by the name Ryan Wilson - which reached the Youth Cup semi-final in 1990. He did not make his senior debut until joining Bolton, though, playing a few games when they were promoted to (the new) Division 1 in 1993. He became more of a regular, either at centre back or right back, after a sizeable fee took him to Blackpool (so missing the end of the campaign that saw Bolton reach the top flight). However, he had spent the first half of the season at Scarborough when signed on loan by Dale just before the 1999 transfer deadline. He figured in most of the remaining games, either in central defence or in midfield, and between his two clubs made 41 appearances during the season, but was not retained by either, Scarborough having been relegated to the Conference. Later he was employed back at Spotland as a coach to the junior sides. Jason's cousin Dan Lydiate is a Welsh intenational rugby union player.

Graham Hicks 1997-2002

Born: Oldham A. 17.2.81 5'11" 13st
Defender
FL Apps/Gls 1/0
Total Apps/Gls 2/0
Career: North Chadderton HS, Boundary Park Juniors, Dale as 1994, yts 5.97, pro 21.1.99 [1/-], Chorley loan 2001, Chorley 2002, Castleton Gabriels 11.02 to 2007-08, Bolton W. Community Football coach, Dale Centre of Excellence coach, Football in the Community coach*
Cricket for Crompton, Rochdale CC
Honours: Oldham Boys

The son of former Dale player Keith, the Centre of Excellence director, Graham played in the club's first under-14s side with Stephen Bywater. He played in the youth team from 1996-97 to 1998-99, winning the youth player of the year award, and was unused substitute a couple of times before making his league debut at right back in the final game of the latter season. Having been given a three and a half year contract, his only start the following term was at centre back in the FA Cup tie against Burton, and though appearing in reserve games for the next two seasons (even deputising for the injured Gilks in goal), he made no further senior appearances. Subsequently turning out for Castleton Gabriels, he moved into coaching when still in his mid-twenties and teamed up with his father at the Centre of Excellence. A very useful club cricketer, he played as wicketkeeper for Crompton 1st XI when he was only 15.

Gareth Stoker 1998-2000

Born; Bishop Auckland 22.2.73
5'9" 11st4
Midfield
FL Apps/Gls 11+1/1
Total Apps/Gls 13+1/1
Career: Leeds U. jnr, app 1989, pro 8.90, Ipswich T. trial 7.91, Hull C. 13.9.91 to cs.93 [24+6/2], Bishop Auckland, Hereford U. 16.3.95 [65+5/6], Cardiff C. 29.1.97 £80,000 [29+8/4], Dale loan 16.2.99, signed 4.3.99 [11+1/1], Scarborough loan 13.9.99, signed 8.12.99 [125+15/6 Conf], Forest Green Rovers 6.03 [24/- Conf] Leigh RMI 7.04 [22/5 Conf], Scarborough trial 7.06, Wakefield 10.06 player-assistant manager, player-manager 1.07, reverted to player 9.07, Ossett T. assistant manager 12.07, Leigh Genesis 6.09

Gareth was Graham Barrow's final signing and though given a contract until 2001, did not figure in Steve Parkin's plans and moved on to Scarborough only a few weeks into the new season, giving them excellent service over the next four years in the Conference. A midfielder with something of a hardman reputation, sent off on his Hull debut, he had been a regular at Hereford, earning a £80,000 move to Cardiff - also being sent off when the Bluebirds met his former club – but suffered a cruciate injury. He later went into non-league management and worked in sports coaching companies.

		Page	Season	To	FL	FAC	FLC	AMC	PO	ExpL	LSC	Other	Total
Alan	Ainscow	85	1989-90		19+1/0	+1/0	2/0	+1/0			1+1/1		22+4/1
Dave	Ainsworth	23	1975-76		+2/0								+2/0
Carl	Alford	80	1988-89	1989-90	+4/0								+4/0
Vernon	Allatt	48	1983-84		40/8	3/1	2/0	1/0			2+1/1		48+1/10
Dave	Allen	78	1988-89								+0/0		+0/0
Jason	Anders	91	1990-91	1993-94	2+15/1	+1/0		+2/0			+1/0		2+19/1
Andy	Armitage	76	1988-89		33+3/0	2/0		1/0			3/0	1/0	42+3/0
Steve	Arnold	13	1973-74		37+3/1	2/0	1/0						40+3/1
Jackie	Ashurst	98	1992-93		1/0		1/0						2/0
Neil	Ashworth	59	1984-85	1985-86	1/0		+1/0				1/0		2+1/0
Phil	Ashworth	30	1978-79		9+2/0		2/1						11+2/1
Graeme	Atkinson	122	1997-98	2001/02	45+12/5	3+1/1	2/0	4+1/0					54+14/6
Mark	Bailey	118	1996-97	1998-99	49+18/1	1+1/0	3+1/0	4/0					57+20/1
Ian	Bannon	24	1976-77	1979-80	112+10/0	6/0	7/0						125+10/0
Andy	Barlow	119	1997-98	1998-99	60+7/1	1+1/0	1/0	2/0					64+8/1
Neil	Barlow	114	1995-96		1+1/0								1+1/0
Dave	Bayliss	108	1994-95	2005-06	172+17/9	5+2/0	11/0	12+1/0			1+3/0		201+23/9
Chris	Beaumont	79	1988-89		31+3/7	2/1	+1/1	2/0					35+4/9
Tony	Beever	99	1992-93	1993-94	+1/0			1/0					1+1/0
Billy	Bell	21	1974-75		5+1/0								5+1/0
Jimmy	Blake	50	1983-84		2/0								2/0
Chris	Blundell	89	1990-91		10+4/0		2/0	2+1/0					14+5/0
Billy	Boslem	22	1975-76	1977-78	42+3/1	4/0	+2/0						46+5/1
Jon	Bowden	95	1991-92	1994-95	73+33/17	8/1	2+1/0	5/0			4+1/1		92+35/19
John	Bramhall	64	1986-87	1987-88	86/13	2/0	8/0	6/1			5/0		107/14
Paul	Brears	14	1973-74	1975-76	26+1/0	4/1							30+1/1
Micky	Brennan	14	1973-74	1974-75	35+2/4	1+2/0	2/0				1/0		39+4/4
Malcolm	Brown	80	1988-89	1991-92	29/1	3/0	2/0	2/0	1/0				37/1
Micky	Brown	117	1996-97		5/0								5/0
Richard	Brown	99	1992-93					+0/0					+0/0
Tony	Brown	86	1989-90	1992-93	111+3/0	8/0	8+1/0	5/0	1/0		9/0		142+4/0
Ian	Bryson	120	1997-98	1998-99	43+11/1	5/2	1/0	2/0					51+11/3
Ian	Buckley	16	1973-74		6/0								6/0
Peter	Burke	36	1980-81	1981-82	68/2	3/1	2/0					+1/0	73+1/3
Willie	Burns	84	1989-90	1990-91	68+4/2	6/0	5/1	4/1			6/1		89+4/5
Jimmy	Burt	14	1973-74		4/0								4/0
Paul	Butler	88	1990-91	1995-96	151+7/10	6+2/0	8+1/0	12+1/0			6/0	+1/0	183+12/10
Stephen	Bywater	120	1997-98					1					1
Paul	Carden	123	1997-98	1999-00	30+15/0	3+1/0	+1/0	3+1/0			+2/0		36+20/0
Steve	Carney	63	1985-86		4/0			1/0					5/0
Everton	Carr	46	1982-83		9/0								9/0
Dave	Carrick	17	1973-74		25+1/4	4/1	1/0						30+1/5
Mark	Carter	119	1997-98		7+4/2		1+1/0						8+5/2
John	Cavanah	54	1984-85		14+3/0	1/0		2+1/0					17+4/0
Mike	Cecere	116	1996-97		2+2/1	1/0	+1/0	1/0			1/0		5+3/1
Phil	Chambers	61	1985-86		9+1/0		2/0						11+1/0
Les	Chapman	47	1983-84	1984-85	87+1/0	3/0	4/0	4/0			6/1	1/0	105+1/1
Vince	Chapman	82	1989-90	1990-91	23+1/1			1/0			3/0		27+1/1
Chris	Clarke	105	1994-95	1995-96	30	1	2	3			2+1	1	39+1
Tim	Clarke	99	1992-93		2								2
Eddie	Cliff	34	1979-80	1980-81	25+1/0								25+1/0
John	Cohen	35	1979-80		+0/0								+0/0
Neil	Colbourne	35	1979-80		1								1
David	Cole	82	1989-90	1990-91	73+11/7	7/0	5/0	4/0			4+1/0		93+12/7
Tony	Colleton	91	1990-91		+1/0								+1/0
Doug	Collins	33	1978-79	1979-80	6+2/0								6+2/0
Paul	Comstive	42	1982-83		9/2		1/0						10/2
Peter	Conning	65	1986-87		40/1	2/0	2/1	2+2/1			2+1 0		48+3/3
Steve	Conroy	46	1983-84	1984-85	49	3	4	1			6	1	64
Joe	Cooke	52	1984-85	1985-86	75/4	5/0	4/1	2/0			3/0	1/0	90/5
Gary	Cooper	15	1973-74	1976-77	81+11/14	7+1/0	1/0						89+12/14
Terry	Cooper	38	1981-82		35/2	3/0	2/1					1/0	41/3
Simon	Copeland	76	1988-89		27+1/0	2/0	2/0	2/0			3/0	1/0	37+1/0
Steve	Corbett	78	1988-89								+0		+0
Peter	Costello	89	1990-91		31+3/10	2/2	4/1	3/0			2/1		42+3/14
Barry	Cowdrill	96	1991-92		15/1								15/1
Ronnie	Coyle	72	1987-88		23+1/1	1/0	4/1	2/0					30+1/2

First	Last	Page	Season	To	FL	FAC	FLC	AMC	PO	ExpL	LSC	Other	Total
Graeme	Crawford	37	1980-81	1982-83	70	1	1				1	1	74
Peter	Creamer	31	1978-79		18+2/0								18+2/0
Mark	Creighton	105	1993-94	1994-95	+0								+0
Danny	Crerand	76	1987-88	1988-89	3/0								3/0
Paul	Cuddy	27	1977-78		+1/0								+1/0
Jason	Dawson	85	1989-90	1990-91	37+18/8	6/1	1+1/0	3+1/0			1+1/0		48+21/9
Miguel	de Souza	126	1998-99		5/0								5/0
Andy	Dean	51	1983-84		1/0								1/0
Kevin	Dearden	94	1991-92		2								2
John	Deary	110	1994-95	1996-97	90+1/10	5/3	3/1	7/1			2/0		107+1/15
Roger	Denton	16	1973-74		2/0								2/0
Barry	Diamond	53	1984-85	1985-86	50+2/16	2/0	3+1/1	2/0			6/2	1/0	64+3/19
Izzy	Diaz	125	1998-99		12+2/2	1+2/0	1/0						14+4/2
Matt	Dickens	108	1994-95		4			1					5
Terry	Dolan	38	1981-82		42+1/1	3/1	1/0					1/0	47+1/2
Wayne	Dowell	114	1996-97		6+1/0						2/0		8+1/0
Jamie	Doyle	71	1987-88								3/0		3/0
Mike	Doyle	48	1983-84		24/1	2/0	2/0	1/0			3/0		32/1
Steve	Doyle	90	1990-91	1994-95	115+6/1	4/0	8/0	7/0		1/0	7/0		142+6/1
Chris	Duffey	22	1975-76		2/0								2/0
Andy	Duggan	74	1987-88	1990-91	4/0		1/0	1/0					6/0
Neil	Dunford	103	1993-94	1994-95	2	1							3
John	Dungworth	24	1976-77		14/3								14/3
Lee	Duxbury	87	1989-90		9+1/0		1/0						10+1/0
Phil	Dwyer	59	1984-85		15-Jan								15-Jan
Neil	Edmunds	79	1988-89	1989-90	36+7/8	3/1		2/0			+1/0		41+8/9
Neil	Edwards	121	1997-98	2004-05	239	16+1	9	10	2		1	3	280+1
Steve	Edwards	51	1984-85		4/0		2/0				3/0	1/0	10/0
Steve	Elliott	86	1989-90	1990-91	46+6/9	2/0	3/1	3+1/0			1+1/0		55+8/10
Tom	English	54	1984-85		3/1								3/1
Mark	Ennis	50	1983-84		1/0								1/0
Dave	Esser	26	1977-78	1981-82	169+11/24	9+1/2	7+2/1					1/0	186+14/27
David	Fairclough	65	1986-87								1/1		1/1
Andy	Farrell	115	1996-97	1998-99	113+5/2	5+1/0	6/0	5/0			4/0		133+6/2
Peter	Farrell	41	1982-83	1984-85	71+2/16	2/1	6/0	1/0			5/1	1/0	86+2/18
Dave	Felgate	31	1978-79	1979-80	47								47
Andy	Fensome	114	1996-97	1997-98	80+2/0	3/0	4/0	3/0			2/0		92+2/0
Mike	Ferguson	18	1974-75	1975-76	68+1/4	10/1	3/0						81+1/5
Mike	Fielding	55	1984-85		6/0	1/0							7/0
Bobby	Finc	30	1977-78		+1/0								+1/0
Alan	Finley	104	1993-94		1/0								1/0
Andy	Flounders	93	1991-92	1993-94	82+3/31	6/1	8+1/1	4/0		1/0	7+1/3		108+5/36
Kevin	Formby	105	1993-94	1996-97	59+8/1	5/0	5/0	10/0			4/0	1/0	84+8/1
Geoff	Forster	31	1978-79		+1/0								+1/0
Ashley	Fothergill	79	1988-89		8+1/0			1/0					9+1/0
Dave	Frain	77	1988-89		42/12	2/1	2/0	2/0			3/0	1/0	52/13
Micky	French	41	1982-83		35+1/11	1/0	3/0				3/1		42+1/12
Frank	Gamble	57	1984-85	1985-86	41+5/9	2/0	1/0	3+2/1			2+1/0		49+8/10
Willie	Garner	42	1982-83		4/0		1/0						5/0
Mark	Gavin	71	1987-88		23/6	1/0	3/0	2/0			3/0		32/6
Simon	Gibson	64	1986-87		3+2/0	1/0	2/0	1/0			2/0		9+2/0
Wayne	Goodison	82	1989-90	1990-91	78+1/4	5/1	3+1/2	4+1/0			5/0		95+3/7
Dave	Goodwin	39	1981-82		34+5/6	1/0	1/0					1/0	37+5/6
Andy	Gouck	116	1996-97	1997-98	58+8/8	2/0	2/0	1+1/0			2/0		65+9/8
Jimmy	Graham	86	1989-90	1993-94	131+6/1	12/0	13+1/0	9/1		1/0	9/0		175+7/2
Dave	Grant	59	1984-85	1986-87	97/2	6/0	5/0	5/0			5/0		118/2
David	Gray	124	1997-98	1998-99	+3/0						+1/0		+4/0
Gareth	Gray	88	1990-91	1991-92	6	2	3	2					13
Ian	Gray	109	1994-95	1996-97	78	5	4	7			3		97
Kevin	Gray	116	1996-97								1/0		1/0
Roy	Greaves	43	1982-83		19+2/0	1/0							20+2/0
Adie	Green	28	1977-78		7/0								7/0
Brian	Greenhoff	45	1982-83		15+1/0	2/0		1/0					18+1/0
Jimmy	Greenhoff	45	1982-83	1983-84	16/0		1/0				1/0		18/0
Ian	Griffiths	48	1983-84	1984-85	40+2/5	2/0	2+1/1	1/0			2/0		47+3/6
Jim	Grummett	16	1973-74	1974-75	32+1/2		1/0						33+1/2
Gary	Haire	62	1985-86		3/0								3/0

First	Last	Page	Season	To	FL	FAC	FLC	AMC	PO	ExpL	LSC	Other	Total
Derek	Hall	107	1994-95	1995-96	14+9/2		1+1/0	1+2/0				+1/0	16+13/2
Paul	Hallows	17	1974-75	1979-80	197/2	15/0	11/0				3/0		223/2
John	Halpin	94	1991-92		22+9/1	3/1	3/0	2/0		1/1	3/0		34+9/3
Neville	Hamilton	39	1981-82	1983-84	72+2/5	3+1/0	5+2/0	1/0			6/0	+1/0	87+6/5
George	Hampstead	24	1976-77		3+1/0								3+1/0
Peter	Hampton	71	1987-88		19/1	1/0	4/0	2/0			3/0		29/1
Paul	Hancox	75	1987-88	1988-89	+2/0								+2/0
Keith	Hanvey	13	1973-74	1984-85	136/10	14/1	7/0				3/0	1/0	161/11
Jason	Hardy	111	1995-96		5+2/0								5+2/0
Carl	Harris	75	1987-88	1988-89	24+1/3		2/0	1/0				+1/0	27+2/3
Brian	Hart	29	1977-78	1979-80	73+5/0	6/2	2/0						81+5/2
Jason	Hasford	85	1989-90		+1/0						+1/0		+2/0
Gary	Haworth	53	1984-85		1/0						+1/0		1+1/0
Paul	Heaton	50	1983-84	1985-86	85+4/9	5/1	2+1/0	5/0			5/0	1/0	103+5/10
Dave	Helliwell	23	1976-77		20+11/3	2/1	1/0						23+11/4
Gary	Henshaw	87	1989-90		8+1/1								8+1/1
Paul	Herring	91	1990-91		+1/0								+1/0
Graham	Hicks	128	1998-99	2001-02	1/0	1/0							2/0
Keith	Hicks	60	1985-86	1986-87	32/1	4/0		2/0			6/0		44/1
Andy	Higgins	46	1982-83	1983-84	31+2/6	2/0	2/0				3/2		38+2/8
Bob	Higgins	37	1980-81		4+1/0	1/0							5+1/0
Ronnie	Hildersley	61	1985-86		12+4/0								12+4/0
Mark	Hilditch	29	1977-78	1991-92	196+17/42	11+1/3	12/1	+2/0			2/0	+1/1	221+21/47
Jon	Hill	84	1989-90	1990-91	25+11/1	1+2/0	2+1/0	1/0			+2/0		29+17/1
Keith	Hill	115	1996-97	2000-01	171+5/6	8/0	10/0	6/1			2/0		197+5/7
Martin	Hodge	101	1993-94	1994-95	42	2	4	1			4+1		53+1
Simon	Holden	53	1984-85	1987-88	35+14/4	+1/0	1/0	2+1/0			1+1/0		39+17/4
Micky	Holmes	83	1989-90	1990-91	47+7/7	6/0	5+1/1	3/1			6/0		67+8/9
Michael	Holt	126	1998-99	1999-00	25+13/7	1+1/0	1+1/0	3+2/2					30+17/9
Stan	Horne	15	1973-74	1974-75	48/5	4/0	1/0						53/5
Andy	Howard	98	1992-93	1993-94	4+16/3	+1/0	1/0	2/0			+1/0		7+18/3
Bobby	Hoy	28	1977-78	1980-81	61+5/12	1/0	2/0						64+5/12
Carl	Hudson	66	1986-87		13+2/1	2/0	2/0	1/1					18+2/2
John	Hudson	70	1986-87		18+1/1								18+1/1
Carl	Hughes	63	1985-86		+0/0								+0/0
Phil	Hughes	91	1991-92								3		3
Zac	Hughes	73	1987-88	1989-90	2/0		1/0	3/0					6/0
Gary	Hulmes	19	1974-75	1975-76	4+6/1	+1/0							4+7/1
Steve	Humphreys	51	1983-84		6/0								6/0
Mark	Hunt	70	1986-87	1987-88	1+1/1		1/0	1/0			+1/0		3+2/1
Graham	Hurst	60	1984-85	1985-86	+1/0								+1/0
Rob	Hutchinson	20	1974-75		2/1								2/1
Nick	Irwin	120	1997-98		+0/0								+0/0
Alan	Johnson	117	1996-97	1999-00	59+3/4	3/1	4/0	1/0			2/0		69+3/5
Ian	Johnson	56	1984-85	1986-87	74+7/1	2/1	6/0	7/0			6/1		95+7/3
Steve	Johnson	49	1983-84	1989-90	40+9/12	6+1/4	2/1	3/0			+1/0		51+11/17
Alan	Jones	36	1980-81		40+4/5	1/1	2/0						43+4/6
Alex	Jones	93	1991-92	1993-94	43+3/2	4+1/0	5/0	5/0		1/0	5/1		63+4/3
Chris	Jones	32	1978-79	1979-80	51+5/19	1+2/1	2/1						54+7/21
Gary	Jones	123	1997-98	2011-12	449+21/74	20+3/0	15+1/3	15+2/3	5/0		2/0	2/0	508+27/80
Paul B.	Jones	81	1988-89		14/2								14/2
Paul S.	Jones	15	1973-74		+0/0								+0/0
Steve	Jordan	105	1993-94		+0								+0
Eamon	Kavanagh	15	1973-74		2+2/0								2+2/0
Ged	Keegan	52	1984-85		2/0		1/0				3/0	1/0	7/0
Gerry	Keenan	41	1982-83	1983-84	35/1	1/0	2/0						38/1
Lance	Key	113	1995-96	1998-99	33	3					1		37
Andy	Kilner	96	1991-92		3/0								3/0
Steve	Kinsey	96	1991-92		3+3/1	1+1/0							4+4/1
Tony	Lacey	21	1975-76	1976-77	83/0	9/0	4/0						96/0
Graham	Lancashire	121	1997-98	2000-01	54+29/23	+1/0	3+1/1	3+3/1			2/3		62+34/28
Dave	Lancaster	101	1993-94	1996-97	51+9/16	2/0	5/1	1/0			2+1/1		61+10/18
Les	Lawrence	52	1984-85		15/4	1/0	2/1				2/0	1/0	21/5
Chris	Lee	89	1990-91		24+2/2	2/0	4/1	3/0			3/1		36+2/4
Mark	Leonard	97	1991-92	1998-99	83+6/7	2/0	5/0	1/0			5+1/0		96+7/7
Phil	Lockett	88	1989-90	1991-92	1+2/0								1+2/0
Geoff	Lomax	70	1987-88	1988-89	70+1/0	1/0	5/0	2+1/0			6/0	1/0	85+2/0

First	Last	Page	Season	To	FL	FAC	FLC	AMC	PO	ExpL	LSC	Other	Total
Chris	Lucketti	81	1988-89	1989-90	1/0						2/0		3/0
Noel	Luke	100	1992-93		2+1/0								2+1/0
Jason	Lydiate	127	1998-99		14/1								14/1
Paul	Lyons	114	1995-96		1+2/0								1+2/0
Paul	Malcolm	54	1984-85		24	1		2					27
Dean	Martin	110	1994-95	1996-97	45+8/0	4/1	+1/0	2+1/0			4/1		55+10/2
Harold	Martin	19	1974-75		11+2/0								11+2/0
Lee	Martin	118	1996-97		+0								+0
Eui	Martinez	37	1980-81	1982-83	110+6/16	5/0	5+1/1				+2/0	1/0	121+9/17
Stuart	Mason	24	1976-77		2/0								2/0
Neil	Matthews	101	1993-94	1994-95	15+4/0	1/0	1/0	6/0			3+1/0	1/0	27+5/0
Don	McAlister	57	1984-85		3/0			1/0					4/0
Jim	McCluskie	51	1983-84	1985-86	14+4/0			+1/0			1/0		15+6/0
Matt	McCormack	99	1992-93		+0/0								+0/0
John	McDermott	34	1979-80		5+3/1								5+3/1
Gerry	McElhinney	44	1982-83		20/1								20/1
Paddy	McGeeney	68	1986-87		3/0								3/0
Roy	McHale	66	1986-87		6+1/0	1/0	2/0				1+1/0		10+2/0
Ian	McInerny	90	1990-91		4/1								4/1
Joe	McIntyre	81	1988-89		2+2/0								2+2/0
Ian	McMahon	49	1983-84	1985-86	89+2/8	4/0	3/0	6/0			3+3/0		105+5/8
Ian	Measham	63	1985-86		12/0								12/0
Stuart	Mellish	74	1987-88	1988-89	24+3/1	+1/0						+1/0	24+5/1
Larry	Milligan	34	1979-80		8+1/0								8+1/0
Steve	Milligan	87	1989-90	1990-91	5/1								5/1
Neil	Mills	64	1986-87		4+6/0	2/1	2/1				3/0		11+6/2
Mike	Milne	33	1978-79		1+1/0								1+1/0
Andy	Milner	86	1989-90	1993-94	103+24/25	7+5/1	8+1/5	4/2		+1/0	7/0		129+31/33
Neil	Mitchell	112	1995-96		3+1/0								3+1/0
Mark	Monington	125	1998-99	2000-01	90+5/12	8/1		8/3			1/0		107+5/16
John	Moore	74	1987-88		10/2								10/2
Ronnie	Moore	60	1985-86		43/9	4/1	2/0	1/0			3/0		53/10
Tony	Moore	55	1984-85		1+2/0								1+2/0
Steve	Morgan	91	1990-91	1991-92	12+11/3		+1/0				+2/0		12+14/3
Tony	Morrin	25	1977-78	1978-79	29+1/0	1/0	3/0						33+1/0
Andy	Morris	126	1998-99	1999-00	26+6/7		1+1/0	3/1					30+7/8
Ernie	Moss	75	1987-88		10/2								10/2
Dave	Mossman	62	1985-86		8/0			2/0					10/0
Paul	Moulden	111	1995-96		6+10/1	3/2		2/3					11+10/6
Bob	Mountford	20	1974-75	1977-78	97+1/36	8/3	6/1						111+1/40
Jimmy	Mullen	25	1976-77		6+2/1								6+2/1
Phil	Mullington	22	1975-76	1978-79	67+8/6	5/1	4/0						76+8/7
Steve	Mulrain	99	1992-93	1993-94	3+5/2			1/0					4+5/2
Dick	Mulvaney	19	1974-75	1976-77	72+1/4	9/0	+1/0						81+2/4
Joe	Murty	20	1974-75	1975-76	15+6/2	+1/0							15+7/2
David	Mycock	73	1987-88	1988-89	19+3/0	1/0		2/0					22+3/0
Peter	Nicholson	44	1982-83		7/0								7/0
Dave	Norton	89	1990-91		9/0			2/0					11/0
Bob	Oates	47	1983-84		42/1	1+1/0	2/0	1/0			3/0		49+1/1
Malcolm	O'Connor	46	1982-83	1983-84	12+4/3	1/0		+1/0			1/1		14+5/4
Brian	Oliver	22	1975-76		3	1							4
Darren	Oliver	103	1993-94	1994-95	22+6/0	1/0		1/0			1/0		25+6/0
Ted	Oliver	27	1977-78	1979-80	19+3/1		1/0						20+3/1
Nigel	O'Loughlin	23	1976-77	1981-82	242+3/18	11/1	13/1					1/0	267+3/20
Steve	O'Shaughnessy	78	1988-89	1990-91	101+8/16	9/2	5/3	7/0			2+2/0	+1/0	124+11/21
Terry	Owen	27	1977-78	1978-79	80+3/21	2/2	2/0						84+3/23
Don	Page	100	1992-93		3+1/1								3+1/1
Robbie	Painter	117	1996-97	1998-99	101+11/30	7/0	3/1	4+2/0			1+1/0		116+14/31
Leigh	Palin	95	1991-92		3/0								3/0
Carl	Parker	97	1991-92	1992-93	9+7/1	+2/0		3/0			+1/0		12+10/1
Derrick	Parker	73	1987-88		6+1/1		1/1	1/0					8+1/2
Derek	Parlane	69	1986-87	1987-88	42/10	1/0	3/1	4/0			2/0		52/11
Mark	Payne	93	1991-92	1992-93	58+4/8	5/0	3+1/0	2+1/0	+1/0		4/1		72+7/9
Jason	Peake	104	1993-94	1999-00	165+11/17	12/3	7/0	13/1			6/3	1/0	204+11/24
Chris	Pearce	36	1980-81	1982-83	41	1	6				2		50
John	Pemberton	54	1984-85		1/0								1/0
John	Pender	122	1997-98		14/0	+1/0		2/0					16+1/0

First	Last	Page	Season	To	FL	FAC	FLC	AMC	PO	ExpL	LSC	Other	Total
Owen	Pickard	107	1994-95									+1/0	+1/0
Kevin	Pilkington	112	1995-96		6								6
Frannie	Powell	113	1995-96		+2/0								+2/0
James	Price	112	1995-96	1996-97	3/0								3/0
John	Price	30	1977-78	1978-79	10+2/0	1/0							11+2/0
Phil	Priestley	127	1998-99	2000-01	2+1			1					3+1
James	Proctor	112	1995-96		1+2/0								1+2/0
Gordon	Rayner	67	1986-87								+0/0		+0/0
Dave	Redfern	58	1984-85	1987-88	87	6	6	5			6		110
Adam	Reed	122	1997-98		10/0			02-Jan					12-Jan
Mark	Rees	68	1986-87		2+1/0								2+1/0
Alan	Reeves	92	1991-92	1994-95	119+2/9	6/0	12/1	5/0		1/0	9/1	1/0	153+2/11
Shaun	Reid	50	1983-84	1994-95	232+8/14	10/2	18/2	20+1/2			22+1/2	2/0	304+10/22
Stuart	Rimmer	107	1994-95		3/0								3/0
Billy	Roberts	80	1988-89		1/0								1/0
Peter	Robinson	59	1984-85		9+3/0								9+3/0
Glenn	Robson	118	1996-97	1997-98	+10/0								+10/0
Kevin	Rose	90	1990-91	1992-93	71	4	2	4			2		83
Alex	Russell	106	1994-95	1997-98	83+19/14	1+1/0	5/1	2+3/0			1+2/0	+1/0	92+26/15
Darren	Ryan	106	1994-95	1995-96	19+13/2	1+3/0		1+5/0			1+3/0	+1/0	23+27/2
John	Ryan	92	1991-92	1993-94	64+6/2	7/0	8/3	5/0		1/0	6/1		91+6/6
Bobby	Scaife	27	1977-78	1979-80	95+3/9	4/2	2+2/0						101+5/11
Andy	Scott	119	1997-98		1+2/0								1+2/0
Bob	Scott	26	1977-78	1978-79	71/3	2/0	5/0						78/3
Jimmy	Seal	35	1979-80	1980-81	44+9/5	5/0	+1/0						49+10/5
John	Seasman	56	1984-85	1987-88	94+1/4	6/0	8/0	4+1/1			6+1/0		118+3/5
Dave	Seddon	16	1973-74	1974-75	18+3/0	3/0							21+3/0
Ian	Seddon	26	1977-78		30+1/3			3/0					33+1/3
Richard	Sharpe	108	1994-95		9+7/2	+1/0		6/1					15+8/3
Graham	Shaw	110	1994-95	1995-96	13+9/0	+3/0	1/1	1+1/0			2/0		17+13/1
Steve	Shaw	28	1977-78		6/0	1/0							7/0
Peter	Shearer	67	1986-87		1/0			1/2					2/2
Gary	Shelton	104	1993-94		3/0								3/0
Philip	Shore	109	1994-95		+0								+0
Chris	Shyne	25	1976-77	1978-79	20	1							21
Lyndon	Simmonds	70	1986-87	1987-88	65/22	1/0	4/1	3/2			3/0		76/25
Andy	Slack	29	1977-78	1978-79	15		2						17
Colin	Small	83	1989-90		5+2/0						2/0		7+2/0
Jason	Smart	63	1985-86	1988-89	116+1/4	3/0	9+1/0	6/0			6/0	1/0	141+2/4
Craig	Smith	120	1997-98		1+2/0		+1/0						1+3/0
Mark	Smith	77	1988-89		26+1/7	2/0	2/0	2/0			1+1/0	1/1	34+2/8
Eric	Snookes	30	1978-79	1982-83	183/1	10/0	11/0				3/0	1/0	208/1
Trevor	Snowden	100	1992-93	1993-94	8+6/0						+2/0		8+8/0
Paul	Sparrow	124	1998-99		21+4/2	4/0	1/0	1+1/0			2/0		29+5/2
Andy	Stafford	41	1982-83		1/1						2/0		3/1
Brian	Stanton	69	1986-87	1987-88	42+7/4		+3/0	4/0			1/0		47+10/4
John	Stiles	97	1991-92		2+2/0								2+2/0
Gareth	Stoker	128	1998-99		11+1/1			2/0					13+1/1
Dean	Stokes	124	1998-99	1999-00	28+2/0	3/0	4/0	3/0			2/0		40+2/0
Kevin	Stonehouse	84	1989-90		13+1/2	1/1	2/0	1+1/0			3/1		20+2/4
Les	Strong	55	1984-85		1/0								1/0
Mark	Stuart	102	1993-94	1998-99	166+36/41	10/1	9+1/1	6+4/2			10+1/2	1/0	202+42/47
Bill	Summerscales	21	1975-76	1976-77	87/4	9/0	4/0						100/4
Dave	Sutton	76	1988-89		28/2	2/0	2/0	2/0			3/0	1/1	38/3
Carl	Swan	43	1982-83		3/0	1/0							4/0
Andy	Sweeney	21	1975-76		12+5/0	1/0	2/0						15+5/0
Steve	Tapley	58	1984-85		1/0								1/0
Alan	Tarbuck	23	1976-77	1977-78	48/1	3/1	5/1						56/3
Alan	Taylor	13	1973-74	1974-75	55/8	3/1	3/1				1/0		62/10
Brian	Taylor	32	1978-79	1982-83	152+2/10	7/0	6/0					1/0	166+2/10
Jamie	Taylor	102	1993-94	1996-97	10+26/4	+1/0		+2/1			+2/0		10+31/5
John	Taylor	19	1974-75		3								3
Steve	Taylor	56	1984-85	1988-89	100+1/46	4/5	6/3	4/2			6/0		120+1/56
Andy	Thackeray	98	1992-93	1996-97	161+4/13	7+1/1	8+1/0	10+3/2			9+2/2	1/0	196+11/18
Geoff	Thomas	43	1982-83	1983-84	10+1/1			+1/0					10+2/1

		Page	Season	To	FL	FAC	FLC	AMC	PO	ExpL	LSC	Other	Total
Chris	Thompson	92	1991-92								2/0		2/0
Dave	Thompson	40	1981-82	1996-97	237+29/24	11+2/0	11+2/0	16+1/0			11/3	2/0	288+34/27
Nigel	Thompson	72	1987-88		3+2/0		+1/0						3+3/0
Stuart	Thompson	44	1981-82	1983-84	23+8/8	1/0							24+8/8
Ian	Thompstone	111	1995-96		11+14/1	2+2/0	1/1	1+1/0			1/0		16+17/2
Don	Tobin	14	1973-74	1975-76	46+2/5	4/1					1/0		51+2/6
Dave	Tong	62	1985-86		+2/0								+2/0
Tony	Towers	58	1984-85		1+1/0								1+1/0
Tony	Towner	62	1985-86		4+1/0	2+1/0							6+2/0
George	Townsend	20	1974-75	1975-76	31+1/0	2/0	2/0						35+1/0
Jack	Trainer	40	1982-83		7/0		2/0				3/0		12/0
Peter	Valentine	109	1994-95	1995-96	49+1/2	4/0	2/0	1/0			2/0		58+1/2
Robbie	Wakenshaw	68	1986-87		28+1/5	2/2	2/0	4/2					36+1/9
Colin	Waldron	35	1979-80		19/0	3/0							22/0
Dean	Walling	72	1987-88	1989-90	43+22/8	+1/0	3/0	1+1/0			4/2	1/0	52+24/10
Dennis	Wann	34	1979-80	1980-81	66+1/7	5/0	4/0						75+1/7
Peter	Ward	83	1989-90	1990-91	83+1/10	7/1	5/0	5/0			4/0		104+1/11
Lee	Warren	74	1987-88	1988-89	31/1	1/0		2/0			3/0	1/0	38/1
Steve	Warriner	39	1981-82	1982-83	11+1/1		2/0				3/0		16+1/1
Ian	Watson	33	1979-80		33	5	2						40
Steve	Watson	66	1986-87								+0/0		+0/0
Alan	Weir	33	1979-80	1982-83	96+10/3	7/0	6/0				3/0	1/0	113+10/3
Keith	Welch	69	1986-87		205	10	12	12			12	1	252
Barry	Wellings	37	1980-81	1982-83	111+5/31	5/1	8/3				3/1	1/0	128+5/36
Tony	Whelan	17	1974-75	1976-77	124/20	14/1	5/0						143/21
Robbie	Whellans	84	1989-90		5+6/1		+1/0				2/0		7+7/1
Winston	White	68	1986-87		4/0								4/0
Steve	Whitehall	94	1991-92	1996-97	212+26/75	13+2/3	10+3/4	15/10		1/0	10+4/2	1/1	262+35/95
Craig	Whitington	109	1994-95		1/0								1/0
Steve	Wilkinson	78	1988-89								2/0	+1/0	2+1/0
Bill	Williams	39	1981-82	1984-85	89+6/2	4/0	9/0	2/0			1+2/0		105+8/2
David	Williams	95	1991-92		6		1			1			8
Mark	Williams	125	1998-99		11+3/1	4/0							15+3/1
Paul	Williams	103	1993-94	1995-96	22+15/7	1/0	2/0	2+1/0			3+1/2	1/1	31+17/10
Dave	Windridge	79	1988-89		5/0								5/0
Paul	Wood	79	1988-89		2+3/0			+2/0					2+5/0
Micky	Woods	66	1986-87		5+1/3	+1/0		2+1/0			+1/0		7+4/3
Alan	Young	67	1986-87	1987-88	19+9/2		2/0	2/1			1/0		24+9/3
Neil	Young	18	1974-75		8+5/4	3/1	1/0						12+5/5

ADDITIONS AND CORRECTIONS TO WHO'S WHO 1907-1939 AND 1939-1973

After the previous parts of the Who's Who were published, further details/corrections have been noted, in particular details of additional honours, mostly (but not always) where only a handful of games were played. As in the main text, promotions are in brackets if the player had left the club in question before the end of the season.

Additional honours: 1907-1939

J.R. Craven Division 2 champions 1909
J. Blackett Division 2 promotion 1908
F. Bracey Division 2 promotion 1908
E. Birnie Division 2 promotion 1907
R. Watson Division 2 promotion 1902, 1904
F. Heap Division 2 promotion 1924
A. Rawlings Division 3N promotion 1928
J. Swann Division 2 champions 1910
G. Kay Division 2 promotion 1911
T. Kay (Division 2 promotion 1922)
T. Hampson Division 2 promotion 1923
J. Peart Division 2 champions 1914
D. Ross Division 2 champions 1910
E. Connor Division 1 champions 1911
T. Bamford Division 2 promotion 1913
F. Taylor Division 2 promotion 1912
E. Whiteside Div. 2 champions 1909, promotion 1911
G. Wall Division 2 promotion 1906

J. Clarke Division 2 promotion 1921
A. Whitehurst Division 2 promotion 1922
C. Quinn (Division 3S champions 1924)
J. Milsom Division 2 promotion 1935
G. Stott Division 3N champions 1933
R. Butler Division 2 promotion 1924
J. Everest Division 3N champions 1939
L.H. Baker Division 2 champions 1924
W. Benton Division 2 champions 1930
F. Twine Division 2 champions 1927
D. Bain Division 1 champions 128
W. Gardner Division 3N champions 1926
S. Elliott Division 2 promotion 1930
W. Marshall Division 3N champions 1930
G.T. Jones Division 3N champions 1937
A. Dawson Division 3N champions 1936
F. Wilson Division 2 promotion 1934

Additional honours: 1939-73

J.S.D. Rawlings (Division 2 promotion 1934)
J. Connor Division 2 promotion 1935
J.T. Taylor Division 3N champions 1937
F. Gallimore Division 2 promotion 1934
E. Toser Division 3S champions 1938
J. Barker Division 2 champions 1938
H. Lowe Div. 2 champions 1931, promotion 1934, Division 1 champions 1932
P. Molloy Division 3S champions 1932
E. Toseland Division 1 champions 1936
R. Neilson Division 1 champions 1936
E. Eastwood (Division 2 champions 1947)
J. Robinson (Division 2 champions 1947)
A. Davies Division 3N champions 1948
D. Boxshall Division 3S champions 1935
G. Eastham Division 2 promotion 1935
H. Anders Division 4 promotion 1961
A. Morton Division 2 promotion 1950
H. Jackson Division 3N champion 1953

F. Lord Division 4 promotion 1963, Division 4 champion 1967
T. Todd Scottish Junior Cup winners 1944
H. Rudman Division 2 champions 1947
F..M. Hussey Div. 3N champions 1958
C.R. Barnes Division 4 promotion 1966
B. Birch (Division 1 champions 1952)
J. Martin Div. 2 champions 1956, 1959
A. Moulden Division 3 champions 1961
R. Ridge Division 2 promotion 1961
P. Phoenix (Division 4 promotion 1964)
L. Calloway Division 4 promotion 1975
B. Handley Division 2 champions 1960
J. Heath Division 3 champions 1961
J. Pennington (Division 4 promotion 1963)
B. Richardson Division 2 promotion 1961
W. Russell Division 2 promotion 1961
B. Wheatley Division 4 promotion 1963
P. Crossley (Division 4 promotion 1976)

There are minor corrections to the following entries from Volume 2:
A. Robinson: the text should read "400 games for Bury and Burnley", not "Bury and Blackburn".
W.R. John: delete "Swansea T. guest 11.44 [1 WL]" (he was still on their books from before the war).
A. Hanson: in career details, Dale WL appearances should be 17.
J. McClelland: in career details, Dale appearances should be 24.
L. Calloway: first spell(s) with San Jose Earthquakes should be 4.74 to 8.74 and 6.75 to 1977.

Note that appearance records included herein supersede those reported in the appearance 'grids' in the author's previous works. In particular, for anyone trying to match the two, the following appearances had missed inclusion in *Rochdale AFC, The Official History 1907-2001*:

1930-31: appearance given as 'Woods' (match 28), should be an additional appearance for Ward.
1970-71: in Rose Bowl, number 14 should be Blair, not Clarke.
1973-74: add Kavanagh at 12 in match 15 (replacing number 6).
1974-75: add Cooper at 12 in match 26 (replacing number 4).
1975-76: Tobin number 11 in match 44, not Mullington.
1976-77: add Mullington at number 10 in match 17.
1977-78: add Boslem at number 5 in match 34.
1985-86: add McCluskie at 12 in match 4 (replacing number 5).
1989-90: add Walling at 12 in matches 29, 30, 31 (replacing number 9 each time).
1990-91: add Burns at 12 in match 15 (replacing number 7).
1991-92: add Morgan at 14 in FL Cup first round, second leg (replacing number 11).
1991-92: add C.D. Jones at number 2 in first two Lancashire Cup games.
1995-96: add Clarke at number 1 in match 46.
1998-99: Holt at number 11 in all three AWS games, not Lydiate.

The following typos in the previous grids may also be noted

1942-43: in match 7, 'Baker' should be Barker.
1945-46: Hargreaves one goal (not 2) in FA Cup round 1, second leg.
1951-52: delete Betts 2(1p) from Lancashire Cup scorers.
1952-53: Murray one goal (not 2) in match 41.
1957-58: missing scorer in match 6 is Ferguson.
1967-68: Lancashire Cup, first match, scorer 'Mutchinson' should be Hutchinson
1976-77: Cooper 2 goals in match 23.
1994-95: Hodge at 1 (not 11) in Lancashire Cup, second game.
1995-96: in match 9 scorers, o.g. should refer to Schofield, not Stuart.
1999-00: Jones at 4 (not 14) in AWS NQF.
2000-01: Gilks at 13 (not 3) in match 35.

BY THE SAME AUTHOR:

ROCHDALE AFC WHO'S WHO 1907-1939 (ISBN 978-1-905891-64-1)
ROCHDALE AFC WHO'S WHO 1939-1973 (ISBN 978-1-905891-83-2)

In two companion volumes to the one you are holding, Steven Phillipps traces the career of over 1,000 men that played for the club up to 1973. Starting in the Manchester League, the club also had spells in the Lancashire Combination and the Central League, before becoming a founder member of the Football League Northern Section in 1921. The books also includes biographies of players that played during the two World Wars. Illustrated with many photographs, the books can be obtained from the publisher at the address on the title page. The price of each volume is £12.

All Rochdale's Football League players, team line-ups, and goal scorers will be found in the English National Football Archive at www.enfa.co.uk